THE SAUCE BOOK

THE SAUCE BOOK

LINDA COLLISTER

Photography by Patrice de Villiers

General Editor Jenni Muir

conran
OCTOPUS

To Alan

First published in 1997 by
Conran Octopus Limited
37 Shelton Street
London WC2H 9HN

Text © Linda Collister 1997
Photography © Patrice de Villiers 1997
Design and layout © Conran Octopus 1997

A catalogue record of this book is available from the British Library.
ISBN 1-85029-921-8

EDITORIAL DIRECTOR: Suzannah Gough
MANAGING/GENERAL EDITOR: Jenni Muir
IN-HOUSE EDITOR: Helen Ridge
ART EDITOR: Sue Storey
HOME ECONOMIST: Meg Jansz
PHOTOGRAPHIC STYLIST: Hilary Guy
PROOFREADER: Victoria Richards
EDITORIAL ASSISTANT: Tanya Robinson
PRODUCTION: Julian Deeming
INDEX: Laura Hicks

Printed in Hong Kong by Wing King Tong Co Ltd
Produced by Chroma Graphics (Overseas) Pte Ltd

CONTENTS

FOREWORD

Above: the craft is in making a balanced and well-seasoned sauce so that it does not overwhelm the food it is to accompany.

What is the point of a sauce? It is not a dish in its own right but enhances and embellishes, adds interest and moisture, complements or contrasts with the flavour, colour, texture and even temperature of the other food. It is the counterpoint to the melody on the plate. The art of sauce making is choosing the right one for the principal ingredient of the dish. The craft is making it so well-balanced, so perfectly seasoned that it matches yet does not overwhelm the food it is to accompany.

A sauce can be as simple or as contrived as you choose. Gravy is often the first sauce people come across. At its best, made from the meat cooking juices, it should be a good glossy translucent brown, richly flavoured but not greasy – and it should move on the plate. No real skill is needed just to spoon off the fat then whisk up the concentrated juices and sediment in the roasting pan. Taste, add salt and pepper and you have a perfectly good sauce for a Sunday roast.

Taste. There is the nub of it. Here every recipe tells you to add salt and pepper to taste. I cannot teach you how to season your sauces, I can only tell you how essential it is to taste the sauce as you prepare it, and again before and after adding the seasoning ingredients. Keep tasting, stirring and adding until you are happy with the result. Never add a touch of salt and pepper, let alone chilli, then serve without retasting – that way lies disaster. A meal where the salt cellar and sugar pot have been confused is not easily forgotten. The more you taste, the more experienced you become and the finer your sauce will be. It is worth building a collection of seasonings so that you have just the right ingredient when you most need it.

$\mathscr{T}$YPES OF $\mathscr{S}$AUCE

Baste: a butter or oil-based mixture used to spoon or brush over meat, fish or vegetables during roasting, grilling or on a barbecue, to prevent them drying out and to add flavour.

Butter Sauces: *beurre blanc* or white butter sauce is a light, delicate emulsion of white wine, vinegar, shallots and cold butter. For *beurre noir* the butter is cooked until brown.

Coulis: the strained juice from puréed fruit, such as berries or tomatoes, usually uncooked, unthickened and served cold.

Egg Emulsions: rich yet light sauces based on butter and egg yolks whisked over a low heat. The best-known hot emulsions are the French *hollandaise* and *béarnaise* sauces. *Mayonnaise* is a cold emulsification of oil and egg yolks plus vinegar or lemon juice.

Below, clockwise from left: Tomato Salsa, Sorrel Sauce, Gravy, Béchamel Sauce, Pesto Genovese.

Gravy: made from the meat juices left in the roasting or frying pan after cooking. The excess fat is removed and stock or wine added to make a *jus* or thin gravy. Flour can be mixed into the fat, browned, then stock or wine added to make a thick gravy.

Ketchup: a sweet-sour preserved sauce with a smooth, thick pouring consistency.

Marinade: a well-flavoured combination of oil and wine or fruit juice, plus herbs or spices, designed to tenderize and flavour food before cooking as well as to prevent it becoming dry during cooking. Sometimes made with yogurt, marinades can be uncooked or cooked, or dry mixtures of herbs and spices rubbed onto the food.

Mousseline: a light, fluffy sauce that is made by vigorous whisking of the mixture, or by folding in some whipped cream.

Purée: similar to a coulis. Vegetables or fruit are cooked until very soft then pushed through a sieve to make a smooth sauce.

Raita: a cooling, thick yogurt-based sauce to accompany curries.

Roux-based Sauces: the roux is a mixture of equal quantities of butter and flour used to thicken a sauce. *Bèchamel* is made from the roux and flavoured milk; for a *velouté* the roux is cooked until it is a light straw colour then stock is whisked in; for a traditional *brown sauce* the roux is slowly cooked to a chestnut brown before the stock is added to give the final sauce its dark colour.

Sabayon: made by whisking egg yolks, sugar and wine. White wine is used for the

Above, clockwise from left: Barbecue Ketchup, Fresh Mint Raita, Lemon Vinaigrette, Zabaglione, Raspberry Coulis (Melba Sauce).

French sabayon and Marsala for the Italian version, *zabaglione*.

Salsa: the word means sauce in Italian, Mexican and Spanish. In modern cooking the term usually indicates an uncooked sauce, typically made from nuts, or from herbs, olive oil and breadcrumbs, or a spicy relish made from diced onions, chilli, lime juice, coriander and tomatoes or sweeter fruits.

Syrup: sugar dissolved in water or fruit juice to make a thin or thick sauce which can be flavoured with herbs and spices.

Vinaigrettes: made from oil and an acidic ingredient such as vinegar or lemon juice, flavoured with mustard, seasonings and often herbs. Can be used raw or cooked.

$\mathscr{M}$ AKING $\mathscr{S}$ TOCKS

When I was training to be a cook it was drummed into me that stock forms the basis of savoury cooking (the French word for stock is *fond* or 'foundation'). Indeed, it was hard to progress until you had proved you could make good stock. It is not used in its own right but as the basis for sauces and soups. Today it is easy to buy cartons of fresh stock, so there is no need to resort to a stock cube, but it is still worthwhile making your own stock once in a while then freezing it in small quantities ready for use.

Stock is made from meat or fish bones and lean trimmings plus vegetables simmered, not boiled, in water. Beef and chicken are most commonly used (veal used to be *de rigueur* for stocks); lamb, pork and duck tend to be too fatty and strong for making stocks suitable for general use. Meat used to be the main ingredient but these days bones, chopped by the butcher to fit your stock pot, make an excellent though less rich stock. Whole peppercorns (ground pepper turns bitter during prolonged cooking and makes the stock cloudy) and a bouquet garni provide even more flavour. If you like herbs, make sure the bouquet garni is large and contains a couple of fresh bay leaves, a good-sized bunch of thyme, plenty of parsley (leaves and lots of stalks) and a sprig of tarragon. Salt is not added initially because the final stock, if well reduced, could be unpalatable.

Remember, it is important to use good quality fresh ingredients for stock making: it is not a way of clearing out the refrigerator.

Basic Beef or Chicken Stock

This is a pale stock suitable for light sauces, veloutés, soups and subtly flavoured dishes.

MAKES 2.5 LITRES/4½ PINTS

1.5kg/3lb 5oz beef bones, chopped, or raw chicken carcasses, or a mixture of wings, backs and necks, or 1 boiling fowl
2 large onions, halved and studded with 2 cloves
2 large carrots, quartered
2 stalks celery, sliced
1 large bouquet garni
1 teaspoon black peppercorns

Rinse the beef bones, carcasses or chicken then put them into the stock pot and cover generously with water from the tap. Bring to a boil and simmer for 2-3 minutes.

Drain the blanched bones or chicken in a colander, discarding the water, and quickly rinse under the cold tap. Return the bones or chicken to the rinsed-out pot, add the vegetables, bouquet garni and peppercorns and enough cold water to cover them well – about 3 litres/5¼ pints.

Bring the stock to a boil, skim it carefully using a slotted spoon then cover and simmer gently: 3 hours for beef stock, 1½ hours for chicken stock. Skim from time to time.

Strain the stock to remove the bones and vegetables. If you are using a whole chicken or chicken pieces, the meat can be reserved and used for soups, pies or served with a sauce made from the reduced stock.

Remove as much fat as possible from the stock. If there is time, chill the stock quickly

Right: straining the Basic Chicken Stock to remove the flavourings. You can save the meat from the chicken wings to use in another recipe.

first so that the fat collects on top and is easy to skim off.

The stock can then be boiled vigorously until it has reduced by half. This will give a well-flavoured liquid that sets to a jelly as it cools. The stock must be cooled as quickly as possible then chilled or frozen. It can be kept in the refrigerator for up to 36 hours.

Variations: the meat or poultry bones and vegetables can be roasted in the oven before making the stock to give the liquid a good brown colour and stronger taste.

You can add up to 100g/3½oz of chopped mushroom stalks and peelings, and, for a beef stock, 1-2 seeded tomatoes. For extra flavour, you can deglaze the roasting pan with 100-200ml/3½-7fl oz of red or white wine or Madeira made up to 350ml/12fl oz with water, then add this to the stock pot.

Game Stock
Use the bones and trimmings from duck, grouse, partridge or pheasants, or make the stock with venison bones. Deglaze the roasting pan with red or white wine, or port.

Lamb Stock
Use lamb bones roasted with the onion and carrot, and add a chopped leek to the stock pot. For a stronger flavour, deglaze the roasting pan with a 350ml/12fl oz mixture of wine and water then add this to the stock. Lamb stock should not be simmered for more than 1½ hours and, as it tends to be greasy, it is important to remove all the fat.

Fish Stock

Fish stock or *fumet* must not simmer for more than 20 minutes or it will taste bitter. The vegetables are therefore sweated in butter to extract the maximum flavour before the bones are added. Shellfish add a good flavour but oily fish are unsuitable as they make the stock greasy and too strong.

MAKES 2 LITRES/3½ PINTS

20g/¾oz unsalted butter
1 large onion or 6 shallots, finely chopped
1 leek, white part only, sliced
2 slices fennel
1.5kg/3lb 5oz white fish bones and trimmings
350ml/12fl oz white wine, or a mixture of wine and water, or 350ml/12fl oz water plus 2 slices lemon
½ teaspoon peppercorns
1 large bouquet garni

Heat the butter in a stock pot and add the vegetables. Stir well then cover with a circle of dampened greaseproof paper and the lid. Cook very gently for about 20 minutes or until the vegetables are really tender but not coloured. Stir the vegetables frequently.

Meanwhile, rinse the fish bones and trimmings under the cold tap and drain thoroughly. Chop the bones and any large heads into pieces. When the vegetables are ready, add the fish to the pan and stir over a low heat for 3-4 minutes.

Add the wine and leave to simmer for 5 minutes, then add 2 litres/3½ pints of cold water to the pot and bring it to the boil. Skim the surface of the stock then add the peppercorns, bouquet garni and lemon (if using). Simmer the stock gently, uncovered, for 20 minutes, skimming from time to time.

Strain the stock through a fine-meshed conical sieve. It can then be reduced and used immediately, or cooled and refrigerated for up to 24 hours. It can also be frozen.

Vegetable Stock

Vary the vegetables given here to suit the season and the final dish. Avoid cabbage, however, as it tends to dominate the flavour; potatoes and other starchy root vegetables can make the stock cloudy and heavy.

MAKES 1 LITRE/1¾ PINTS

2 medium carrots, finely sliced
1 parsnip, finely sliced
2 medium onions, finely sliced
1 stalk celery, sliced
2 slices fennel
1 small leek, sliced
1 courgette, sliced, or 3-4 green beans
½ teaspoon peppercorns
1 large bouquet garni
2 garlic cloves, unpeeled
250ml/9fl oz dry white wine
1.5 litres/2¾ pints cold water

Put all the ingredients into a stock pot and bring them to a boil. Simmer, uncovered, for 30 minutes, skimming as necessary.

Strain the stock through a fine-meshed conical sieve then leave to cool and store in the refrigerator, or freeze.

Variations: for a darker vegetable stock, add up to 100g/3½oz of sliced mushrooms or mushroom peelings and a couple of juicy ripe tomatoes, roughly chopped.

Kitchen Bouillon

This is not a recipe you will find in a chef's book. Few cooks admit to this cheat's method of making stock but the result is suitable for soups, gravies and well-flavoured everyday sauces. An easy, tasty opaque broth of indeterminate colour, this recipe is an excellent way to recycle the remains of a roasted joint or cooked chicken carcass. However, it is not a way of using items only fit for the dustbin – all the ingredients should be fresh and of good quality.

leftover bones and carcasses, chopped
lean raw meat trimmings
2 onions, quartered
2 carrots, quartered
2 celery stalks, sliced
1 leek, white part only, sliced
1 large bouquet garni
1 teaspoon peppercorns

Put all the ingredients into a stock pot, cover with cold water and bring to a boil. Skim thoroughly then simmer very gently, uncovered, for no more than 1 hour, topping up the pan if necessary with cold water.

Strain the stock, discarding the solids, then skim off the fat. The broth can then be reduced as necessary. Cool it as quickly as possible then chill or freeze immediately. Do not leave it hanging around a warm kitchen.

Oriental Chicken Stock

You can use this, my favourite stock, for stir-fries and curries as well as soups.

MAKES 2.5 LITRES/4½ PINTS

1kg/2lb 4oz chicken wings
2 medium onions, sliced
1 carrot, quartered
1 stick celery, chopped
1 teaspoon black peppercorns
3.5cm/1½in piece root ginger, unpeeled and thickly sliced
few parsley or coriander stalks, lightly crushed

Put all the ingredients into a stock pot with enough cold water to cover – you will need 2.5-3 litres/4½-5¼ pints. Bring the stock to a boil and skim the surface well. Cover the pot and simmer gently (do not let it boil) for 1 hour, skimming from time to time.

Strain the stock through a fine-meshed conical sieve. Reserve the chicken wings so that you can use their meat in the final dish but discard the other bits and pieces. Remove as much fat as possible from the stock then reduce it if necessary. The stock can be cooled then frozen or stored in the refrigerator for up to 2 days.

Variation: you can include 1-2 drumsticks with the chicken wings if you like but do not use drumsticks exclusively.

Dashi

Dashi is a richly flavoured stock for Japanese soups and noodle dishes. It is made from kombu seaweed and shavings of bonito tuna. The ingredients can usually be found in Oriental grocers, specialist food shops and health food stores.

MAKES 1 LITRE/1¾ PINTS

30g/1oz kombu seaweed
1 litre/1¾ pints cold water
30g/1oz dried bonito flakes
TO MAKE DASHI BROTH:
6 tablespoons Japanese soy sauce
4 tablespoons mirin

Put the kombu into a stock pot with the cold water and heat very slowly, stirring often, until the mixture just comes to a boil.

Remove the pot from the heat and lift out the kombu with a slotted spoon. Add the bonito flakes to the stock, stir well then return the pot to the heat and bring the liquid to a full rolling boil.

Remove the pot from the heat and leave the stock to stand for about 5 minutes. Skim the surface to remove any scum then strain the liquid through a conical sieve lined with a piece of muslin, clean linen tea towel or paper coffee filter. Leave the stock to cool.

The stock can be diluted to suit the dish. Store in the refrigerator and use within 24 hours, or freeze. The strained kombu and bonito can be used to make a second batch of dashi, which will taste more concentrated.

To make dashi broth, add the soy sauce and mirin to the dashi stock just before use.

Left: Dashi can be used to make a healthy bowl of Teriyaki Salmon and Japanese Noodles (see page 98) as well as other Oriental dishes.

OTHER INGREDIENTS

I like to cook with as many organic (and free range) foods as possible. They not only have, in most cases, much more flavour but more vitamins and minerals than intensively produced food, and they are produced with more care to the welfare of animals and the land. Whatever your choice, throughout this book it is assumed you will scrub or wash all fruit, vegetables and herbs as necessary.

Butter: fresh (check the best-before date) unsalted butter is best for cooking. Salted butter is often very salty, which can alter the balance of a sauce. It also has a less creamy, more greasy flavour than unsalted butter and burns more easily. Normandy butter is considered the best. It freezes well so take advantage of special offers.

Chocolate: the quality and depth of taste is determined, not by price, but by the quantity and quality of the cocoa solids used in production. This is given on the packet – look for a cocoa solids content of 70 per cent. Avoid cooking chocolate and plain chocolate confectionery bars as they often contain as little as 30 per cent cocoa solids; the rest is sugar, fats and flavourings.

Cream: cream for whipping should be fresh and well chilled. If overwhipped, it will turn grainy then separate. Cream can also separate if it is added to acidic ingredients, for instance to a fresh tomato sauce, or if overheated. Crème fraîche has a distinct nutty, slightly sour flavour and rich texture. It is less likely to separate on heating but it is not suitable for whipping, nor is cream that has been labelled 'extra-thick'.

Eggs: choose organic or free range and check the date on the pack for freshness. Remember that uncooked or partially

cooked eggs should not be served to the very young, the elderly, pregnant women and anyone frail or vulnerable to infection.

Flour: use plain white flour rather than self-raising or wholemeal for making sauces. Cornflour is used in Chinese dishes. Potato flour *(fecule)* or arrowroot are often used to thicken sauces at the end of cooking.

Herbs: fresh herbs are always used in this book unless otherwise specified. Always wash and thoroughly dry them before use.

Lemons: always use unwaxed fruit if you will be using the rind or zest in a recipe. The same applies to oranges.

Mustard: try to have a selection of mustards in the kitchen. French and German mustards have a good depth of flavour but English mustard is too fiery to add to most sauces. Mustard turns a sauce very bitter if allowed to boil, so always add it off the heat.

Nuts: their high fat content makes nuts quickly taste stale and rancid when exposed to the air, so use the freshest possible and store opened packets in the freezer.

Oils: avoid blended salad or vegetable oils. The best quality, most interesting oils for flavouring are made from the first (low temperature) pressing of a single fruit, grain or nut. The flavour of olive oil ranges from sweet and delicate through fruity to the powerfully robust, so select an oil suitable for the finished dish. Groundnut oil is mild and excellent for frying as it has a high smoking point. Nut oils tend to be expensive and are unsuitable for cooking at high temperatures, but can be excellent on their own or combined with a mild oil for salads.

For Oriental cooking, choose a sesame oil made from roasted sesame seeds.

Salt and Pepper: these seasonings should always be added to taste unless otherwise specified in the recipe.

Soy Sauce: choose naturally brewed soy sauce from Japan – the flavour is very different from non-brewed soy made by chemically hydrolysing vegetable proteins and adding caramel, salt and sugar. Large bottles of Japanese soy sauce tend to be much cheaper at Oriental stores.

Tomatoes: choose ripe, well-flavoured tomatoes, otherwise look out for good quality tinned plum tomatoes: a 400g/14oz can should have a drained weight of 250g/9oz. Tomato purée can be very salty so add it before seasoning. Sun-dried tomato purée has a rounder, richer flavour.

Vegetables: in this book it is assumed that you will wash, dry and trim all vegetables before use. Where vegetables such as carrots, onions and potatoes are commonly peeled you should do so unless specified in the recipe. It is assumed that you will not peel aubergines, courgettes or peppers.

Vinegars: white and red wine vinegars are the ones most often used in vinaigrettes and salads. Cider vinegar and tarragon vinegar are interesting alternatives. Raspberry vinegar makes a distinctive dressing and can be used for deglazing. Balsamic and sherry vinegars are expensive but useful in the kitchen. Malt vinegar is far too pungent to be used in cooking except for preserving and as a condiment for fish and chips. Japanese and Chinese rice vinegars tend to be mild and even slightly sweet.

EQUIPMENT

You do not need much in the way of specialized equipment for making sauces, but you will need a good small to medium-sized saucepan with sloping sides. The classic pan for making sauces is copper and lined with tin, nickel or stainless steel. Copper is a good conductor of heat and using this sort of pan helps to avoid scorching a sauce as it cooks. The clever design of these pans ensures the whisk can reach every part of the pan, and that it does not wobble around on the stove as the sauce is whisked, or topple over when the whisk is leant against the side. These pans need to be used carefully as metal implements can scratch the lining.

The next best choice, and probably the most practical for home cooks, would be a heavy-based, well-balanced, good quality stainless steel pan, again with sloping sides. Many cookware shops and large department stores now stock these semi-professional pans. Try to avoid using aluminium pans, which can react with acidic ingredients such as wine, vinegar and lemon juice, and also toughened glass, which can result in a sauce that sticks and catches.

A small to medium-sized straight-sided pan is useful for making sugar syrup and for keeping sauces warm in a bain-marie.

A deep roasting tin makes a good bain-marie. It should be filled one-third full with warm water and set over a low heat.

A large stock pot, again non-aluminium, is always useful and not just for making stock; it can also be used for poaching chickens, cooking pasta or soup making.

A colander, with a long handle and sturdy legs, and a conical strainer with small holes, a coarse wire mesh chinois or conical sieve and a fine-meshed conical sieve or tamis for making smooth, glossy sauces, are all very useful. Stainless steel is best for these.

A stainless steel wire whisk with a large, thick handle is vital. You should choose a size appropriate to the size of your pan. Small coiled wire sauce whisks are also very good, and inexpensive. Avoid using large balloon whisks for sauce making: they are better for whisking cream and egg whites. Rotary whisks are not a good choice either.

Several wooden spoons, with long handles and shallow bowls, are good for stirring creamy sauces and vegetable mixtures where you do not need a foamy or frothy texture, however I think a whisk is more efficient at dispersing lumps. A flat wooden spatula is a good buy: it also does not conduct heat so can be used for stir-frying and slow-cooked dishes. A flexible plastic spatula is handy for scraping out pans.

A small ladle, stainless steel, with a long handle can be used with a chinois for straining sauces or pushing them through a sieve. A large metal ladle, again with a long handle, can be used for transferring liquids from pan to processor and back again.

A food processor, with a large bowl, or a heavy-duty blender make light work of puréeing sauces and can be used for making hollandaise and mayonnaise very speedily. These machines can also be used for pestos and nut sauces.

Old-fashioned pestles and mortars are also useful for crushing spices, pestos and other thick sauces. Choose a heavy, fairly large one with a non-reactive inner surface.

A measuring jug made from toughened glass is vital for accurate measuring, as are a set of measuring spoons.

Right (from left to right): straight-sided stainless steel saucepan, balloon whisk, large metal ladle, coiled wire whisk, tin-lined copper saucepan, measuring spoons, conical strainer with small holes, fine-meshed conical sieve, blender.

$\mathscr{E}$QUIPMENT

$\mathcal{T}$HICKENING $\mathcal{S}$AUCES

Making sauces well requires skill, of course, but experience and judgement are more important. The correct thickness for a sauce depends on how it is to be used and what it is to accompany. There are several ways to adjust the consistency to your liking.

MOUNTING WITH BUTTER

Adding pieces of icy-cold butter to a sauce just before serving gives the sauce a fine, glossy quality and a richer, creamier flavour as well as making it slightly thicker. This method can also make a slightly harsh sauce smoother in flavour.

It is important to use well-chilled unsalted butter that has been cut into small cubes. Salted butter will give an undesirable salty, slightly greasy finish to the sauce.

Bring the sauce to a boil, then take it off the heat and gradually whisk in the pieces of butter so they quickly melt and thicken the sauce. Once a sauce has been mounted with butter it should be served as soon as possible, without reheating.

BEURRE MANIÉ

This is one of the quickest, easiest ways to thicken a sauce. Also known as kneaded butter, it is primarily used for hearty stews and casseroles if they are too thin at the end of cooking. The beurre manié is added just before serving, though a sauce thickened this way can be kept warm or even reheated.

Mash equal quantities of very soft unsalted butter and plain flour together with a fork or palette knife to give a smooth paste. Whisk or stir small pieces of this paste into the boiling sauce – it works instantly so you can keep adding the paste until the sauce is of the right consistency. Let the sauce boil gently for 2-3 minutes before serving in order to cook out the taste of the flour.

CORNFLOUR

This is another simple, quick way to thicken a sauce and is commonly used in Chinese cooking and for making low-fat sauces.

In a small bowl, mix 1 tablespoon of cornflour with an equal quantity of cold water, stock or other cold liquid to make a smooth, pourable paste (this process is known as slaking). Pour the paste into the boiling sauce while stirring or whisking vigorously – as the sauce boils it will thicken and become slightly opaque.

If necessary, add more of the cornflour mixture to get the right consistency. The finished sauce should coat the back of a spoon; too much cornflour will give a jelly-like finish. Gently boil the sauce for 1 minute to cook the cornflour. A sauce thickened in this way can be kept hot or reheated and will not thin if re-boiled.

ARROWROOT AND POTATO FLOUR (FECULE)

These are also added at the end of cooking and have an advantage over cornflour in that they give a fine, glossy, transparent finish to the sauce. However, sauces that have been thickened in this way cannot be cooked further: the sauce will instantly thicken on boiling but will become thin again if allowed to simmer for more than 1 minute.

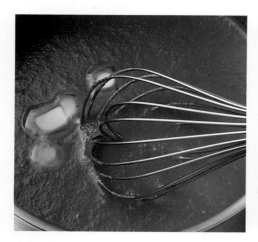

Mounting with butter: *take the boiling sauce off the heat and gradually whisk in the cubes of butter so they melt and thicken the sauce.*

Beurre Manié: *gradually add small pieces of the flour and butter paste to the sauce, stirring well after each addition, until thick.*

Cornflour: *pour the mixture of cornflour and water into the boiling sauce while whisking vigorously then cook the sauce for 1 minute.*

Thickening Sauces

Mix 1 tablespoon of arrowroot or potato flour with an equal quantity of cold water or stock to make a smooth, pourable paste, then whisk it into the boiling sauce. As soon as the sauce thickens, remove it from the heat and serve immediately.

EGG YOLKS AND CREAM
Added at the end of cooking, this mixture will enrich and thicken a sauce, giving it a luxurious, rich, creamy taste and a velvety smooth texture. Velouté sauces are often finished in this way, but egg yolks and cream can also be used to enrich béchamel sauces and soups. Remember, the eggs will curdle if the mixture is boiled, and the sauce cannot be reheated.

Lightly whisk the egg yolks with an equal quantity of cream (or even creamy milk) in a heatproof bowl until just combined. Bring the sauce to a boil then remove it from the heat. Add some of the hot sauce to the egg mixture, stirring constantly (this gently heats the egg mixture so it is less likely to curdle when it meets the very hot sauce). Stir this mixture into the sauce off the heat then stir it over a low heat until the sauce thickens enough to lightly coat the back of a spoon.

Do not overheat the sauce or allow it to boil as it will curdle. Serve immediately.

REDUCTION
A thin, runny sauce, or one that is lacking in flavour, can be carefully boiled over a medium-high heat (do not let it scorch around the edges) until enough of the liquid has evaporated to make it thicker and more concentrated in flavour. Gravy and stock-based sauces are often thickened this way to intensify the flavour and give a mellow result; it is best to reduce them before you add any other thickening agent in order to avoid the sauce catching on the bottom of the pan or scorching. Take care that the sauce does not boil too hard or it will become cloudy and taste bitter.

As the stock or sauce reduces, skim off any froth on the surface using a small ladle or slotted spoon. Check the consistency from time to time by pouring a little of the sauce over the back of a spoon – it can be as thin as milk, like single cream, thicker cream or a rich, thick, sticky sauce known as demi-glace. Sauces such as these are always seasoned after they have been reduced or the flavour may be too intense.

Quick cream sauces can also be made using this method. The cream is brought to a boil in a pan with flavourings such as wine, herbs and cooking juices and simmered until thick. Cream can also be boiled until it has reduced by about a third, then added to a hot sauce to thicken it. Choose double cream or UHT cream; crème fraîche tends to curdle when used in this way.

PURÉES
A gravy or casserole that is slightly too thin can be thickened by mashing a cooked potato and stirring it into the sauce before serving. A casserole made with beans or lentils can be thickened by puréeing a cup or so of the mixture then stirring it into the pot.

Breadcrumbs can be stirred in to thicken hearty casseroles and soups, but the sauce then needs to be cooked for 10 minutes or so, stirring frequently, before serving.

Some sauces are thickened simply by puréeing the ingredients in a blender or food processor, or by pushing them through a sieve. This method is often used for sauces made from raw or cooked fruit or from cooked vegetables and is an excellent means of producing velvety-textured low-fat sauces.

Arrowroot or Potato Flour: *whisk the paste of water and arrowroot or potato flour into the boiling sauce then remove it from the heat.*

Egg Yolks and Cream: *combine the yolks and cream in a bowl and add a little of the sauce. Stir this mixture into the pan off the heat.*

Reduction: *boil the sauce for several minutes or until enough liquid has evaporated to give a lightly thickened consistency.*

ℛoux ℬases

A roux is a cooked mixture of equal amounts of butter and flour. Unlike other methods of thickening a sauce, it is used at the very beginning of the recipe as the base of the sauce. The darker the roux, the more colour the final sauce will have. Once the roux has been cooked to the desired colour, the pan is removed from the heat and the liquid is added. The sauce is then simmered until it reaches the correct consistency. You will need 20g/¾oz each of butter and flour to make 400ml/14fl oz of sauce of a medium thickness. Some cooks prefer to clarify the butter first, however you will find that fresh unsalted butter gives a perfectly satisfactory result and, of course, saves time.

WATCHPOINTS

- *Use a heavy-based saucepan to prevent the roux catching on the base of the pan and scorching.*
- *To avoid lumps in the finished sauce, spread the roux out over the base of the saucepan so that it cooks evenly.*
- *Cook the roux over a very low heat so that it bubbles gently.*
- *Do not allow the roux to scorch or turn dark brown or the sauce will taste bitter.*
- *If lumps do form in the sauce, pour it through a fine sieve into a clean pan.*

1 A white roux, which can be used for béchamel and velouté sauces, is cooked for just 1-2 minutes over a low heat so the mixture remains pale in colour. The resulting sauce made from milk or a pale stock will also be lightly coloured. The cooled roux can be stored covered in the refrigerator for 3 days if desired.

2 If the roux is cooked for 3-5 minutes the flour in the mixture will start to turn a golden colour. This is known as a blond or straw-coloured roux and is also used for béchamel and velouté sauces. The extra time has the advantage of helping to cook out the raw taste of the flour.

3 Bacon or ham and vegetables, as well as butter and flour, are included in a brown roux, which is cooked very gently on the stovetop for 10-20 minutes or until the flour turns a rich brown colour. Some cooks choose to bake the roux in the oven, which can take as long as 45 minutes. Brown roux is the basis of a traditionally-made brown sauce as well as many Cajun recipes such as gumbo.

$\mathcal{S}$AUCE $\mathcal{C}$ONSISTENCY

The consistency you want a sauce to achieve depends on its final use. A thin, delicate pouring sauce is best for fish or vegetables as it will not overwhelm them. It can also be used as the basis of soups or other sauces. A sauce of a medium coating consistency will cover the surface of more robust ingredients and is best for gratins and pasta dishes. The thickest sauces are practically solid and used as the base for soufflés and for binding together the ingredients for crêpe fillings, croquettes and fish cakes. If a sauce is too thick, work in a little extra milk or stock then adjust the seasoning. Sauces thicken slightly on reheating, so make them thinner than usual if you are preparing them in advance.

1 A sauce has reached pouring consistency when it lightly coats the back of a spoon and, when you draw your finger across the spoon, the trail left in the sauce slowly runs back together. This is the best consistency for sauces that you wish to simply moisten the food and is ideal for flooding the serving plate for a grand presentation.

2 When the sauce is a coating consistency it will cling to the back of the spoon and a clear trail will be left when you draw your finger across it. This type of sauce will similarly cling to the food, oozing across the top and down the sides.

3 A sauce of a binding consistency is made with a higher proportion of butter and flour to liquid. The finished sauce will be very thick and will only drop from the spoon when the handle is tapped on the side of the pan. This is the consistency required to hold solid ingredients together when making croquettes, soufflés and similar dishes.

ℳAKING ℐOMATO ℐAUCE

A good tomato sauce, such as this fine, smooth version, is highly versatile and healthy. Use it for pasta dishes such as cannelloni, ravioli or simply with spaghetti, add it to casseroles and stews, or serve it alongside grilled meats. To make a tomato soup, add vegetable stock or single cream until the mixture is of the right consistency.

Tomato Sauce

MAKES 1 LITRE/1¾ PINTS

2 tablespoons olive oil
1 large onion, chopped
2 cloves garlic, chopped
1 stick celery, chopped
1 medium carrot, finely sliced
1kg/2lb 4oz tomatoes, chopped
salt and black pepper

EQUIPMENT
• **Large heavy pan or frying pan with lid**
• **Wooden spoon**
• **Conical sieve, food processor or blender**

1 Heat the oil in a heavy pan and add the chopped onion. Cover the pan and cook very slowly for about 15 minutes or until the onions are soft and golden.

2 Stir in the garlic, celery and carrot then cover the pan and continue cooking the vegetables for another 5 minutes. Add the chopped tomatoes and seasoning and cook the mixture gently for a further 20 minutes.

3 Strain the sauce through a conical sieve, pressing down on the solids to extract as much flavour as possible. Alternatively, process the mixture until smooth in a food processor or blender. Taste and adjust the seasoning. The cooled sauce can be stored in the refrigerator for up to 5 days.

WATCHPOINTS
•*Use ripe, well-flavoured tomatoes to avoid a watery-tasting, thin sauce.*
•*Stir frequently to avoid the sauce catching on the base of the pan.*

FOR STEAK ADD: LEMON JUICE
WHOLEGRAIN MUSTARD
FRESH PARSLEY.

MAKING MAYONNAISE

Mayonnaise is a cold, thick, delicious emulsion of egg yolks and oil, nicely acidified and flavoured with salt, pepper and mustard. The oil can be a delicate vegetable one such as safflower or sunflower, light olive oil or the richest extra virgin olive oil depending on how the mayonnaise is to be used: a combination often works best.

Mayonnaise

MAKES 200ML/7FL OZ

1 large egg yolk, at room temperature
1 teaspoon Dijon *(ENGLISH)* mustard, or to taste
juice of ½ lemon, or 2 tablespoons white wine
   vinegar
salt and pepper
170ml/6fl oz vegetable ~~or olive oil, or a mixture~~

EQUIPMENT
• Small bowl
• Damp cloth
• Whisk
• Measuring jug

1 Put the egg yolk, mustard, half the lemon juice or wine vinegar and a little salt and pepper into a small bowl. Stand the bowl on a damp cloth to stop it wobbling while you whisk the ingredients until they are creamy.

WATCHPOINTS
•*Add the oil very slowly. If the mixture starts to separate, stir in 1 tablespoon of warm water.*
•*If the mixture curdles, place a fresh yolk in another bowl then slowly whisk in the curdled mixture. Adjust the seasoning before serving.*

2 Very slowly whisk in the oil, drop by drop. Then, as the mayonnaise starts to thicken, begin adding the oil in a thin, steady stream, whisking constantly.

3 When all the oil has been incorporated, taste and stir in more of the lemon juice or vinegar and more seasoning as required. Stir gently before use. Mayonnaise can be kept covered in the refrigerator for 2 days.

Blender Mayonnaise: to make mayonnaise in a food processor, blender, or a food mixer fitted with a whisk attachment, put the egg yolk, mustard, lemon juice or vinegar, salt and pepper into the bowl and process them briefly, just until they are combined.

Then, with the machine running, gradually pour in the oil through the feed tube (or wherever appropriate) in a thin, steady stream until you have a thick, emulsified mixture. Taste the mayonnaise and adjust the flavourings as necessary.

Making Béchamel Sauce

Béchamel sauce is infinitely adaptable and versatile. It can be used plain or as a base for several other flavoured sauces. When made to a thin consistency it can be used in soups; a medium thickness is best for coating pasta, vegetables, fish and eggs; and thick béchamel is ideal for binding ingredients together to make fish cakes and croquettes. Make sure the milk is full-fat and thoroughly infused with the onion, bay leaf, parsley, mace and peppercorns. The sauce should be whisked constantly as it comes to the boil to eliminate lumps and give a silky texture, then cooked a full 20 minutes so the flour no longer tastes raw. Béchamel can be kept hot in a bain-marie if necessary and freezes well.

Béchamel Sauce

MAKES 400ML/14FL OZ MEDIUM-THICKNESS
SAUCE

400ml/14fl oz whole milk
¼ teaspoon peppercorns
1 bay leaf
2 slices onion
1 blade mace
2 parsley stalks, crushed
20g/¾oz unsalted butter
20g/¾oz plain flour
salt and white pepper
freshly grated nutmeg

EQUIPMENT
• **Heavy saucepan**
• **Wire whisk**
• **Wooden spoon (optional)**

1 Heat the milk with the peppercorns, bay leaf, onion, mace and parsley stalks in a medium-sized, heavy-based saucepan. As the milk comes up to boiling point, cover the pan, remove it from the heat and leave to stand for 20 minutes to allow the flavours to infuse (leave it for up to 1 hour if possible). Strain the milk into a jug and discard the flavourings. Rinse out the saucepan.

2 Gently melt the butter in the saucepan. Stir in the flour using a wooden spoon or wire whisk to make a smooth paste. Cook gently, stirring, over a very low heat so the roux bubbles as it cooks.

Making Béchamel Sauce

3 Remove the pan from the heat and, using a wire whisk, gradually whisk in the infused milk to make a smooth liquid.

4 Set the pan over a medium heat and whisk rapidly as the mixture comes to a boil. It should thicken but remain smooth.

5 Reduce the heat so the sauce barely simmers, then leave it to cook very gently for 20 minutes, stirring frequently.

6 The correct consistency is reached when the mixture coats the back of a spoon and a clear trail can be drawn through the sauce. When it is ready, give it a final whisk then season with salt, pepper and nutmeg.

7 To keep the sauce warm in a bain-marie, press a circle of dampened greaseproof paper onto the surface of the sauce, or dot the surface with butter, then cover the pan with a lid. The cooled sauce can be stored in the refrigerator for up to 3 days or frozen.

WATCHPOINTS

• *For the best flavour use good ingredients: full-fat milk and butter are preferable to skimmed milk and margarine.*
• *Take care not to catch the sauce on the base of the pan; milk easily scorches, making the sauce taste unpleasant.*
• *If there are any lumps, whisk the sauce vigorously, strain it through a sieve or process it in a blender or food processor.*

Variations: *Simple White Sauce*
Follow the recipe for Medium-Thickness Béchamel as given but do not infuse the milk with the flavourings.

Thin Béchamel
Follow the recipe for Medium-Thickness Béchamel but use 15g/½oz each of butter and flour. The correct consistency is reached when the sauce is the thickness of single cream: it will only lightly cover the back of a spoon and you will not be able to draw a clear trail through the sauce.

Thick Béchamel
Follow the recipe for Medium-Thickness Béchamel but use 30g/1¼oz each of butter and flour. The correct consistency is reached when the sauce is semi-solid and drops off the spoon only when the spoon is tapped on the rim of the saucepan.

Cream Sauce
Adding crème fraîche, double or single cream to the recipe for Medium-Thickness Béchamel instantly changes the taste and texture, making the sauce velvety smooth and rich. Whisk 4-5 tablespoons of cream into the heated béchamel and simmer gently, whisking until the sauce reaches the correct consistency. Taste and adjust the seasoning if necessary. Use cream sauce to coat steamed vegetables, simply poached fish and plain poultry dishes.

Making Hollandaise Sauce

Hollandaise sauce is one of the lightest and yet richest sauces you can make. A smooth emulsification of egg yolks and butter sharpened with lemon juice, it has to be made with care and attention otherwise it may curdle. A non-aluminium pan is essential to prevent discoloration of the sauce. Using clarified unsalted butter gives the smoothest result as well as the best creamy flavour, and freshly squeezed lemon juice is a must. Hollandaise is served warm to accompany fish, vegetables or egg dishes and can be flavoured to suit the dish it is to accompany – herbs, mustard and orange juice are popular additions. The finished sauce cannot be reheated but can be kept warm for a short time.

Hollandaise Sauce

MAKES 300ML/½ PINT

225g/8oz unsalted butter
3 medium egg yolks
2 tablespoons water
salt and white pepper
juice of ½ lemon

EQUIPMENT
• **Small, heavy, non-aluminium saucepan**
• **Whisk**
• **Jug**

1 To clarify the butter, very gently melt it in a small pan. Skim the froth from the surface using a small spoon then carefully tip the melted butter into a clean pan or jug leaving the milky sediment at the bottom behind. Set aside the melted butter until it is tepid and discard the sediment.

2 Put the egg yolks and water into a small, heavy-based, non-aluminium saucepan and whisk them together, off the heat, until frothy.

Making Hollandaise Sauce

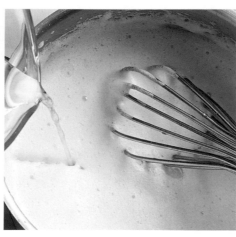

WATCHPOINTS
• Keep the heat very low. If the mixture of yolks and water gets too hot the eggs will scramble and you will have to start again.
• Add the butter very slowly and make sure that it is tepid, otherwise the sauce will split or separate.
• There is no need to throw a curdled sauce away: it can often be saved by vigorously whisking in an ice cube. If that fails, start again with 2 egg yolks and 2 tablespoons of water whisked to a mousse, then gradually whisk in the curdled mixture.

3 Set the pan over a very low heat and whisk constantly for 5 minutes or until the mixture is very thick and mousse-like.

4 Remove from the heat and, whisking constantly, pour in the melted butter in a slow, steady stream to make a thick sauce.

Variations: for a really light sauce, use 2 yolks for each 225g/8oz of butter – this can be a bit tricky as the mixture easily splits. Use 4 egg yolks to make a richer, thicker hollandaise.

Sauce Mousseline
Fold 60ml/2fl oz of crème fraîche or lightly whipped double cream into the hollandaise then taste and adjust the seasonings as necessary. Use to accompany vegetables, chicken and delicate white fish.

Sauce Moutarde
Make the hollandaise as given then stir in 1 tablespoon of Dijon mustard and season to taste. Add more mustard for a really piquant sauce. This goes well with crab and stronger flavoured fish, as well as grilled cutlets of meat or poultry.

5 Whisk the seasonings and lemon juice into the thickened sauce and serve as soon as possible. You can keep the sauce warm for 15 minutes or so by covering it and keeping it in a tepid water bath or bain-marie. Do not even think about using a microwave oven to reheat hollandaise.

Blender Hollandaise: Put the egg yolks (at room temperature) into the bowl of a food processor or blender with the water, lemon juice, salt and pepper and process briefly until just combined. Heat the clarified butter but do not allow it to boil. While the motor is running, pour the butter through the feed tube in a thin, steady stream. When the sauce is creamy and thick, adjust the seasoning to taste and serve.

ℳaking Crème ℳnglaise

Otherwise known as posh custard, this vanilla-flavoured dessert sauce is best made from egg yolks and rich, creamy milk – use Channel Islands milk or a combination of ordinary milk and single cream. Crème anglaise can be served warm, at room temperature, or chilled with a variety of sweet dishes but it particularly complements fruit and sponge puddings. If you prefer, the sauce can be flavoured as necessary with a variety of interesting ingredients including melted chocolate, coffee, cardamom and nutmeg. To make ice-cream, chill the finished custard then combine it with an equal quantity of whipped cream before freezing the mixture in an ice-cream machine.

Crème Anglaise

SERVES 4-6

1 vanilla pod
150ml/5fl oz very creamy milk
3 large egg yolks
25g/1oz caster sugar

EQUIPMENT
• Heavy pan with lid
• Small pointed knife
• Wooden spoon
• Large bowl
• Sieve

WATCHPOINTS
• *The sauce must be well-flavoured with vanilla otherwise it will taste insipid.*
• *Take care not to overheat the egg mixture or the eggs will scramble and the custard will be ruined.*

1 Split the vanilla pod in half lengthways, then put it into a heavy-based saucepan with the milk. Heat until scalding hot, then remove the pan from the heat, cover, and leave the milk to infuse for 15 minutes.

2 Remove the vanilla, but scrape the tiny black seeds from inside the pod back into the milk with the point of a small knife; the milk should look speckled.

Making Crème Anglaise

3 With a wooden spoon, beat the egg yolks and sugar together in a large bowl until the mixture is thick and pale.

4 Slowly pour the hot milk onto the yolk mixture, stirring constantly. Stand the bowl on a damp cloth to keep it stable.

Variations: *Chocolate Custard*
Add 50g/1¾oz of dark chocolate, very finely chopped, to the milk when you remove the vanilla. Stir until melted (you may need to warm it), then follow the recipe as given.

Espresso Custard
Replace the vanilla pod with 1½ tablespoons of very finely ground espresso coffee.

Cardamom Custard
Replace the vanilla with 5 lightly crushed green cardamom pods.

Apricot or Peach Custard
In a food processor, purée the flesh of 4 ripe apricots or 1 peach then pour in the custard and process until thoroughly combined.

5 Rinse out the milk pan, then pour the mixture back into it and cook over a very low heat, stirring constantly with a wooden spoon, until the custard thickens enough to coat the back of the spoon. This process may take 5 minutes, but do not be tempted to hurry it; if the custard boils, it will curdle and cannot be used.

6 Using a fine-meshed sieve, strain the thickened custard into a serving jug to give a completely smooth sauce. Serve it warm, if you like, or leave it to cool.

7 If you wish to keep the sauce, sprinkle the surface with a little sugar to prevent a skin forming. Leave it to cool, then cover and chill. Use the custard within 2 days.

Making Caramel Sauce

A shiny, lustrous sauce the colour of rich amber. The secret to making caramel successfully is patience. Watch it carefully and test regularly as demonstrated here – the simple sugar and water mixture can sometimes turn quicker than expected and, unfortunately, there is no saving a burnt caramel. You will find the result is worth a little trouble, however. The intermittent stages of sugar syrup are as versatile as the finished sauce and can be used for fruit salads and pouring over cakes. When completed, the caramel sauce can be served warm, at room temperature or chilled, with ice creams, creamy desserts like parfaits, mousses and bavarois, or with fresh fruit such as juicy sliced oranges or bananas.

Caramel Sauce

MAKES 300ML/½ PINT

240g/9oz granulated sugar
300ml/½ pint water

EQUIPMENT
• Scales
• Measuring jug
• Medium-sized saucepan
• Wooden spoon
• Natural bristle pastry brush
• Sugar thermometer (optional)
• Metal spoon
• Bowl of iced water
• White saucer
• Oven glove or tea towel

1 Put the sugar and 150ml/5fl oz of the water into a medium-sized heavy pan. Set over a low heat and stir frequently with a wooden spoon until the sugar dissolves. Do not let the mixture boil at this stage. From time to time, brush down the sides of the pan with a pastry brush dipped in hot water to dissolve any sugar crystals stuck to the side of the pan as these could cause crystallization. As soon as all the grains of sugar have dissolved, stop stirring and remove the wooden spoon.

2 Bring the syrup to a boil (you can add a sugar thermometer at this stage). Depending on the heat and size of the pan, the syrup will reach small thread stage (102°C/215°F) in about 30 seconds. To test this stage without a thermometer, let some syrup fall from a metal spoon: it should fall in a thin, short thread. Left at this stage, the syrup can be used for poaching fruit and when cooled can be kept in the refrigerator for up to 2 months.

Making Caramel Sauce

3 Boil the syrup for a further 2 minutes to reach soft ball stage (115°C/238°F). To test without a thermometer, drop about half a teaspoonful of the syrup into a bowl of ice cubes and water. You should then be able to roll it into a soft, pliable ball with your fingers. At this stage the syrup can be used to make fondant paste.

Continue boiling the syrup a further 3-4 minutes to achieve hard crack stage (157°C/315°F). The syrup is now pale gold. It will set hard if a little is dropped in iced water and will snap in two with a crack. At this stage it can be used for decorating cakes when a strong, distinct taste is not needed. Otherwise, continue boiling the syrup to produce a caramel.

WATCHPOINTS
- *Caution: hot caramel causes bad burns if it touches the skin.*
- *Do not use a tin-lined copper saucepan or a non-stick pan as the melting point of the lining may be below that of the caramel.*
- *Use a natural bristle brush rather than a nylon brush as the syrup will be very hot.*
- *Have a large bowl filled with icy-cold water at the ready. If the caramel is cooking too fast, stop it turning darker by immersing the base of the pan in very cold water.*
- *For accuracy, use a sugar thermometer. To prevent it cracking, put it into the syrup as soon as the sugar has dissolved. Cool the thermometer before washing it.*
- *If you don't have a thermometer, drop the syrup on a white plate to check the colour.*

4 At 160°C/320°F the caramel is a pale amber colour and has a mild flavour. It can be used for pouring over croque-embouche or meringue cakes and for spun sugar. Medium caramel (170°C/340°F) is a darker amber colour with a deep, rich taste. This is the stage required for caramel sauce or for crème caramel, where the caramel is poured into the base of a cooking mould.

5 To finish making the caramel sauce, remove the pan from the heat as soon as it reaches 170°C/340°F – the caramel could easily overcook and burn. Leave it to cool for a few seconds, or until it stops bubbling. Cover your hand with an oven glove or tea towel and pour in the remaining 150ml/5fl oz of water – take care as the caramel will boil up and splutter.

6 Cook gently until the caramel dissolves. For a thicker sauce, boil until syrupy. The sauce, once cold, can be kept in the refrigerator for up to 1 week.

Variations: *Creamy Caramel Sauce*
Replace the final 150ml/5fl oz of water with 150ml/5fl oz of cream.

Coffee Caramel Sauce
Replace the final 150ml/5fl oz of water with freshly brewed black coffee.

QUICK AND SIMPLE

The recipes featured in this chapter are the speediest, easiest ways to add interest to simply cooked meat, fish and vegetables. No real effort or special skills are needed, just some imaginative ingredients to create fresh, delicious, lively food that can be cooked in less time than it takes to order a takeaway.

We start with a selection of speedy dinners which incorporate the caramelized cooking juices of pan-fried meat, chicken and fish into an instant sauce. This method, known as deglazing, is perhaps the simplest way to make a sauce: you just stir in a little wine, brandy, cream or stock and other flavourings as desired. Gravies are also made in this fashion.

Some softened butter mashed with plenty of well-flavoured ingredients can be kept in the refrigerator to add to steamed vegetables, grilled meat or fish, even drained hot pasta. Again, the result is instant flavour and interest for very little effort.

Barbecues are now possible year-round thanks to gas barbecues, indoor stove grills and cast-iron grill pans, so I have included in this chapter some simple recipes for marinades, spice rubs, flavoured oils and barbecue bastes.

Use these ideas to make quick meals as enjoyable as any well-planned, highly organized dinner party.

Left (clockwise from right): Lime and Chilli Oil, Tomato and Onion Baste, Pistachio Butter and Mustard Butter.

Entrecôte Steak

This is one of the simplest of all sauces for beef but it is important that you use a good-quality jellied stock or tinned consommé.

SERVES 4

50g/1¾oz butter
4 beef rib steaks
100ml/3½fl oz well-reduced stock or canned beef consommé
100ml/3½fl oz red wine

Heat the butter in a large, heavy frying pan and, when it is sizzling, add the steak and cook for 3-5 minutes on each side. When the meat is done to your liking, remove it to a plate and keep warm.

Add the stock and wine to the pan to deglaze it: bring the liquid to a boil, stirring constantly to scrape up the caramelized cooking juices and incorporate them into the sauce. Simmer the sauce vigorously until it has reduced to a pouring consistency then pour it over the steaks and serve.

Variation: fry a shallot in the butter before adding the stock and red wine.

Deglazing a pan: pour in the liquid and stir vigorously, scraping the caramelized meat juices from the bottom of the pan and simmering until they dissolve to make a slightly thickened sauce.

Brandied Ginger Steak

SERVES 2

1-2 teaspoons ground ginger
2 beef fillet steaks
black pepper
1 teaspoon salt
25g/1oz butter
2 tablespoons brandy
1 tablespoon lemon juice
½ teaspoon Worcestershire sauce
1 tablespoon chopped parsley

Rub the ginger evenly into both sides of each steak, sprinkle them with black pepper and leave to stand for 10 minutes.

Sprinkle the salt evenly over the base of the frying pan and heat until it is lightly browned. Add the steaks to the pan and cook for 3 minutes over a fairly high heat. Turn the steaks then add the butter to the pan and continue cooking for 3-5 minutes or until the meat is done to your liking.

Add the brandy, lemon juice and the Worcestershire sauce to the pan and stir well, scraping up any sediment and moistening both sides of the steak with the pan juices. When the sauce is hot, serve it and the meat sprinkled with the parsley.

Devilled Steak

SERVES 2

2 beef fillet steaks
black pepper
150g/5½oz butter
1 clove garlic, crushed
2 tablespoons Worcestershire sauce
2 tablespoons chopped parsley

Lightly season each side of the steaks with black pepper. In a large frying pan, melt the butter and heat until sizzling. Add the steak and cook for 2-3 minutes. While the first side is cooking, rub the crushed garlic into

the top of each steak. Turn the steak over and continue cooking on the other side.

Deglaze the pan with the Worcestershire sauce and swirl the steaks round in it. When the meat is cooked to your liking, sprinkle it with chopped parsley and serve.

Pepper Steaks with Cream and Mushrooms

SERVES 4

2 tablespoons mixed peppercorns, crushed
4 beef fillet steaks
1 tablespoon olive oil
25g/1oz butter
1 clove garlic, crushed
200g/7oz mushrooms, sliced
2 tablespoons brandy
150ml/5fl oz single cream
salt

Press the crushed peppercorns into the steaks. Heat the oil and butter in a large frying pan, add the steaks and cook them over a high heat to your liking. Remove the steaks from the pan and keep them warm while you make the sauce.

Add the garlic and mushrooms to the pan and cook them briefly in the cooking juices. Deglaze the pan with the brandy and simmer it for 1 minute, then add the cream and cook the sauce over a low heat until it thickens. Season to taste with salt and pour the sauce over the steaks.

Pork Piccata

SERVES 2

25g/1oz butter
2 pork escalopes
juice of 1 lemon or 80ml/3fl oz marsala
salt and black pepper

*P*AN *S*AUCES

In a heavy frying pan, melt the butter until sizzling and add the pork escalopes. Cook them for 2-3 minutes on each side, then remove from the pan and keep warm.

Add the lemon juice or marsala to the pan and bring to a boil, stirring constantly to incorporate the caramelized cooking juices. When the sauce has reduced by a third, season it to taste then serve with the veal.

Pork Fillet with Cognac

A useful recipe for those times when you need to cook a smart dinner really quickly with the minimum of effort.

SERVES 4

2 small pork fillets, about 650g/1lb 7oz in total
½ teaspoon coarsely ground black pepper
50g/2oz unsalted butter
2 medium shallots, finely chopped
2 small cloves garlic, crushed
4 tablespoons cognac
4 tablespoons vegetable or chicken stock
salt

Cut the pork fillets into thick rounds about 2cm/¾in wide, then toss them in the black pepper until evenly coated. Heat the butter in a large, heavy frying pan and cook the pork in batches for 3-4 minutes over a moderate heat until browned on each side and cooked through – the meat should not be pink. Transfer the pork to a warm serving dish and keep it hot while making the sauce.

Add the shallot and garlic to the pan and fry, stirring constantly, for 2-3 minutes until soft and golden. Add the cognac and stock to the pan and stir vigorously over a medium heat to scrape off and dissolve all the caramelized cooking juices stuck on the bottom of the pan. Simmer the sauce for a few seconds then taste and add salt as necessary. Spoon the sauce over the pork and serve immediately.

Lamb with Marsala, Tomato and Olive Sauce

SERVES 4

2 tablespoons olive oil
4 lamb chops or steaks
1 small shallot, finely chopped
1 clove garlic, crushed
4 tablespoons marsala
2 plum tomatoes, peeled, seeded and sliced
1 rounded tablespoon chopped black olives
black pepper

Heat the oil in a large, heavy frying pan and cook the meat to your liking. Remove to a plate and keep warm.

Add the shallot and garlic to the pan and stir over a low heat until softened. Pour in the marsala and stir well to incorporate the caramelized cooking juices.

Bring the mixture to a boil, add the tomatoes and simmer for 2 minutes. Remove the pan from the heat and stir in the olives, then add pepper to taste. Stir any juices that have collected from the meat into the sauce and serve immediately.

Variation: beef or pork steaks and chops can be used instead of lamb.

Below: Pork Fillet with Cognac makes a quick but classy dinner party dish, here stylishly presented with wild rice and sugar snap peas.

Sole Meunière

A *meunière* is a miller's wife, so this sauce, at once incredibly easy and very satisfying, involves coating the fish in flour before cooking it in butter. Once on the plate, the fish is doused in lemon juice, chopped parsley and the nut-brown pan juices. If you are cooking for more than two, you may have to fry the fish in batches or use two pans, which is why I am giving the quantities per person. You need to work quickly at the end, so have all the ingredients ready.

SERVES 1

½ tablespoon plain flour
salt and pepper
1 small whole sole or 2 small sole fillets,
    cleaned, skinned and trimmed
35g/1½oz clarified butter
juice of ½ lemon
½ tablespoon finely chopped fresh parsley
lemon wedge

Spread the flour out on a large plate and season it thoroughly with salt and pepper. Coat the fish on both sides with the flour, making sure it is generously coated, then shake to remove any excess.

Heat the butter in a large, heavy frying pan and, when it is starting to turn light golden brown in colour, add the fish (if you are cooking fillets, place them in the pan skin-side uppermost). Cook the sole fillets for 2-2½ minutes on each side, a whole fish for 4-5 minutes on each side, depending on the size and thickness.

Remove the cooked fish to a warm serving plate. Quickly pour the lemon juice over the fish, sprinkle it with the chopped parsley and then pour over the hot pan juices – the butter should be a nice nut-brown or *noisette*. Add the lemon wedge to garnish and serve immediately.

Variations: fish such as trout and plaice can be used instead of sole.

Above: Sole Meunière is a fast French favourite in which lemon and parsley add piquancy to a buttery sauce for pan-fried fish.

Cod in Oatmeal with Mild Mustard Sauce

SERVES 4

4 cod fillets, about 200g/7oz each, skinned
2 tablespoons seasoned flour
1 egg, beaten
140g/5oz medium oatmeal
1 tablespoon vegetable oil

25g/1oz unsalted butter
4 tablespoons single cream
1 tablespoon wholegrain mustard
1 tablespoon lemon juice
salt and pepper

Pan Sauces

Roll the fish fillets in the flour, dusting off the excess, then dip them in the egg to coat evenly. Drain off the excess then coat in the oatmeal, pressing it on well. Chill the fish for 15 minutes or until ready to cook.

Heat the oil and butter in a large, heavy frying pan. Cook the fish for 3-4 minutes on each side or until brown and cooked through. Drain on kitchen paper and keep warm.

Pour off all but 2 tablespoons of fat from the pan. Stir in the cream, mustard, lemon juice and seasoning to taste. Heat the sauce thoroughly but do not allow it to boil or it will turn bitter. Taste and adjust the seasoning as necessary then serve with the fish.

Variations: use halibut instead of cod or replace the fish with skinned boneless chicken breasts, turkey escalopes or pork.

Salmon with Roasted Garlic and Coriander

SERVES 4

1 whole bulb garlic
2 tablespoons olive oil
4 salmon steaks
3 tablespoons red wine
2 tablespoons chopped coriander
salt and pepper

Preheat the oven to 190°C/375°F/Gas 5. Separate the garlic cloves but leave them unpeeled. Put them in a baking dish and roast in the hot oven for 15 minutes or until soft and golden. Allow to cool slightly.

Meanwhile, heat the oil in a large, heavy frying pan and cook the salmon to your liking. Remove from the pan and keep warm.

Lower the heat and squeeze the garlic cloves from their skins into the pan. Stir gently to break up the garlic then add the wine and simmer for 2-3 minutes, stirring constantly, to make a thick sauce.

Stir in the coriander then taste and season as necessary. Add any juices from the fish to the sauce and serve immediately.

Variations: this dish can be made with roast lamb or beef, pan-fried meats and with well-flavoured fish such as cod and halibut. Vary the herb to suit the meat or fish.

Chicken with Green Peppercorn Sauce

SERVES 2

40g/1½oz unsalted butter
2 chicken breast fillets, skinned
1 tablespoon lemon juice
2 tablespoons canned green peppercorns, drained and rinsed
2 egg yolks, beaten
100ml/3½fl oz crème fraîche
1 teaspoon Dijon mustard
salt and pepper

Melt the butter in a large, heavy frying pan. Add the chicken and cook it for 4 minutes on each side or until thoroughly cooked. Remove from the pan and keep warm.

Add the lemon juice and peppercorns to the pan and cook for 1 minute. Stir in the remaining ingredients and cook the sauce over a low heat until it thickens. Adjust the seasonings as necessary and serve the sauce immediately with the chicken.

Chestnut Cream Chicken

SERVES 2

1 tablespoon olive oil
2 chicken breast fillets, skinned
1 tablespoon unsweetened chestnut purée
4 tablespoons double cream
salt and pepper

Heat the oil in a heavy-based frying pan and cook the chicken breasts over a medium-high heat for 4 minutes on each side, or until thoroughly cooked. Remove the chicken from the pan and keep warm.

Add the chestnut purée and the cream to the pan and stir vigorously to break down the purée and incorporate the caramelized cooking juices from the chicken into the sauce. When the sauce is smooth, allow it to simmer gently for 1 minute then taste and season as necessary with salt and plenty of pepper. If the sauce is too thick, stir in more cream. Serve the sauce with the chicken.

Variations: this dish can also be made with turkey escalopes or with pork chops, which also suit the sweet flavour of the sauce.

Chorizo with Onions and Sherry Vinegar

SERVES 2

4 chorizo frying sausages
2 medium onions, sliced
2-3 tablespoons sherry vinegar

Place the chorizo in a small-medium frying pan over a gentle heat and cook them slowly until the sausages exude enough fat to fry the onions. Add the onions to the pan and continue cooking, stirring occasionally, until the onions are softened and beginning to caramelize. Turn the sausages regularly so that they brown evenly.

Remove the chorizo and onions to serving plates and add the vinegar to the pan. Raise the heat and bring the liquid to a vigorous boil, stirring constantly to incorporate the caramelized pan juices. Pour the sauce over the chorizo and onions and serve.

Variation: stir 1-2 tablespoons of cream into the sauce at the last minute, if desired.

Traditional Gravy

The best gravy is made simply from the meat juices left behind in the roasting pan after the roasted meat or poultry has been transferred to a carving board. Old-fashioned gravy is thickened with flour so the gravy lightly coats the back of a spoon, however today's thin, flourless gravy tends to be called jus as it is made just from the meat juices deglazed with a little stock or wine. In each case the gravy must have a good flavour, neither watery and weak, nor so strong and sticky it overwhelms the taste of the meat. It should moisten and enhance. This recipe is suitable for any roast joint or bird – beef, lamb, pork, venison, chicken, turkey, pheasant and other game.

SERVES 4-6

2 tablespoons plain flour
450ml/16fl oz stock
salt and pepper

Transfer the cooked meat or bird to a carving board or warmed serving plate, cover loosely with kitchen foil and leave to stand for 15 minutes before carving for the meat juices to settle.

Carefully remove the excess fat from the roasting tin but retain all the meat juices. Leave a couple of spoonfuls of fat in the pan to make the gravy. Put the roasting tin on top of the stove and stir in the flour, blending it well into the fat and meat juices. Cook for 2-3 minutes over a medium heat, stirring constantly until the flour is golden.

Stir in the stock and bring the mixture to a boil, stirring constantly to make a smooth thickened gravy. Simmer for 2-3 minutes then taste and season with salt and pepper.

Strain the gravy into a warmed sauceboat and serve piping hot. It is important that gravy is quickly cooled then chilled or frozen if it is not being used immediately. It can be kept in the refrigerator for 2 days, or in the freezer for up to 1 month.

Variations: *Flavoured Gravies*
For roast chicken and turkey, add 1-2 tablespoons of good cranberry jelly along with the stock or add 1 tablespoon of finely chopped fresh thyme after straining.

For pork, add 1-2 teaspoons of finely chopped sage with the stock. Alternatively, add the pared rind of 1 lemon along with the stock, then 1 tablespoon of finely chopped coriander after straining. If necessary, add a squeeze of lemon juice with the seasoning.

Unthickened Gravy/Jus
Follow the recipe for Traditional Gravy but discard all the fat and omit the flour. Add the stock and deglaze the roasting pan over a fairly high heat to dislodge and dissolve all the caramelized meat juices.

Rosemary Gravy

This gravy for roast lamb is quick to make providing the herb-flavoured stock is prepared in advance.

MAKES 175ML/6FL OZ

2 tablespoons red wine
1 tablespoon redcurrant jelly
1 tablespoon arrowroot or potato flour (fecule)
1 tablespoon cold water
salt and pepper
FOR THE STOCK:
500g/1lb 2oz lamb bones and trimmings
handful of rosemary sprigs
1 medium onion, quartered
2 carrots, thickly sliced
½ teaspoon peppercorns
1.7 litres/3 pints cold water

To make the stock, preheat the oven to 200°C/400°F/Gas 6. Put the lamb bones in a roasting tin and cook them in the hot oven for 30 minutes or until well browned.

In a large saucepan or stockpot, put the roasted bones, meat trimmings, rosemary, vegetables, peppercorns and cold water and bring to a boil. Thoroughly skim the stock then simmer it gently for 2 hours.

Cool the stock then strain it and discard the flavourings. Chill overnight and, next day, remove all the fat from the surface.

Pour the stock into a medium-sized, heavy-based pan and boil until it has reduced to 150ml/¼ pint. At this point the stock can be cooled and stored in the refrigerator for 2 days or frozen for up to 1 month.

Once the meat has been roasted, remove it from the roasting tin and keep warm. Skim all the fat from the tin, reserving the meat juices, then add the wine and deglaze the pan over a medium heat. Add the stock and the redcurrant jelly and simmer gently for 2 minutes, stirring.

Mix the arrowroot or potato flour with the tablespoon of water then pour the mixture into the sauce, stirring constantly. It should thicken instantly. Remove it from the heat, taste and season as necessary. Add any juices that have collected around the meat then strain into a warm sauce boat and serve.

Onion Gravy

Although this is a traditional, homely sauce, it nonetheless demands attention to detail.

SERVES 4-6

1 tablespoon vegetable oil
25g/1oz unsalted butter
500g/1lb 2oz onions, finely sliced
large pinch of fresh or dried thyme leaves or
   chopped fresh sage
1 clove garlic, crushed (optional)
1 tablespoon plain flour
350ml/12fl oz stock
salt and ground black pepper

Heat the oil and butter in a large, heavy frying pan. Add the onions, herbs and garlic, if using, and stir well. Cover the onions with

*G*RAVIES

Old-fashioned Liver and Bacon·

Lamb's liver and well-produced smoked back bacon are a classic team.

SERVES 4

500g/1lb 2oz lamb's liver
3 tablespoons seasoned flour
400g/14oz onions, finely sliced
3 tablespoons vegetable oil
250g/9oz back bacon, rind removed
300ml/½ pint beef stock
1 tablespoon lemon juice
salt and pepper
4 tablespoons extra stock or red wine

Trim the liver, removing any membranes and cutting out any ducts with kitchen scissors. Cut the meat into wide strips and toss in the seasoned flour. Shake off any excess and set the liver and flour aside separately.

Cook the onions in 2 tablespoons of the oil in a large, heavy frying pan for about 20 minutes or until soft and slightly golden, then raise the heat and fry the onions, stirring, until they are a rich golden brown. Drain the onions and keep them warm. Meanwhile, grill the bacon and keep it warm.

Heat the remaining tablespoon of oil in the pan and quickly fry the liver on both sides until cooked to your liking; do not overcook it or it will turn hard and gritty. Remove the liver from the pan and keep it warm.

Remove the frying pan from the heat and sprinkle in the reserved flour. Gradually stir in the stock followed by the lemon juice and seasoning. Return to the heat, bring the mixture to a boil, stirring constantly, then simmer for 2-3 minutes. The sauce should coat the back of a spoon. Taste and adjust the seasoning, adding the extra stock or red wine if the mixture is too thick.

Spoon the onions onto a warmed plate, arrange the liver and bacon on top and serve the gravy separately.

Above: succulent grilled sausages are topped with a rich Onion Gravy and accompanied by creamy mashed potatoes to make a warming meal.

a lid or a disc of dampened greaseproof paper then cook very gently for 25 minutes or until meltingly soft, stirring occasionally.

Remove the lid, raise the heat under the pan and continue cooking the onions, stirring frequently, until they are a dark chestnut brown but not burned. Stir in the flour and cook, stirring constantly, until the flour is light brown in colour.

Add the stock and bring the mixture to a boil, stirring constantly to give a thickened gravy. Simmer gently for about 10 minutes, stirring frequently. Season to taste with salt and pepper and serve the gravy piping hot.

Variations: for a stronger flavour, replace 100ml/3½fl oz of the stock with an equal quantity of red wine, white wine or beer.

Serve with good grilled sausages, fried liver, toad-in-the-hole or roast beef. You can make an onion soup by adding some extra stock.

Flavoured Butters and Oils

Maître d'Hôtel Butter (Parsley Butter)

SERVES 4-6

¼ teaspoon sea salt
1½ tablespoons finely chopped parsley
juice of ½ lemon
100g/3½oz unsalted butter, softened
black pepper

In a small bowl, beat the sea salt, parsley and lemon juice into the butter until well combined, then add black pepper to taste.

   Place the butter on a piece of greaseproof paper, or kitchen foil, and use the paper to help shape the butter into a cylinder about 3cm/1¼in across. When tightly wrapped, chill until firm. Store in the refrigerator for up to 1 week or freeze for 1 month.

This classic butter is traditionally served with grilled meat and fish or vegetable dishes.

Anchovy Butter

SERVES 4-6

8 anchovy fillets, finely chopped
100g/3½oz unsalted butter, softened
squeeze lemon juice
pinch cayenne pepper
black pepper

Pound the anchovies to a paste in a mortar. Thoroughly blend the anchovy with the softened butter then work in the remaining ingredients to taste. Shape and store as for the Maître d'Hôtel Butter (see left).

Variations: *Smoked Salmon Butter*
Replace the anchovies with 60g/2¼oz of pounded smoked salmon.

Pistachio Butter
For an attractive topping for fish, chicken or rice, omit the lemon juice and cayenne pepper and replace the anchovies with 1 tablespoon of pounded pistachio nuts.

Serve with fish, pasta and potatoes. I use anchovy butter to make the roux when preparing a béchamel sauce for fish pies.

Four Pepper Butter

SERVES 4-6

¼ teaspoon crushed sea salt
⅛ teaspoon cayenne pepper
½ teaspoon paprika
¼ teaspoon ground black pepper
1 teaspoon very finely chopped red chilli
100g/3½oz unsalted butter, softened

In a small bowl, beat the sea salt, cayenne pepper, paprika, black pepper and chopped red chilli with the butter until thoroughly combined. Shape and store as for the Maître d'Hôtel Butter (see left).

Variation: *Ginger and Lemongrass Butter*
Add 1 teaspoon of very finely chopped lemongrass, 1 teaspoon of finely grated root ginger and ¼ teaspoon of finely grated lime rind to the butter instead using the salt, cayenne, paprika, black pepper and chilli.

Grilled meats and fish, pasta and rice or vegetable dishes go well with this butter.

Left (from left to right): Four Pepper, Pistachio, Wholegrain Mustard and Smoked Salmon butters are as delicious as they are colourful.

Horseradish Butter

SERVES 4-6

¼ teaspoon crushed sea salt
1 tablespoon finely grated fresh horseradish
100g/3½oz unsalted butter, softened
black pepper

Beat the salt and horseradish into the butter, adding the pepper to taste. Shape and store as for the Maître d'Hôtel Butter (see left).

Variations: replace the horseradish with 4 teaspoons of wholegrain mustard, or with 1½ tablespoons of Pernod.

To go with steaks, cold beef sandwiches, hot smoked fish and grilled trout.

Aromatic Oil

Peanut oil is specified for this recipe as it works best at high temperatures.

MAKES 125ML/4FL OZ

125ml/4fl oz peanut oil
4 cloves garlic, peeled
1 large sprig thyme
1 large sprig rosemary
2 small dried chillies
½ teaspoon sea salt
¼ teaspoon ground black pepper

Put all the ingredients into a large, screw-topped jar, replace the lid and shake well to combine. Leave the oil at room temperature for several hours before use or store it in the refrigerator for no more than 3 days.

Use Aromatic Oil to roast, barbecue or grill vegetables. This very handy mixture can also be used for roasting or grilling meat and fish, or as a quick salad dressing.

Lime and Chilli Oil

MAKES 350ML/12FL OZ

pared rind of 1 lime
350ml/12fl oz virgin olive oil
3 red chillies
handful of basil leaves
1 tablespoon mixed peppercorns

Stir all the ingredients together then pour them into a bottle or jug and leave to infuse for at least 30 minutes before use. Store in the refrigerator for no more than 3 days.

Above: fresh herb sprigs, chilli and garlic are marinated in peanut oil to give an Aromatic Oil suitable for roasting and grilling fresh vegetables.

Variation: for a Thai flavour, add a stalk of lemongrass, lightly crushed with a rolling pin, to the bottle.

You will find this zesty mixture a very good basting oil for fresh seafood, especially meaty fish such as grilled or barbecued salmon, swordfish or tuna steaks.

Simple Soy Baste

FOR 2-6 SERVINGS

2 tablespoons Japanese soy sauce
2 tablespoons unsalted butter, melted

In a small bowl, mix together the soy sauce and melted butter and brush the liquid onto the food before grilling.

What treatment could be simpler for meat, fish and vegetables?

Tikka Marinade

FOR 4 SERVINGS OF MEAT OR POULTRY

3 cloves garlic, chopped
1 medium red onion, chopped
1.5cm/½in piece root ginger, chopped
1 heaped tablespoon blanched almonds
1 teaspoon ground coriander
½ teaspoon ground cumin
½ teaspoon garam masala
½ teaspoon sea salt
juice of 1 lemon
3 tablespoons plain set whole milk yogurt

Place all the ingredients for the marinade in the bowl of a food processor and process to make a thick, almost smooth paste, scraping down the sides of the bowl frequently.

Pour the marinade over your choice of meat or poultry and mix thoroughly. Cover and leave to marinate for 1-12 hours in the refrigerator.

Variations: for a hotter effect, replace the garam masala with chilli powder.

My preference is to use chicken thighs as they stay moist and juicy during grilling, and they have the best flavour. Chicken breasts, turkey meat or lean leg of lamb can also be used. Cut the meat into generous cubes before marinating. When ready to cook, loosely thread the cubes of meat onto metal skewers – if the pieces are placed too tightly together they will not cook evenly. Place under a very hot grill until cooked through, turning the skewers frequently. They can be served hot or cold, with naan bread or warm pitta and salad.

Red Spicy Marinade

By adjusting the amount of Tabasco, this marinade for grilled and oven-roasted meat can be mildly flavoured or hot and fiery.

FOR 4 SERVINGS OF MEAT OR POULTRY

1 tablespoon sweet paprika
1 tablespoon ground coriander
¼ teaspoon garam masala
4 drops Tabasco, or more to taste
3 cloves garlic, crushed
¼ teaspoon freshly ground black pepper
¼ teaspoon sea salt
juice of 1 lemon
1 tablespoon olive oil

Combine all the ingredients to make a thick paste then smear it all over the meat, in each and every crevice. Cover and leave to marinate on a non-metallic plate in the refrigerator for at least 1 hour and for up to 12 hours.

For the best flavour and texture, I prefer to use large boneless chicken thighs with the skin left on, as the darker meat of the chicken remains moist even when thoroughly cooked. You could also use meaty spare rib pork chops. Grill the marinated pieces of chicken or pork, or you can cook them in a greased non-metallic baking dish in a hot oven, basting the meat occasionally with the marinade. Dot with butter for a richer taste.

Apricot Marinade with Yogurt Sauce

The idea for this unusual recipe comes from South Africa, where its sunny flavours are a favourite with barbecued meats.

FOR 4 SERVINGS OF MEAT OR POULTRY

1 tablespoon olive oil
1 small onion, chopped
2 bay leaves
2 cloves garlic, chopped
½ teaspoon ground cinnamon
½ teaspoon ground coriander
½ teaspoon ground cumin
½ teaspoon turmeric
1 teaspoon chilli powder
juice of 1 lemon
4 tablespoons sherry
2 tablespoons brown sugar
100g/3½oz apricot jam
FOR THE SAUCE:
4 rashers bacon
75ml/2½fl oz Greek yogurt

Heat the oil in a frying pan, add the onion and bay leaves and cook over a low heat, stirring frequently, for 5 minutes. Add the garlic to the pan and continue cooking for another 5 minutes or until the onion is softened but not browned.

Add the spices, lemon juice, sherry, sugar and jam to the pan then bring to a boil and simmer for 5 minutes, stirring occasionally. Transfer the mixture to a large bowl and leave it to cool before adding your choice of meat. Cover and marinate the meat in the refrigerator.for a minimum of 2 hours and a maximum of 24 hours

Meanwhile, grill or fry the bacon until very crisp, then leave it to cool. Crumble the bacon into a small bowl and set it aside.

When ready to cook the meat, remove it from the marinade, allowing the excess to drip back into the bowl. Transfer the marinade to a small saucepan. Bring it to a

$\mathscr{M}$ARINADES AND $\mathscr{B}$ASTES

boil and simmer for 2-3 minutes until thick. Remove the sauce from the heat and stir in the yogurt and bacon. Serve with the meat.

———— 🥄 ————

This marinade is suitable for chicken, lamb or pork, barbecued or grilled. Marinate them as whole portions or, to make kebabs, dice the flesh before marinating.

Tomato and Onion Baste

FOR 6-8 SERVINGS OF MEAT OR POULTRY

50ml/2fl oz tomato ketchup
50g/2oz onion, finely chopped
2 tablespoons Worcestershire Sauce
2 tablespoons cider vinegar
½ teaspoon English mustard powder
2-3 drops Tabasco Sauce, or to taste

In a medium bowl, stir all the ingredients together then allow the mixture to stand for 30 minutes before use.

The sauce can be kept covered in the refrigerator for up to 3 weeks.

———— 🥄 ————

Use as a baste for chicken, lamb and pork.

Five-Spice Marinade

FOR 4 SERVINGS OF MEAT OR POULTRY

1 tablespoon five-spice powder
2 tablespoons rice wine
2 tablespoons honey
2 tablespoons soy sauce
1 teaspoon sesame oil
2 cloves garlic, crushed
2cm/¾in piece root ginger, grated

Combine all the ingredients in a large bowl, then add your choice of meat or poultry and turn until thoroughly coated in the mixture. Cover and leave at room temperature for 30 minutes, or cover and marinate in the refrigerator for up to 6 hours.

When you are ready to cook the meat or poultry, remove it from the marinade, allowing any excess to drip back into the bowl. Bring the leftover marinade to a boil in a small pan, then brush the hot marinade onto the meat as it cooks.

———— 🥄 ————

I particularly like this marinade with meaty, well-flavoured pork spare rib chops, but it can also be used to enhance skinless chicken breasts, beef steaks and kebabs. The meat can be cooked on a barbecue, under a grill or on a cast-iron grill pan.

Left: brushing the hot Five-Spice Marinade, with its peppery sweet-and-sour flavour, onto pork spare ribs during cooking will give a thick, tasty coat to the meat and keep it moist.

Marinades and Bastes

Spicy Lemon Marinade

You'll find this marinade works well on both roast lamb and chicken, giving a crisp, fragrantly spicy exterior while helping to keep the meat moist during cooking.

FOR 1 JOINT OF MEAT OR WHOLE CHICKEN

1 lemon
½ tablespoon sea salt
½ teaspoon freshly ground black pepper
½ teaspoon ground cumin
½ teaspoon garam masala
1 tablespoon olive oil

Grate the rind from the lemon and then squeeze the juice. Mix them together in a small bowl with the other ingredients.

Below: crispy roast chicken is enhanced by a Spicy Lemon Marinade, made from a mixture of lemon, oil and aromatic spices.

Brush the marinade over a leg or shoulder of lamb, or a whole chicken, then leave, uncovered if possible, in a cool spot (not the refrigerator) for 1-2 hours before roasting. The excess marinade can be used to baste the meat during cooking.

Saffron Marinade

Saffron works particularly well with fish.

FOR 4 SERVINGS OF FISH

½ teaspoon saffron threads
4 tablespoons boiling water
4 tablespoons dry white wine
125ml/4fl oz virgin olive oil
sea salt and pepper

Crumble the saffron into a small heatproof bowl and pour over the boiling water. Cover

and leave to soak for 15 minutes or, if possible, overnight. Stir the wine, oil and seasonings into the saffron. Brush the marinade over both sides of the fish until it is well coated. Keep any leftover marinade to brush over the fish during baking.

Leave the fish to marinate for 20 minutes at room temperature (unless the weather is very hot), or for up to 12 hours in the refrigerator, well-covered. Bake in a hot oven until the fish is opaque.

Almost any fish fillets can be used with this marinade: thick skinless cod or haddock, large plaice, lemon sole, chunky pieces of monkfish, John Dory, halibut. Serve with small potatoes baked in an earthenware pot with unpeeled garlic, shallots and thyme.

Lime Marinade

This is a sweet citrus-flavoured marinade for chicken or fish.

FOR 4 SERVINGS OF CHICKEN OR FISH

grated rind and juice of 2 large limes
½ teaspoon sea salt, or to taste
freshly ground black pepper
4 teaspoons demerara sugar
4 teaspoons olive oil

Mix all the ingredients together in a non-metallic shallow dish. Add the chicken or fish and coat it thoroughly with the mixture. Cover and leave to marinate for 10-20 minutes at room temperature or cover and marinate for up to 12 hours in the refrigerator.

When ready to cook, lift the chicken or fish out of the marinade and cook under a heated grill or on a barbecue, using the leftover marinade to baste it as it cooks.

Variation: add 1 teaspoon of finely chopped fresh coriander to the marinade.

Marinades and Bastes

Excellent for thick steaks of fresh tuna, as well as salmon, halibut, cutlets of cod, or skinned and boned chicken pieces.

Rosemary Marinade

A robust marinade that doubles as a simple sauce. Use freshly squeezed fruit juices and fresh rosemary for the best result.

FOR 4 SERVINGS OF FISH

1 small red onion, finely chopped
1 heaped tablespoon finely chopped rosemary
1 large clove garlic, crushed
strip of pared lemon rind
125ml/4fl oz lemon juice
125ml/4fl oz orange juice
125ml/4fl oz dry white wine
50ml/2fl oz soy sauce
¼ teaspoon coarsely ground black pepper

Put all the ingredients into a non-aluminium saucepan and slowly bring to a boil. Remove the pan from the heat and leave the mixture to cool completely before use.

When ready, pour the cooled marinade over the fish and turn it in the mixture until thoroughly coated. Cover the dish and leave to marinate for 30 minutes. If you wish to leave the fish in the marinade for longer, you can refrigerate it for up to 4 hours.

To make a sauce from the marinade, return it to the pan and boil the mixture rapidly until it has reduced to a syrupy sauce. Keep the sauce warm until needed then serve it alongside the fish.

Firm-fleshed, well-flavoured fish steaks such as halibut, salmon, shark, swordfish and tuna work best with this marinade but it is also delicious with small whole fish like sardines and mackerel that have been slashed several times on each side before marinating. You may need to brush the fish, the grill pan or the barbecue with oil before cooking to prevent it sticking.

Herb Marinade

An excellent European-style marinade for beef featuring chopped fresh green herbs, red wine vinegar and crushed garlic.

FOR 4 SERVINGS OF BEEF

6 tablespoons olive oil
6 tablespoons red wine vinegar
4 large cloves garlic, crushed
freshly ground black pepper
4 tablespoons finely chopped mixed herbs such as basil, oregano, parsley and thyme

Combine all the ingredients in a shallow non-metallic dish. Add the meat and coat it thoroughly in the marinade. Cover the dish

Above: Rosemary Marinade is used to flavour kebabs made from tender cubes of fresh halibut, grilled and then drizzled with the reduced sauce.

and leave the meat to marinate for up to 2 hours in the refrigerator or, preferably, for up to 2 days.

When ready to cook, remove the meat from the marinade, reserving any liquid left in the dish to use as a baste during cooking.

Use this marinade for grilled and barbecued beef steaks or for roasted joints. For maximum flavour, aim to marinate the meat for as long as possible.

$\mathscr{S}$UMMER $\mathscr{S}$AUCES

Warm weather food should employ the wealth of gorgeous produce in the market – it is hard to resist snatching up the first bundle of asparagus, or tiny purple globe artichokes, or broad beans the size of a small fingernail. This is the time to make vibrant vegetables the focus of the meal, and relegate meat and fish to the sidelines.

Salad dressings and vinaigrettes should add flavour and moisture without overwhelming the principal ingredients of the dish. Choose a delicate dressing of extra virgin olive oil, white wine vinegar and seasoning for mild, tender green leaves; cold cooked tiny leeks can support a more robust mixture including a little garlic and plenty of herbs. Crunchy, hearty leaves or potatoes benefit from a thicker, more intensely flavoured dressing.

Dips and spreads, made ahead then chilled, are ideal for outdoor eating and picnics. Add a bowl of colourful sliced vegetables, some really interesting breads, a couple of cheeses, perhaps a pâté, and there you have lunch.

For cooler evenings, when appetites are flagging, warm salads are a happy medium between a hot meal and a snack.

Left (from left to right): Tartare Sauce, Cottage Cheese and Walnut Dip, Dressing for Crispy Duck Salad, Lemon Vinaigrette.

Basic Vinaigrette

This is the easiest, quickest sauce you can make, yet it really makes a salad come alive. Vinaigrette is infinitely variable, so you can add herbs, spices and other flavourings to suit your meal. The usual proportions of vinaigrette are one part vinegar to three parts oil but I find this too sharp, and prefer the mellower flavour that comes with increasing the oil.

MAKES 150ML/5FL OZ

2 tablespoons vinegar
2 teaspoons Dijon mustard
salt and pepper
125ml/4fl oz oil

Put all the ingredients into a screw-topped jar, fasten it tightly then shake well. Taste and adjust the flavour-balance as necessary: if the dressing is too oily, add a teaspoon more vinegar and a little extra seasoning; if it is too sharp, add another 1-2 teaspoons of oil and a large pinch of salt.

The vinaigrette can be kept chilled in the refrigerator for up to 1 week. Bring it back to room temperature and shake the jar well before using.

Variation: for a herb vinaigrette, allow 2 tablespoons of freshly chopped herbs, and add them just before using.

Lime or Lemon Vinaigrette

A dash of sugar enhances the citrus flavour.

MAKES 175ML/6FL OZ

1 lime or lemon
salt and pepper
½ teaspoon sugar
4 tablespoons extra virgin olive oil
4 tablespoons sunflower oil

Wash, dry and finely grate the rind of the lime or lemon and squeeze the juice from the fruit. Combine the grated rind with 2 tablespoons of the juice in a mixing bowl. Add a little salt, pepper and the sugar, then whisk in the two oils. Taste and add more lime juice if necessary. The dressing should taste quite sharp.

Below: the sweet-sour flavour of a zesty Lime Vinaigrette makes a lively dressing for this tropical Avocado, Papaya and Watercress Salad.

Avocado, Papaya and Watercress Salad

A real taste of the tropics, this salad combines a tangy vinaigrette with the rich flavours of exotic papaya and avocado.

SERVES 4

large bunch watercress
2 avocados
2 papayas
175ml/6fl oz Lime Vinaigrette (see left)

$\mathscr{V}$ INAIGRETTES

Rinse the watercress and trim off the coarse stalks. Halve, stone and peel the avocados, then slice them widthways. Halve the papayas and remove the black seeds. Peel the skin off with a sharp knife and cut the flesh into slices crossways.

Arrange the slices of papaya and avocado and the sprigs of watercress on four plates or combine them gently in a bowl. Pour the dressing over the top and serve immediately.

Variation: fresh, ripe mangoes can be substituted for the papayas.

Lime and Walnut Dressing

Walnuts are one of the most versatile nuts, suitable for a wide range of sweet and savoury dishes, however they do turn rancid quickly. You can keep walnuts at their best by storing them in the freezer.

MAKES 175ML/6FL OZ

50g/1¾oz walnuts
1 lime
2 tablespoons walnut oil
2 tablespoons olive oil
1 teaspoon Dijon mustard
salt and pepper

Finely chop the walnuts and squeeze the juice from the lime. Place all the ingredients together in a small bowl and whisk until thoroughly combined. Season to taste with salt and pepper.

Combine this dressing with some crisp green salad leaves and your choice of chicken or seafood. Fillets or pieces of grilled mackerel or lightly poached trout are a particularly good match with the walnuts and lime. For a slightly different flavour, try toasting the walnuts in a frying pan before chopping them.

Lime Pickle Dressing

Choose your favourite brand of lime pickle (or even better, use home-made) for this simple but unusual combination.

MAKES 100ML/3½FL OZ

1 tablespoon lime pickle
½ lime
4 tablespoons olive oil
salt and pepper

If the lime pickle is chunky, chop it finely. Squeeze the juice from the lime half and place it in a small bowl with the pickle and olive oil. Whisk until thoroughly combined and season to taste with salt and pepper.

An excellent accompaniment to simply roast duck, this dressing can also be served with poached or grilled chicken and turkey. It makes an interesting Indian-style salad when combined with freshly grated carrot.

Lemon and Cumin Dressing

This unusual and richly flavoured dressing takes inspiration from the cooking of Middle Eastern countries in its use of ground cumin, coriander and lemon juice.

MAKES 125ML/4FL OZ

2 cloves garlic
1 lemon
½ teaspoon ground cumin
½ teaspoon ground coriander
4 tablespoons olive oil

Finely chop or crush the garlic and squeeze the juice from the lemon. Combine them in a small bowl with the cumin and coriander to make a paste. Gradually whisk in the olive oil until the mixture is smooth.

Serve over freshly grilled or barbecued shellfish such as prawns and squid, or stirred into rice salads.

Poppyseed Dressing

MAKES 100ML/3½FL OZ

1 tablespoon freshly squeezed lemon juice
1 teaspoon honey
5 tablespoons groundnut oil
1 tablespoon poppyseeds
salt and pepper

Stir the lemon juice into the honey then add the oil, whisking to make a smooth, thickened vinaigrette. Stir in the poppyseeds then taste and add salt and pepper as necessary. If the taste of the poppyseeds is too strong, add a little more honey.

Best served with cos lettuce and some well-flavoured vegetables.

Orange and Sesame Dressing

MAKES 130ML/4½FL OZ

3 tablespoons freshly squeezed orange juice
4 tablespoons groundnut oil
2 tablespoons toasted sesame seeds
salt and pepper

Put all the ingredients into a screw-topped jar and shake well. Taste and adjust the seasonings as necessary. Chill the dressing thoroughly before use.

The fresh orange flavour of this dressing works particularly well with grated carrots.

COOKED SALAD DRESSINGS

Crispy Duck Salad

A really fast, well-flavoured and substantial warm salad that makes a main dish for two or a first course for four. Choose boneless duck breasts – they don't need to be any fancy breed – and some crisp salad leaves.

SERVES 2-4

2 boneless duck breasts, about 300g/10½oz
1 tablespoon vegetable oil
1 small bulb fennel, cut into thin wedges
1 small cos or iceberg lettuce
½ radicchio
1 small bunch watercress
FOR THE MARINADE AND DRESSING:
1 tablespoon soy sauce
2 tablespoons freshly squeezed orange juice, or to taste
1 teaspoon sesame oil
½ teaspoon ground roasted Sichuan peppercorns

Wipe the duck breasts and prick the skin well with a fork. Mix together the soy sauce, orange juice, sesame oil and Sichuan peppercorns in a shallow dish and marinate the duck in the mixture, uncovered, for 20 minutes at room temperature. Meanwhile, preheat the oven to 220°C/425°F/Gas 7.

Remove the duck from the marinade, reserving the liquid, and pat it dry on kitchen paper. Using a pan or small roasting dish that can be used in the oven as well as on top of the stove, heat the vegetable oil. Put the duck in the pan skin-side down, and cook for 3-4 minutes until browned. Turn the duck over, then put the dish in the oven for 20 minutes until the meat is cooked and the juices run clear when the meat is pierced.

Meanwhile, prepare the fennel, lettuce, radicchio and watercress and put them into a large salad bowl. When the duck is cooked, remove the breasts to a carving board and leave them to rest for 5 minutes.

Put the roasting pan on the stove over a medium heat and add the reserved marinade

to the cooking juices. Bring the mixture to a boil, scraping and stirring with a spoon to dissolve all the caramelized juices in the bottom of the pan. When the sauce is well blended, taste and add a little more orange juice as necessary – the dressing should be highly flavoured.

Cut the duck breasts, on the diagonal, into thin slices and place them on top of the salad. Spoon over the hot dressing, toss the salad quickly and serve immediately.

Variations: change the mix of salad leaves as you desire, including chicory or Chinese leaves if they are available.

Above: soy sauce, fresh orange juice and the caramelized cooking juices of tender duck breasts make a warm dressing for Crispy Duck Salad.

Lemon Chilli Dressing

SERVES 4-6

5 tablespoons olive oil
1 red chilli, cored, seeded and finely chopped
1 shallot, finely chopped
2 cloves garlic, crushed
juice of 1 lemon
salt and pepper

COOKED SALAD DRESSINGS

Heat the olive oil in a small, heavy saucepan and fry the chilli and shallot until soft, stirring occasionally. Add the garlic to the pan and cook gently without letting it burn.

Remove the pan from the heat and whisk in the lemon juice. Season to taste with salt and pepper and serve immediately.

———— 🥄 ————

This dressing is delicious with a salad of fresh prawns. You could also stir it into cooked pasta or some grilled mushrooms.

Lemon, Anchovy and Coriander Dressing

If your anchovies have been preserved in brine and not oil, rinse them in a little water or milk before using to remove some of the salty flavour.

SERVES 4

4 tablespoons extra virgin olive oil
15g/½oz tinned or bottled anchovies, drained
2 tablespoons chopped coriander
2 tablespoons lemon juice
black pepper

In a small, heavy saucepan, gently heat the olive oil. Chop the anchovies to a thick paste then gently and slowly cook them in the oil, stirring frequently, for about 10 minutes or until the mixture is thick and sauce-like.

Allow the anchovy mixture to cool slightly then stir in the coriander and lemon juice. Taste and season as necessary with plenty of black pepper. The dressing can be stored in a jar in the refrigerator for up to 4 days.

———— 🥄 ————

Good with robust green vegetables such as artichokes, French beans or broccoli. A nice combination is French beans, new potatoes and red peppers: toss the vegetables in the dressing then season.

Sauce Vierge

SERVES 6

1 clove garlic
8 coriander seeds, crushed
2 tablespoons water
3 tablespoons virgin olive oil
1 tablespoon sherry vinegar
225g/8oz tomatoes, peeled, seeded and diced
2 tablespoons chopped chervil
1 tablespoon chopped parsley
1 tablespoon chopped tarragon
salt and black pepper

Place the garlic, coriander seeds, water, olive oil and vinegar in a small saucepan and heat them gently for 5 minutes to encourage the flavours to infuse. Strain the mixture through a sieve and discard the flavourings.

Add the diced tomato, chervil, parsley and tarragon to the dressing then season to taste with salt and black pepper.

———— 🥄 ————

Serve with poached or grilled fish, chicken, or with ham, salads or soft creamy cheeses.

Caesar Salad

SERVES 4-6

1 large cos or romaine lettuce
4 large cloves garlic, sliced
4 tablespoons extra virgin olive oil
3 thick slices white bread, crusts removed
5 tablespoons olive oil or vegetable oil
7 anchovy fillets, drained
3 tablespoons milk
1 large egg
juice of 1 large lemon
60g/2oz Parmesan cheese, grated
black pepper

Put the washed and dried lettuce leaves into a large plastic bag and chill for at least 2 hours to crisp up the leaves.

Place 2 of the sliced garlic cloves into a small bowl with the extra virgin olive oil. Cover and leave to infuse for 2 hours.

Dice the bread. Heat the remaining garlic very gently with the olive or vegetable oil in a frying pan. Discard the garlic when it is golden brown, then raise the heat and fry the diced bread until crisp and golden. Drain the croutons on kitchen paper.

Meanwhile, soak the anchovy fillets in the milk for about 15 minutes, then drain and finely chop the anchovies.

When ready to serve, tear up the lettuce and place it in a large salad bowl. Discard the garlic from the extra virgin oil, then pour the oil over the lettuce. Toss gently. Put the egg into a pan of boiling water, cook it for 1 minute, then break the egg into the salad bowl. Toss the salad, pour over the lemon juice, toss again then add the anchovies and Parmesan and toss well. Add pepper to taste, scatter over the croutons and serve.

Variations: use brioche, challah or sourdough bread to make the croutons.

———— 🥄 ————

Caesar Salad can be served on its own as a main course or as a substantial first course.

Adding the lightly cooked egg: break it directly onto the salad then toss until it coats the leaves, forming the basis of the thick, creamy dressing.

Green Mayonnaise

MAKES 350ML/12FL OZ

150g/5½oz young spinach leaves
200ml/7fl oz Mayonnaise (see page 19)
3 tablespoons crème fraîche
1 clove garlic, or to taste, crushed
salt and pepper
freshly grated nutmeg

Steam the spinach or cook it in the minimum possible quantity of water for just 2 minutes until floppy. Drain thoroughly then squeeze out as much water as possible. Chop the spinach finely then leave it to cool.

Combine the spinach with the mayonnaise, crème fraîche and garlic in a bowl or, for a really smooth and brightly coloured dressing, blend the ingredients together in a food processor. Taste and add salt, pepper and nutmeg as necessary.

Variation: *Green Goddess Dressing*
Add 1 teaspoon of finely chopped anchovy fillets and another clove of garlic to the mixture and serve it with avocados, cold cooked vegetables and seafood.

———— 🥄 ————

To make a delicious potato salad, toss the Green Mayonnaise with 750g/1lb 10oz of boiled new potatoes, halved or quartered and left to cool. Cover and chill the salad for 2 hours before serving.

Watercress Mayonnaise

MAKES 250ML/9FL OZ

1 bunch watercress
200ml/7fl oz Mayonnaise (see page 19)

Twist and remove the leaves from the bunch of watercress and discard the stems. Finely chop the watercress leaves and stir them into the mayonnaise.

Variations: for a lower fat dressing, replace some or all of the mayonnaise with fromage frais. The watercress can be replaced with a large bunch of fresh coriander (the stems, leaves and white roots can all be finely chopped). Add the grated rind and juice of 1 small lime for a really tangy mayonnaise.

———— 🥄 ————

Good with cold salmon and other seafood.

Thousand Island Dressing

MAKES 250ML/9FL OZ

1 tablespoon sun-dried tomato purée
200ml/7fl oz Mayonnaise (see page 19), not
   highly seasoned
1 large hard-boiled egg, chopped
3 heaped tablespoons green olives, chopped
1 tablespoon snipped chives
1 tablespoon lemon juice
pepper

Stir the tomato purée into the mayonnaise then, when thoroughly combined, stir in the remaining ingredients. Taste and add more pepper or lemon juice as needed. Serve the sauce immediately or cover and store in the refrigerator for 1 day. Stir well before use.

———— 🥄 ————

Serve this pinkish, textured mayonnaise as a dressing for crunchy salads and seafood.

Chantilly Mayonnaise

MAKES 250ML/9FL OZ

4 tablespoons double cream, chilled and
   whipped, or 4 tablespoons crème fraîche,
   well-chilled
200ml/7fl oz Mayonnaise (see page 19)
salt and pepper

Fold the cream into the mayonnaise then taste and adjust the seasoning as needed. Use immediately for the best texture.

———— 🥄 ————

Made with whipped cream, this is a light, mild dressing for delicate vegetables such as asparagus. Using crème fraîche gives a heavier dressing for cold shellfish.

Creamy Salad Dressing

MAKES 250ML/9FL OZ

125ml/4fl oz Mayonnaise (see page 19)
100ml/3½fl oz creamy milk
3 tablespoons snipped chives
2-3 drops Tabasco sauce
white wine vinegar, to taste
salt and black pepper

Place the mayonnaise in a large jug and whisk in the milk until the mixture is the consistency of single cream. Whisk the chives and Tabasco into the mixture. Add a little vinegar to taste, then season.

Use the dressing immediately or store it covered in the refrigerator for up to 4 days.

———— 🥄 ————

This dressing goes best with robust salad greens such as cos, spinach or watercress.

Aïoli

A rich garlic mayonnaise, not for the faint hearted. Ensure that the garlic is very fresh.

MAKES 250ML/9FL OZ

200ml/7fl oz Mayonnaise (see page 19), made
   with a high proportion of virgin olive oil
1 tablespoon finely chopped garlic
¼ teaspoon sea salt
freshly ground black pepper

M AYONNAISES

Left: fresh chillies and spring onions are very finely chopped to give a pretty, smooth curried sauce for Coronation Chicken.

Coronation Chicken

This delicious cold chicken salad was invented by Rosemary Hume and Constance Spry in 1953 when they cooked for one of the large Coronation Day luncheons. Since then the dish has been reduced to a rather unpleasant concoction of cheap bottled mayonnaise and either ready-made curry paste or, worse, curry powder straight from the jar. This version uses home-made mayonnaise and fresh herbs and spices to give a lively, fresh taste and appearance.

SERVES 4-6

1 small chicken, or 4 medium chicken pieces, poached

FOR THE SAUCE:

225ml/8fl oz Mayonnaise (see page 19)
1 large mild red chilli, cored, seeded and very finely chopped
1 spring onion, very finely chopped
1 small clove garlic, crushed
2 teaspoons fresh lime juice, or to taste
2 teaspoons finely chopped fresh coriander
large pinch cayenne pepper
1-2 tablespoons crème fraîche, or to taste

Remove the skin and bones from the chicken, keeping the meat in large pieces wherever possible. Cover and chill.

Mix together all the sauce ingredients then taste and add more lime juice as necessary. If the sauce is too strong, add a little more crème fraîche. Cover and chill until needed.

Just before serving, combine the chicken and sauce in a bowl. Any leftovers can be kept, covered, in the refrigerator for 1 day.

Coronation Chicken can be served with green salad and new potatoes, or with pasta salad.

Chill the mayonnaise well. Pound the garlic and salt until smooth using a pestle and mortar then stir them into the mayonnaise. Add pepper to taste. Use immediately or cover tightly and chill for up to 24 hours.

Variation: peel and roughly chop 1 whole head of garlic. Put it into a food processor with ¼ teaspoon of sea salt, a little pepper and 1 large egg yolk and process to a purée. Gradually pour in 200ml/7fl oz of virgin olive oil in a thin, steady stream. Work in the juice of 1 large lemon then taste and adjust the seasonings as necessary.

Use Aïoli in generous quantities with a fish soup such as bourride, salt cod, hard-boiled eggs and cold cooked or raw vegetables.

Tartare Sauce

SERVES 6

200ml/7fl oz Mayonnaise (see page 19)
1 hard-boiled egg, very finely chopped
1 tablespoon capers, very finely chopped
1 tablespoon baby gherkins, very finely chopped
1 tablespoon finely chopped fresh parsley
1 teaspoon finely chopped fresh tarragon
salt and pepper

Combine all the ingredients in a bowl then taste the sauce and adjust the seasoning as necessary. Serve chilled within 12 hours.

Tartare Sauce is the classic accompaniment to breadcrumbed, deep-fried fish and other seafood such as calamari and prawns.

Dill and Mustard Dressing

SERVES 4-6

1 large egg yolk
2 tablespoons mild German or American mustard
1 teaspoon caster sugar
¼ teaspoon sea salt
ground black pepper
2 tablespoons vegetable oil (not olive oil)
2 tablespoons white wine vinegar
1 tablespoon finely chopped dill

Mix the egg yolk and mustard together in a small bowl then stir in the sugar, salt and a little pepper. Gradually stir in the oil, as for mayonnaise, then the vinegar and dill.

Taste the dressing; you may need to add more vinegar, sugar or pepper to suit your palate. Store it tightly covered in the refrigerator for up to 24 hours.

———— 🥄 ————

Usually served with thinly sliced gravad lax, this dressing is also good with smoked salmon or when used to dress a salad of cold poached fresh salmon.

Rouille

A rust-coloured mayonnaise flavoured with fresh red chillies. Rouille is traditionally made using a pestle and mortar, but a food processor will save your weary arm muscles.

MAKES 125ML/4FL OZ

5 large cloves garlic, finely chopped
¼ teaspoon sea salt
½-1 medium-hot red chilli, cored, seeded and finely chopped
2 large egg yolks
125ml/4fl oz virgin olive oil
black pepper
1 teaspoon sun-dried tomato purée

Put the garlic, salt and chilli in the mortar and crush them to a smooth paste. Mix in the egg yolks then slowly and gradually work in the olive oil to make a thick sauce. Stir in a little pepper and the tomato purée. Taste and adjust the seasoning as necessary. Serve immediately or cover tightly and chill for up to 24 hours. Stir well before using.

To make rouille in a food processor, put the garlic, salt, chilli and egg yolks in the bowl of the processor and purée until smooth, scraping down the sides from time to time. With the machine running, pour the oil through the feed tube in a slow, steady stream. Add the tomato purée and some pepper then taste and adjust the seasoning.

———— 🥄 ————

Rouille is commonly served with bouillabaisse and other fish soups.

Guacamole

This popular avocado sauce from Mexico should be thick and full of flavour. Try to use fully ripe, black-skinned avocados.

SERVES 4-6

1 clove garlic, crushed
1 small shallot or spring onion, finely chopped
½ fresh green chilli, seeded and chopped
small bunch fresh coriander, chopped
2 large ripe avocados, at room temperature, halved and stones reserved
juice of 1 lime
2 medium tomatoes, peeled, seeded and diced
few drops Tabasco sauce
sea salt and black pepper

Put the garlic, shallot, chilli, coriander and a pinch of salt in a mortar and crush them to a rough paste. Scoop the flesh from the avocados and add it to the mortar with the lime juice. Work the avocado into the chilli paste until roughly crushed.

Stir in the finely diced tomatoes then taste and add the Tabasco, salt and pepper as needed. Serve immediately or bury the stones in the sauce, cover tightly and chill for up to 4 hours. The surface will turn slightly brown so remove the stones and stir the guacamole well before serving.

———— 🥄 ————

Use as a sauce with grilled fish or poultry, as part of a fajita platter, or as a dip with raw vegetables and tortilla chips.

Gazpacho Dressing

MAKES 250ML/9FL OZ

1 medium red pepper
2 medium tomatoes, peeled, cored and seeded
7.5cm/3in piece cucumber, thickly sliced
1 large spring onion, thickly sliced
1-2 cloves garlic, or to taste, roughly chopped
4 tablespoons olive oil
1 tablespoon red wine vinegar
sea salt and black pepper

Preheat the grill to the highest setting and grill the red pepper until the skin blackens. Cool then peel away the skin and discard the core and seeds. Chop the flesh roughly.

Put the pepper into a food processor or blender with the tomatoes, cucumber, spring onion and garlic and process until smooth. With the motor running, pour in the oil through the feed tube, then the vinegar.

Taste the dressing and adjust the flavourings as needed. Strain through a coarse sieve then cover and chill thoroughly. If the sauce becomes too thick on chilling, stir in an ice cube. It can be kept for up to 1 day in the refrigerator. Stir before serving.

———— 🥄 ————

Best icy cold with warm poached salmon, trout or with a hot chicken salad. Also good with char-grilled vegetables and rice salads.

*P*URÉES

Coriander and Lime Dressing

MAKES 150ML/5FL OZ

125ml/4fl oz virgin olive oil
2½-3 tablespoons fresh lime juice
2 small spring onions, roughly chopped
small bunch coriander
salt and black pepper

Put all the ingredients into a food processor or blender and process until finely chopped. Taste and adjust the seasoning as needed.

The finished dressing can be stored, tightly covered, in the refrigerator for up to 8 hours. Allow it to come back to room temperature then stir well before using.

Grilled oily fish, especially mackerel and trout, and chicken suit this sharp, tangy dressing. You can also whisk it into the pan juices at the end of cooking. Alternatively, use it to dress a crunchy salad.

Salsa Verde

SERVES 4-6

25g/1oz fresh white breadcrumbs
1 tablespoon red wine vinegar
40g/1½oz flat-leafed parsley
15g/½oz tarragon
1 clove garlic
3 anchovies
150ml/¼ pint virgin olive oil
salt and black pepper

Put the breadcrumbs into the bowl of a food processor or blender and moisten them with the vinegar. Leave the breadcrumbs to stand while you prepare the other ingredients.

Pluck the parsley and tarragon leaves from their stems, roughly chop the garlic and anchovies and add them all to the bowl.

Process the mixture just until it is finely chopped then, with the machine still running, add the oil in a thin, steady stream.

Taste and season as necessary. Do not overwork the mixture or it will become gluey. Serve the sauce at room temperature. It can be stored, tightly covered, in the refrigerator for up to 24 hours. Stir well before using.

Variation: for a thin, smooth herb dressing, omit the anchovies and breadcrumbs.

In Italy salsa verde is made to accompany bollito misto, a selection of boiled meats such as beef, chicken, sausage and veal plus boiled carrots and potatoes. In the south of the country, basil is added and the sauce is tossed with pasta. Salsa Verde is delicious with baked ham and ham terrines.

Below: anchovies and red wine vinegar add pungency to Italy's 'green sauce', Salsa Verde.

YOGURT DRESSINGS

Mango, Chilli and Yogurt Dressing

SERVES 4

1 medium fresh mango, peeled and chopped
100ml/3½fl oz Greek yogurt
1 teaspoon wholegrain mustard
small bunch of chives
1 tablespoon finely chopped mild red chilli
black pepper

Purée the mango, yogurt and mustard in a food processor or with a hand blender. When the mixture is smooth, snip in the chives and stir in the red chilli and black pepper to taste. Serve at room temperature or chilled.

———— ✎ ————

Dollop this thick, creamy dressing onto asparagus, salmon salads or potato salads.

Yogurt Salad Dressing

When it comes to plain yogurt, most people have a definite preference for one type or another. Choose your favourite for this well-flavoured dressing – it does not matter if you use a fat-free yogurt or the thick Greek type. After all, it's your salad.

MAKES ABOUT 200ML/7FL OZ

150ml/5fl oz plain yogurt
1 clove garlic, chopped
1 bunch watercress
1 tablespoon olive oil
salt and black pepper
few drops of Tabasco sauce

Put the yogurt and garlic into the bowl of a food processor or blender. Hold the bunch of watercress in your hand, like a bunch of flowers, then twist off the leaves. Add them to the bowl with the oil, a little salt and plenty of black pepper.

Above: watercress adds its peppery flavour and attractive green colour to Yogurt Salad Dressing, here drizzled over a bowl of lightly steamed then cooled new potatoes to make a hearty salad.

Process until the dressing is fairly smooth. Taste and adjust the seasoning, adding a few drops of Tabasco. Cover the dressing and chill until ready to use. It can be kept in the refrigerator for up to 24 hours. Stir well before using.

Variations: reduce the quantity of yogurt to 100ml/3½fl oz to make a dip. If you like, crème fraîche can be used instead of yogurt.

———— ✎ ————

This is not a dressing for delicate leaves but is good on crisp, crunchy salads made from cos and iceberg lettuce. You can use it with sliced ripe tomatoes or as a dressing for potato salad. It is also good with salmon.

Roasted Aubergine and Yogurt Dressing

SERVES 6

1 medium aubergine
125ml/4fl oz Greek yogurt
1 clove garlic, crushed
2-3 tablespoons chopped parsley
salt and black pepper

Roast the aubergine until the skin is charred, preferably over a gas flame, otherwise in a very hot oven. Allow it to cool slightly, then peel and discard the skin.

Put the aubergine flesh into a food processor with the remaining ingredients and process until smooth. Adjust the seasoning to taste and serve at room temperature.

———— ✎ ————

Serve with grilled or barbecued chicken or use as a dip for flat breads and crudités.

ℳILK AND 𝒞HEESE 𝒟RESSINGS

Buttermilk Dressing

Buttermilk can be difficult to find in stores these days, but it makes lovely creamy salad dressings (and good pancakes).

SERVES 4-6

225ml/8fl oz buttermilk, or 50ml/2fl oz crème
    fraîche blended with 175ml/6fl oz milk
1 tablespoon cider, sherry or wine vinegar
1 clove garlic, crushed
1 tablespoon finely chopped mild red chilli
4 tablespoons finely chopped herbs such
    as basil, coriander, oregano and parsley
salt and black pepper

In a small bowl, blend the buttermilk or the mixture of crème fraîche and milk with the remaining ingredients. Taste and season as necessary with salt and black pepper. Chill for 30 minutes before serving.

———— ✧ ————

A thick dressing that is good for crunchy salad leaves tossed with cooked fresh or tinned fish such as salmon and tuna. It can also be used in hearty salads featuring black beans, kidney beans, chicken or tomatoes.

Blue Cheese Dressing

This thick, creamy, grey-blue dressing is usually made with Roquefort cheese, but you can substitute any other blue cheese. The crumbled cheese is mixed with a simple vinaigrette, made with a light vegetable oil rather than olive oil. I like to add honey mustard to soften and mellow the flavour.

SERVES 6

75g/2¾oz Roquefort cheese
1 tablespoon white wine vinegar
4 tablespoons vegetable oil
1½ teaspoons honey mustard
black pepper

Crumble the cheese into a small bowl then whisk in the other ingredients to make a creamy dressing – it need not be entirely smooth. Taste and add plenty of black pepper: you will not need to add salt if the cheese is very tangy. Use immediately or keep tightly covered in the refrigerator for up to 24 hours. Stir well before using.

———— ✧ ————

Pour over robust green salad leaves, use as a dressing for pasta salads or small pieces of cold poached chicken.

Below: Roquefort, white wine vinegar and sweet honey-flavoured mustard combine to make a rich, creamy Blue Cheese Dressing.

White Bean and Rosemary Dip

SERVES 6-8

250g/9oz dried cannellini beans
1 large sprig rosemary, plus 1½ tablespoons
  rosemary leaves, finely chopped
1 onion, peeled but left whole
7 tablespoons extra virgin olive oil
4 cloves garlic, or to taste, finely chopped
juice of 1 lemon, or to taste
salt and coarsely ground black pepper

Soak the beans overnight, or for at least 12 hours, in enough cold water to cover them well. Drain and rinse thoroughly, then pick the beans over before cooking.

In a large pan, cover the beans well with fresh cold water. Bring to the boil, skim the surface, then boil the beans rapidly for 10 minutes. Add the large sprig of rosemary and the onion, then cover and simmer for 45 minutes until the beans are very tender. Drain the beans, reserving the cooking liquid. Discard the rosemary sprig and onion.

In a medium-sized saucepan, gently warm 5 tablespoons of the olive oil with the garlic and 1 tablespoon of the chopped rosemary leaves. Add the beans and cook the mixture, stirring frequently, over a low heat for about 5 minutes.

Mash the cooked bean mixture to a rough paste using a potato masher. Stir in the lemon juice to taste, then season with salt and pepper and beat in just enough of the reserved cooking liquid to make a thick dip.

Drizzle the remaining 2 tablespoons of olive oil over the dip and garnish with the remaining chopped rosemary before serving.

The dip can be cooled and then stored, covered, for up to 3 days in the refrigerator.

Variation: replace the chopped rosemary with a generous spoonful of basil pesto and, if you like, add some finely chopped roasted aubergine or black olives to the mixture.

Offer this as an informal starter course with fresh or roasted vegetables and slices of warmed or toasted Italian bread such as ciabatta or focaccia, flavoured with herbs or olives if you like. When cold, it can be used in sandwiches or stuffed into pitta bread with some green salad to make a healthy lunch.

Above: White Bean and Rosemary Dip, served here with olive-flavoured bread, is garnished with a drizzle of extra virgin olive oil, black pepper and some finely chopped sprigs of rosemary.

I P S

Goats' Cheese Dip

Choose a creamy goats' cheese, as mild or strongly flavoured as you like.

SERVES 4

100g/3½oz soft goats' cheese
juice of ½ lemon
2 tablespoons extra virgin olive oil
2 tablespoons finely chopped fresh herbs
salt and pepper

Beat the cheese until creamy then beat in all the remaining ingredients, adding plenty of pepper but salt may not be necessary if the cheese is particularly strong. Taste and adjust the seasonings as necessary, then cover and chill the dip for up to 4 hours before serving.

Variations: replace the goats' cheese with a creamy cows' milk cheese such as Boursin Naturel. Ricotta is the low-fat choice. Add 100g/3½oz of smoked trout fillet (free of skin and bones) and include plenty of fresh dill with the herbs. Process the mixture until it is smooth then cover and chill as above.

———————— ✎ ————————

This quick, summery dip can be served with raw vegetables, bread sticks, slices of French bread or chicken kebabs.

Cottage Cheese and Walnut Dip

SERVES 4-6

175g/6oz cottage cheese
1 tablespoon grated Parmesan cheese
2 tablespoons virgin olive oil
1 spring onion, chopped
2 tablespoons finely chopped parsley
50g/2oz walnuts, chopped
salt and black pepper

Combine all the ingredients in a medium-sized bowl and stir until thoroughly combined. Taste and adjust the seasoning as necessary. If the mixture seems too thick, add a little water or milk.

Variations: replace the parsley with basil and the cottage cheese with ricotta.

———————— ✎ ————————

Serve with toasted flat breads or crudités.

Hummus

Hummus made with freshly cooked dried chickpeas tastes far nicer than that made with canned legumes, although you do have to plan ahead. The chickpeas should be soaked for 12 hours then boiled until really tender. There are no short cuts in terms of time but the recipe is extremely simple and you can flavour the hummus just as you like: my preference is to have plenty of lemon juice but only a touch of garlic.

MAKES 400ML/14FL OZ

100g/3½oz chickpeas
1 small onion, peeled but left whole
4 cloves garlic, or to taste
juice of 1 large lemon, or to taste
2 tablespoons tahini
2-3 tablespoons virgin olive oil
salt and pepper
1 sprig coriander

Soak the chickpeas in plenty of cold water for 12 hours or overnight. Next day, drain the chickpeas, rinse them with cold water then put them into a medium-sized pan with plenty of fresh cold water to cover. Do not add salt as this will toughen the chickpeas.

Bring the chickpeas to a boil and boil rapidly for 10 minutes. Skim if necessary then add the onion and 2 whole peeled cloves of garlic. Simmer them gently for

1¼-1½ hours or until the chickpeas are really tender, topping up the pan as necessary with hot water to keep the chickpeas well covered during cooking.

Drain the chickpeas, reserving the cooking liquid but discarding the onion and garlic. Tip the drained chickpeas into a food processor and add 1-2 cloves of garlic, the lemon juice, tahini, 1 tablespoon of the olive oil and 2 tablespoons of the reserved cooking liquid. Process the mixture until smooth then taste and add salt and pepper, plus more lemon juice, garlic and tahini as desired. The hummus should be the consistency of whipped cream: if it is too thick add a little more of the reserved cooking liquid.

Tip the hummus into a serving bowl and smooth the surface. Spoon the remaining 1 or 2 tablespoons of virgin olive oil over the top (this also prevents the dip becoming crusty) and garnish with coriander.

The hummus, minus the coriander, can be stored, tightly covered, in the refrigerator for up to 2 days before serving. Stir well before use. The flavour is much improved if the hummus is made 12-24 hours in advance.

Variations: add ½ teaspoon of ground coriander or cumin with the tahini; or stir in 1 tablespoon of finely chopped fresh coriander just before serving; or add half a red chilli pepper, cored, seeded and finely chopped just before serving. For a slightly textured hummus, remove a heaped tablespoon of the cooked chickpeas before processing, chop them roughly by hand or mash with a fork, then stir them into the dip before serving.

———————— ✎ ————————

Warm pitta bread or crunchy raw vegetables are good accompaniments. Hummus makes a great sandwich spread too, layered with chopped fresh dates and coriander leaves. Alternatively, thin down the dip with some more of the cooking liquid to make a runny dressing for cold cooked or raw vegetables.

CLASSIC SAUCES

These are the cook's showpieces. Here, experience and technique, attention to detail and careful seasoning are the difference between success and failure.

Feather-light butter sauces and the gloriously rich emulsions of egg yolk and melted butter are less difficult than the results suggest; with the freshest possible free range eggs and creamy, unsalted butter, a touch of lemon juice and seasoning, you can have a sauce to make the heart, let alone a perfectly poached fish, sing.

The grandest of haute cuisine restaurants take great pride in their sleek, glossy, refined and reduced brown sauces. These are based on carefully-made stock, strained or clarified, then reduced to produce a dark, well-flavoured, slightly syrupy sauce. The trick is to avoid both a watery result and an over-concentrated, gelatinous finish. A sauce should, after all, enhance and not overwhelm.

This may sound like a lot of trouble but, once mastered, these recipes can turn a simple piece of grilled fish, meat or poultry into an elegant dinner party dish.

Left (from left to right): Sauce Meurette, Sorrel Sauce, Saffron Hollandaise.

Parsley Sauce

The intense flavour of this sauce comes from the crushed fresh parsley stalks added to the milk infusion, as well as plenty of chopped leaves added just before serving. If possible, use really fresh organic parsley.

MAKES 550ML/19FL OZ

500ml/18fl oz whole milk
½ teaspoon black peppercorns
1 onion, peeled and studded with 2 cloves
2 bay leaves
40g/1½oz fresh parsley
25g/1oz unsalted butter
25g/1oz plain flour
3 tablespoons single or double cream
salt and white pepper

Put the milk, peppercorns, onion and bay leaves into a medium-sized saucepan. Pick the parsley leaves from the stalks and reserve, then crush the stalks and add them to the milk. Heat the milk slowly until scalding hot but not boiling, then cover the pan, remove it from the heat and leave to infuse for 30-60 minutes. Meanwhile, finely chop the parsley leaves.

Strain the milk and discard the flavourings. Rinse out the saucepan and use it to melt the butter. Stir in the flour and cook over a low heat for 1 minute, stirring constantly. Remove the pan from the heat and gradually add the flavoured milk, whisking constantly.

Set the pan over a medium heat and whisk the mixture briskly until thick. Lower the heat so the sauce barely simmers, then leave it to cook gently for 20 minutes, stirring often. Whisk in the chopped parsley and cream then season the sauce to taste with salt and white pepper. Serve immediately.

Delicious with poached or steamed white fish such as cod, haddock or plaice and with steamed vegetables such as broad beans, cauliflower, Swiss chard or marrow.

Cheese Sauce

In this Sauce Mornay, cheese and egg yolk thicken the thin béchamel considerably.

MAKES 550ML/19FL OZ

400ml/14fl oz Thin Béchamel Sauce (see page 21)
60g/2oz grated cheese such as mature Cheddar, Emmental or Gruyère
2 tablespoons single or double cream
1 large egg yolk
salt and pepper

Bring the sauce to a boil then remove it from the heat and stir in the grated cheese. When it has melted completely, blend the cream with the egg yolk, stir the mixture into the sauce and season to taste. Do not bring the sauce back to a boil or the cheese may turn stringy and the egg may start to scramble.

Variation: when making macaroni cheese, add 1 teaspoon of Dijon mustard to the sauce for a more robust flavour.

Use in gratins, to coat steamed broccoli or cauliflower, or mixed with fish and hard-boiled eggs to make a fish pie.

Onion Sauce

MAKES 550ML/19FL OZ

25g/1oz unsalted butter
3 medium onions, thinly sliced
1 bay leaf
400ml/14fl oz Thick Béchamel Sauce (see page 21), kept warm
2 tablespoons crème fraîche or double cream
salt and pepper

Heat the butter in a heavy pan, add the onions and bay leaf and stir well. Press a circle of dampened greaseproof paper on top of the onions then cover the pan with a lid and cook very gently for about 25 minutes, stirring occasionally, until the onions are meltingly soft but not browned.

Add the onions to the béchamel sauce then cook gently for 5 minutes, stirring constantly. Purée the sauce in a blender or food processor or push it through a fine sieve. Reheat the sauce, stir in the cream, then taste and adjust the seasoning.

Onion Sauce, also known as Sauce Soubise, is good with pork chops and vegetables.

Mushroom Sauce

Small, white button mushrooms will give this sauce a delicate flavour and appearance. For a stronger taste, choose brown cap or wild mushrooms.

MAKES 550ML/19FL OZ

1 small shallot, finely chopped
15g/½oz butter
75g/2¾oz mushrooms, finely sliced
squeeze of lemon juice
2 tablespoons water
400ml/14fl oz Medium Béchamel Sauce (see page 20), kept warm
2 tablespoons crème fraîche or double cream
salt and pepper

Heat the butter in a heavy pan and cook the shallot very gently for a few minutes until softened. Add the mushrooms, lemon juice and water and stir well. Cover the surface with a circle of dampened greaseproof paper then the pan lid and cook gently for 5 minutes until the mushrooms are tender.

Stir the mushroom mixture and any cooking liquid into the béchamel sauce then heat gently, stirring frequently until the sauce is the correct consistency. Stir in the cream then adjust the seasoning as necessary.

Béchamel Sauces

Variations: add 2-3 drops of mushroom ketchup and some chopped fresh herbs; or add 1 tablespoon of vermouth to the mushrooms; or finish with crème fraîche.

———— ⟳ ————

Good with eggs, fish, poultry and vegetables.

Sorrel Sauce

MAKES 550ML/19FL OZ

about 20g/¾oz unsalted butter
150g/5½oz young sorrel leaves, destalked
200ml/7fl oz Medium Béchamel Sauce (see page 20), kept warm
3 tablespoons double cream
salt and pepper
pinch of nutmeg

Heat the butter in a non-aluminium pan, add the sorrel then cook gently for 5-7 minutes, stirring frequently, until very soft. Drain well then roughly chop the leaves.

Stir the sorrel into the sauce along with the cream and gently reheat. Simmer it for 2 minutes then taste and add salt, pepper and nutmeg as necessary. If too sharp or thin, mount with an extra 20g/¾oz of butter.

———— ⟳ ————

Serve with fish or spooned over vegetables.

Tomato Sauce

MAKES ABOUT 550ML/19FL OZ

100ml/3½fl oz tomato passata
400ml/14fl oz Medium Béchamel Sauce (see page 20), kept warm
2-3 tablespoons double cream

Put the passata in a small non-aluminium pan and boil it vigorously until the volume has reduced to about 4 tablespoons of liquid.

Whisk the reduced passata into the sauce then reheat. Add the cream and simmer for 5 minutes. Taste, adding extra passata and seasoning as necessary.

Variation: for a well-flavoured prawn sauce that tastes good with cauliflower or white fish, add a few drops of anchovy essence and 100g/3½oz of cooked prawns to the sauce just before serving.

———— ⟳ ————

A creamy, pink-coloured sauce that can be served with pasta, steamed vegetables, warm hard-boiled eggs or poultry.

Below: Broad Bean and Pancetta Sauce is a pretty variation of Medium Béchamel. Serve it with chicory to give a well-balanced meal.

Broad Bean and Pancetta Sauce

MAKES 550ML/19FL OZ

100g/3½oz pancetta or bacon, diced
400ml/14fl oz Medium Béchamel Sauce (see page 20), kept warm
150g/5½oz broad beans, cooked and skinned
pepper

Put the pancetta or bacon in a cold frying pan and heat it gently to melt the fat. Fry until lightly browned then drain and add it to the sauce with the beans. Gently reheat and season to taste with pepper.

———— ⟳ ————

This sauce is excellent with chicory or leeks as a main dish, or stirred into pasta.

Velouté Sauce

The word *velouté* translates as velvet, and so this sauce should be super-smooth, glossy and rich.

MAKES 400ML/14FL OZ

500ml/18fl oz stock or reduced poaching liquid
25g/1oz unsalted butter
25g/1oz plain flour
squeeze of lemon juice
salt and pepper

Heat the stock if necessary. Melt the butter in a medium-sized heavy pan and stir in the flour to make a roux. Cook gently, stirring constantly, for about 3 minutes until it turns a golden straw colour.

Remove the pan from the heat, cool for 1 minute then whisk in the stock. Return the pan to the heat and whisk as the sauce comes to the boil and thickens. Reduce the heat and simmer very gently, uncovered, for 30 minutes, skimming occasionally.

At the end of the cooking time the sauce should coat the back of a spoon. If it is too thin, reduce by boiling gently. Taste and add lemon juice, salt and pepper as necessary. For a super-glossy, smooth sauce, pass the mixture through a fine-meshed conical sieve.

Variations: add 2 tablespoons of dry sherry to the finished sauce. Alternatively, add 4 tablespoons of crème fraîche, bring back to a boil, whisking constantly, then season.

Sauce Aurore
Add 100ml/3½fl oz of tomato passata after the sauce has simmered for 20 minutes. Continue simmering for another 15 minutes then mount with 25g/1oz of unsalted butter. Add 1½ tablespoons of chopped basil or chervil just before serving, if you like.

Velouté sauce is best served with poultry and steamed vegetables.

Saffron Sauce

The stock for this velouté could be made from fish bones, heads and trimmings, or from shellfish shells and heads.

MAKES 400ML/14FL OZ

400ml/14fl oz Velouté Sauce (see left)
1 rounded teaspoon saffron threads
25g/1oz unsalted butter, chilled and diced

Make the velouté as given left. Meanwhile, preheat the oven to 180°C/350°F/Gas 4, roast the saffron for 10 minutes, then crumble it into a small bowl. Remove 4 tablespoons of the simmering sauce, pour it over the saffron and leave it to soak for 20-30 minutes.

Strain the reduced sauce into a clean pan, stir in the saffron mixture and simmer for 10 minutes. Season to taste then remove the pan from the heat and gradually whisk in the butter. Serve immediately.

Serve this brilliantly coloured sauce with fish and shellfish.

Sauce Allemande

MAKES 450ML/16FL OZ

400ml/14fl oz Velouté Sauce (see left)
60g/2oz mushroom stems, or button
** mushrooms, sliced**
1 shallot, finely chopped
1 large egg yolk
squeeze of lemon juice
salt and pepper
25g/1oz unsalted butter, chilled and diced

Prepare the velouté sauce up to the simmering stage. Add the mushrooms and shallot and simmer for 30 minutes, stirring occasionally. When cooked, the sauce should just coat the back of a spoon.

Strain the sauce through a fine-meshed conical sieve and return it to the rinsed-out pan. In a small heatproof bowl, whisk a ladle or two of the sauce with the egg yolk then whisk this mixture into the hot sauce. Gently reheat the sauce, stirring constantly, so it thickens slightly; do not let it boil.

Remove the pan from the heat and season to taste with lemon juice, salt and pepper. Gradually whisk in the butter, then serve.

Variations: *Sauce Poulette*
Whisk in 1½ tablespoons of finely chopped parsley and the juice of half a lemon, or more. Serve this sauce immediately with the richer poultry and offal dishes.

Sauce Suprême
Omit the shallot and egg yolk. When the sauce has reached coating consistency, stir in 4 tablespoons of crème fraîche or double cream. Serve with poached chicken.

Sauce Allemande is excellent served with vegetables and makes chicken a real treat, especially if you include the stems and trimmings from chanterelles.

Texan Meat Pie

Almost any kind of meat can be used in this pie: beef, lamb, pork, turkey or venison. Lean cuts cook quickly but allow longer for the better-flavoured, cheaper stewing meat.

SERVES 4-6

FOR THE VELOUTÉ SAUCE:
50g/1¾oz unsalted butter
50g/1¾oz plain flour
1-2 teaspoons hot chilli powder, to taste
2 teaspoons ground coriander
2 teaspoons ground cumin
600ml/1 pint beef stock
1 teaspoon dried oregano

Velouté Sauces

simmer the sauce uncovered over a very low heat for 20 minutes, stirring occasionally.

While the sauce is cooking, heat the oil in a heavy frying pan and add the diced meat in batches, frying quickly to seal and brown it on all sides. As the meat is browned, remove it from the pan with a slotted spoon and add it to the velouté sauce.

When all the meat is cooked, add the garlic and onion to the frying pan and stir them over a low heat for a couple of minutes until softened. Add them to the sauce with some salt and pepper then partially cover the pan and simmer gently until the meat is really tender: allow 40 minutes for prime cuts and up to 2 hours for stewing steak. If you want to use a casserole, the sauce can be cooked in the oven at 170°C/325°F/Gas 3.

When the meat is cooked, add the beans and continue cooking, uncovered, for about 15 minutes or until the mixture is slightly thickened. Taste and adjust the seasoning. If necessary, transfer the sauce to a baking dish or pie dish and leave it to cool.

Boil the diced potatoes until just tender, drain thoroughly then mash until smooth. Beat in the butter and just enough milk to make a smooth, spreadable mixture, then season to taste with salt and pepper.

Spread the potato mixture in an even layer on top of the meat sauce. At this point the dish can be left until cold then covered and stored in the refrigerator for up to 3 days or frozen for up to 1 month (defrost the pie overnight in the refrigerator).

To finish the pie, preheat the oven to 180°C/350°F/Gas 4 and cook it uncovered for about 30 minutes or until the sauce is bubbling and piping hot throughout. Serve the pie with a bowl of chilled fresh tomato salsa (see page 102) for extra piquancy.

Variations: the meat sauce used in this dish can be served with rice and salsa as chilli con carne. If you prefer a really hot sauce, use 2 teaspoons of chilli powder.

FOR THE MEAT SAUCE:
2 tablespoons olive oil
700g/1lb 9oz lean braising steak, finely diced
3 cloves garlic, crushed
1 medium onion, finely chopped
salt and black pepper
400g/14oz cooked pinto or borlotti beans
FOR THE TOPPING:
750g/1lb 10oz potatoes, peeled and diced
40g/1½oz unsalted butter, diced
75ml/3fl oz hot milk
salt and pepper

Melt the butter for the sauce in a medium-sized heavy pan or flameproof casserole,

Above: classic Velouté Sauce is given a spicy kick with ground chilli, coriander and cumin, then used to make this hearty Texan Meat Pie.

then remove it from the heat and stir in the flour. Return the pan to the heat and stir over a low heat until the roux becomes the colour of dark straw. Add the spices and cook, stirring constantly, for 1 minute.

Remove the pan from the heat, leave the roux to cool for 1 minute then slowly whisk in the stock. Return the pan to the heat and bring the sauce to a boil, whisking constantly until smooth and thick. Add the oregano then reduce the heat and gently

H OLLANDAISE S AUCES

Grilled Spinach Tarts with Hollandaise

This is a smart yet easy first course or brunch dish that is infinitely adaptable. The individual tarts and their filling of spinach and anchovy can be prepared in advance, then assembled just before serving. For this recipe you will need six 12cm/4½in loose-based tart tins.

SERVES 6

FOR THE PASTRY:
300g/11oz plain flour
¼ teaspoon salt
large pinch of pepper
150g/5½oz unsalted butter, chilled and diced
2 medium egg yolks
2-3 teaspoons icy-cold water
FOR THE FILLING:
500g/1lb 2oz baby spinach leaves
25g/1oz anchovy fillets, drained and chopped
black pepper
FOR THE GLAZE:
**300ml/½ pint Hollandaise Sauce, made with a
    large pinch of cayenne pepper (see page 22)**

To make the pastry, put the flour, salt, pepper and butter into a food processor and process until the mixture resembles fine crumbs. With the machine running, add the egg yolks and water through the feed tube. Mix just until the dough comes together. Remove the dough from the bowl, then wrap and chill it for about 20 minutes until firm.

Roll out the pastry on a floured work surface then cut out 6 circles, each 14cm/5½in in diameter, using a plain cutter or a saucer as a template. Use the rounds of pastry to line the tartlet tins and chill them for 15 minutes. Meanwhile, heat the oven to 200°C/400°F/Gas 6.

Right: cayenne-spiked Hollandaise Sauce provides a creamy topping for these stylishly simple Grilled Spinach Tarts.

Line each pastry case with a round of non-stick baking parchment and fill them with baking beans. Stand the tins on a baking tray and bake the tartlets for 12 minutes or until they are lightly golden and only just firm. Carefully remove the paper and beans from the tartlet cases, then lower the oven temperature to 180°C/350°F/Gas 4 and bake for a further 5-7 minutes until the pastry is completely cooked, light golden and crisp. Cool the tart cases for 1 minute until they are firm enough to unmould, then leave to cool completely on a wire rack.

To make the filling, steam the spinach until wilted, then remove it from the heat and leave to cool. Squeeze out the excess water from the cooked spinach, chop it roughly and mix it with the anchovies and plenty of black pepper.

When ready to finish the dish, arrange the pastry cases on a baking tray and divide the spinach filling between them. Gently warm the tarts through in a low oven while you are making the sauce. Preheat the grill to a very high temperature.

Make the hollandaise sauce as given on page 22, adding a large pinch of cayenne pepper along with the seasoning: be sure not to add too much salt as the anchovies will be salty enough. Spoon the sauce over

CLASSIC SAUCES

Hollandaise Sauces

the filling in each tart then quickly put them under the very hot grill until they are browned on top. Serve immediately.

Variation: the spinach and anchovy filling can be replaced by steamed asparagus spears or broccoli florets, or by spinach combined with crisply cooked bacon and either seared scallops or some hard-boiled quails' eggs, halved.

Saffron Hollandaise

A brilliantly coloured, aromatic version of hollandaise sauce with an intense flavour.

MAKES 300ML/½ PINT

1 rounded teaspoon saffron threads
2 tablespoons warm water
3 medium egg yolks
225g/8oz clarified unsalted butter, tepid
juice of ½ lemon
salt and white pepper

Preheat the oven to 180°C/350°F/Gas 4 then toast the saffron for 10-12 minutes. Put the toasted saffron into a small bowl with the warm water and leave it to soak overnight or for at least 4 hours.

Put the egg yolks and water into a small, heavy, non-aluminium saucepan and whisk them, off the heat, until frothy. Set the pan over a very low heat and whisk constantly for about 5 minutes or until you have a very thick mousse-like mixture.

Remove the saucepan from the heat and, whisking continuously, pour in the melted butter in a slow, steady stream until you have a thickened sauce. Whisk in the lemon juice and seasonings then serve the sauce as soon as possible.

Crab, lobster, scallops and prawns, poached salmon and trout are lovely with this sauce.

Sauce Maltaise

Sauce Maltaise is traditionally made with blood oranges which, though small, contain a fair amount of tart, red juice.

MAKES 300ML/½ PINT

2 small blood oranges
300ml/½ pint Hollandaise Sauce (see page 22)

Grate the zest from one orange and set it aside, then squeeze the juice from both oranges. Put the juice into a small pan and heat until it is tepid. Whisk the juice and zest into the hollandaise just before serving.

This is a good sauce to serve with richer fish such as salmon, salmon trout, red mullet, large prawns, monkfish, or with green vegetables such as lightly steamed asparagus and broccoli.

Hollandaise with Tomato and Basil

Choose tomatoes with plenty of flavour as well as a good colour for this sauce.

MAKES 300ML/½ PINT

2 ripe tomatoes
small bunch of basil
300ml/½ pint Hollandaise Sauce (see page 22)

Blanch and peel the tomatoes then quarter them. Remove the seeds and core then cut the flesh of each quarter into 2 or 3 strips. Pluck the basil leaves from their stems and roughly shred the leaves. Stir the tomatoes and basil into the hollandaise sauce and serve immediately.

Steamed white fish or globe artichokes make ideal partners for this sauce.

Sorrel Hollandaise

MAKES 300ML/½ PINT

125g/4½oz young sorrel leaves
20g/¾oz unsalted butter
300ml/½ pint Hollandaise Sauce (see page 22)

Remove the stalks and centre ribs from the sorrel. Heat the butter in a medium-sized, non-aluminium pan, add the leaves, stir well and cook for 5 minutes or until very soft. Drain the leaves in a colander then chop them thoroughly to give a thick purée. Stir this into the hollandaise, adjust the seasoning as necessary and serve.

A pretty green-coloured sauce for poached monkfish, salmon or turbot.

Almond and Herb Sauce

MAKES 250ML/9FL OZ

3 large egg yolks
1 tablespoon finely chopped parsley
1 tablespoon very finely chopped blanched almonds (not ground)
1 teaspoon grated lemon rind
1 clove garlic, crushed
salt and pepper
175g/6oz clarified unsalted butter, tepid

Mix the yolks, parsley, almonds, lemon rind, garlic and a little seasoning in a heatproof bowl. Stand the bowl in a bain-marie to gently warm the ingredients then remove it from the heat. Pour the melted butter onto the yolk mixture in a thin, steady stream, whisking constantly. Adjust the seasoning as necessary then serve. This sauce can be kept warm or reheated.

An unusual, modern sauce that is delicious served with roast lamb or lamb cutlets.

63

Béarnaise and Beurre Blanc

Sauce Béarnaise

Béarnaise is thicker and more substantial than hollandaise but nevertheless should have the texture of lightly whipped cream.

MAKES 350ML/12FL OZ

15g/½oz tarragon, leaves chopped and stalks crushed
2 shallots, finely chopped
1 teaspoon peppercorns, crushed
1 blade mace
3 tablespoons tarragon vinegar
4 medium egg yolks
2 tablespoons cold water
225g/8oz clarified unsalted butter, tepid
1 tablespoon chopped chervil
pinch of cayenne pepper
squeeze of lemon juice
salt and white pepper

Put the tarragon stalks into a small, heavy saucepan with the shallots, peppercorns, mace and vinegar. Boil the mixture until it has reduced to 1 tablespoon in volume then set it aside to cool.

Strain the reduction into a clean pan, add the yolks and water and whisk the mixture off the heat until it is frothy. Set the pan over a very low heat and whisk it constantly for 5 minutes until very thick and mousse-like.

Remove the pan from the heat and slowly whisk in the clarified butter. Whisk in the chopped tarragon and chervil then season the sauce to taste with cayenne, lemon juice, salt and pepper. Serve at once.

Variations: *Sauce Choron*
Replace the lemon juice with 1½ tablespoons of tomato passata.

Sauce Paloise
Replace the tarragon with fresh mint.

Sauce Ravigote
Stir 2 teaspoons each of snipped chives and finely chopped parsley plus 1 teaspoon of finely chopped capers into the sauce. Add extra lemon juice to make it nicely sharp.

Serve with grilled steaks or roast beef.

Beurre Blanc

This sauce from the Loire must not become too hot or the butter will melt and separate.

SERVES 4-6

40g/1½oz shallots, finely chopped
2 tablespoons white wine vinegar
2 tablespoons dry white wine
2 tablespoons cold water
200g/7oz unsalted butter, chilled and diced
squeeze of lemon juice
salt and pepper

Put the shallots, vinegar and white wine into a small, heavy saucepan and simmer until the liquid has reduced to 1 tablespoon in volume.

Whisk in the water then gradually whisk in the butter, moving the pan on and off the heat until the sauce turns creamy and thick.

Season to taste with a squeeze of lemon juice, salt and pepper. Serve immediately.

Variations: for a smoother sauce, strain through a fine-meshed conical sieve.

Beurre Blanc à la Crème
Replace the water with 2 tablespoons of crème fraîche or double cream.

Sauce Beurre Rouge
Replace the vinegar and the wine with 4 tablespoons of dry red wine and add 2 tablespoons of cream instead of water.

Beurre blanc is the perfect sauce for any steamed or poached fish, however delicate, as well as steamed vegetables.

Sauce Vin Blanc

Here stock is added to flavour the sauce with the main ingredient of the dish.

SERVES 4-6

40g/1½oz shallots, finely chopped
100ml/3½fl oz dry white wine
100ml/3½fl oz chicken, fish or vegetable stock
2 tablespoons crème fraîche or double cream
200g/7oz unsalted butter, chilled and diced
squeeze of lemon juice
salt and pepper

Put the shallots, wine and stock into a small, heavy-based saucepan and boil gently until the liquid has reduced by two-thirds. Add the cream and continue simmering until the mixture has reduced by half.

Gradually whisk in the butter, moving the pan on and off the heat so that the sauce is piping hot but not boiling. Taste and season with a squeeze of lemon juice plus salt and pepper. Serve immediately.

Suitable for chicken, fish or vegetables.

Champagne Beurre Blanc with Fish

SERVES 4

60g/2¼oz shallots, finely chopped
100ml/3½fl oz champagne
100ml/3½fl oz fish stock or water
1 small bouquet garni
4 salmon fillets or steaks
200g/7oz unsalted butter, chilled and diced
50g/1¾oz jar salmon caviar
squeeze of lemon juice or extra champagne
salt and pepper

Put the shallots, champagne, stock or water and bouquet garni into a non-aluminium

*B*EURRE *B*LANC

sauté pan or other shallow pan then cover and simmer gently for 5 minutes. Add the salmon, bring the liquid back to a boil then cover and simmer for 8-10 minutes or until the fish is just cooked. Remove the fish, drain it thoroughly and keep it warm while you are making the sauce.

Gently boil the cooking liquid until it has reduced to about 2 tablespoons of syrupy concentrate. Strain the liquid through a fine-meshed conical sieve into a small, heavy-based saucepan, then reheat it.

Over a low heat, whisk in the butter a few pieces at a time, moving the pan on and off the heat so the sauce is piping hot but not boiling and the texture is glossy.

Very gently stir in the salmon caviar, then taste the sauce and add a squeeze of lemon juice or some extra champagne plus salt and pepper as needed. Serve the sauce immediately with the fish.

Beurre Blanc with Herbs

SERVES 4

50ml/2fl oz white wine vinegar
2 tablespoons dry white wine
25g/1oz shallots, finely chopped
small bunch of herbs, leaves chopped and stalks crushed
2 tablespoons crème fraîche or double cream
100g/3½oz unsalted butter, chilled and diced
salt and white pepper

Put the vinegar, wine, shallots and the stalks of the herbs into a small, heavy pan. Simmer the mixture until it has reduced by two-thirds. Add the cream to the pan and simmer until the mixture has reduced by half.

Strain the reduction, pressing lightly on the shallots and stalks in the sieve. Return the reduction to the pan and reheat it.

Above: tarragon-flavoured Beurre Blanc with Herbs is a good match for salmon, here presented on layers of spinach and steamed, sliced potatoes.

Gradually whisk in the butter, moving the pan on and off the heat so the mixture is very hot but not boiling. Remove the sauce from the heat and season to taste with salt and pepper. Whisk in 1 tablespoon of chopped herbs and serve immediately.

A beurre blanc flavoured with tarragon is lovely with a rich seafood like salmon and scallops. Choose basil for monkfish and chicken; parsley for cod or hake; chervil for delicate fish like sole and plaice. A sauce flavoured with coriander (with or without a little grated root ginger) is good with crab, salmon and large prawns.

$\mathcal{C}$REAM $\mathcal{S}$AUCES

Crab Sauce

Adding wholegrain mustard to this butter sauce finished with cream stops it tasting too rich. Use fresh white crab meat wherever possible for the best flavour.

SERVES 4

60g/2½oz unsalted butter
1 small shallot, finely chopped
200ml/7fl oz dry white wine
100ml/3½fl oz double cream, plus an extra
  50ml/2fl oz, whipped
125g/4½oz white crab meat
scant teaspoon wholegrain mustard
salt and white pepper

Below: fresh is best for this distinctive Crab Sauce flavoured with shallot, wine and mustard. Its rich and unctuous texture comes from a combination of double cream and whipped cream.

Melt 1 tablespoon of the butter in a medium-sized saucepan and cook the shallot over a low heat for 3-4 minutes until it is soft but not coloured. Add the wine, bring to a boil then simmer until it has reduced by half.

Add the 100ml/3½fl oz of double cream, bring the mixture back to a boil and cook gently until the sauce just coats the back of a spoon. Add the crab and cook, stirring, until the sauce just comes to a boil.

Remove the pan from the heat and stir in the remaining butter. When it is thoroughly combined, fold in the whipped cream and mustard. Taste the sauce and add salt and pepper as necessary. Serve immediately.

———————⌐⌐———————

Other types of seafood are an excellent accompaniment to this sauce. Try it with steamed or poached fish steaks, prawns, scallops, or with beef steaks or pasta.

Shallot and Sauternes Sauce

Using sweet white wine in this sauce gives a delicious flavour: the result would simply not be as succulent if a drier wine were used. Sauternes is pricey but there are many good, inexpensive brands of Muscat available.

SERVES 4

4 shallots, finely chopped
1 tablespoon finely chopped carrot
1 tablespoon finely chopped celery
2 tablespoons finely chopped mushroom
25g/1oz butter
200ml/7fl oz sweet white wine such as
  Sauternes or Muscat
200ml/7fl oz chicken or fish stock
150ml/5fl oz double cream
salt and pepper

Cream Sauces

Put the chopped shallots, carrot, celery and mushroom into a medium-sized saucepan with the butter. Cover the pan and sweat the vegetables over a low heat until they are thoroughly softened but not brown.

Raise the heat under the pan, add the sweet wine and stock and bring the mixture to a boil. Boil vigorously until the volume of the liquid has reduced by half.

Lower the heat under the pan a little, add the double cream and simmer the sauce for 2 minutes or until it is thick. Season to taste with salt and pepper and serve.

Variation: for a richer, smoother sauce, pass the mixture through a fine sieve to create a purée then return the sauce to the stove and mount it with 75g/3oz of diced butter, whisking until it is glossy.

Serve the sauce with poached, grilled or roasted chicken or fish, varying your choice of stock to suit the meat.

Leek and Chive Sauce

The flavour of this very easy sauce seems to appeal to everyone.

SERVES 4

50g/1¾oz unsalted butter
2 shallots, finely chopped
2 leeks, finely chopped
90ml/3fl oz dry white wine
250ml/9fl oz double cream
small bunch of chives
salt and pepper

Melt the butter in a small saucepan and add the shallots and leeks. Cook them gently for 5 minutes or until soft but not coloured.

Raise the heat a little, add the white wine, bring to a boil and simmer until the volume of liquid has reduced by half. Pour in the cream, bring the mixture to a boil again and simmer gently until the sauce has reduced to a coating consistency.

Snip the chives into the sauce, stir briefly to combine and then taste and season as necessary with salt and pepper.

This luxurious sauce adds sophistication to hot poached salmon or chicken. You could also serve it with a colourful mixture of steamed vegetables, or as an alternative to hollandaise when making Eggs Benedict.

Whisky Cream Sauce

In this unusual, simple sauce, the traditional reduction of wine is replaced by whisky.

SERVES 4

50g/1¾oz unsalted butter
2 shallots, finely chopped
90ml/3fl oz whisky
2 tablespoons horseradish sauce
250ml/9fl oz double cream
small bunch of dill, chopped
salt and pepper

Melt the butter in a small saucepan, add the shallots and cook them gently over a low heat until they are soft but not coloured. Add the whisky, raise the heat a little and simmer until the volume of liquid has reduced by half. Stir in the horseradish sauce and the cream and simmer gently until the sauce has reduced to a coating consistency.

Add the chopped dill, stir and then season the sauce to taste with salt and pepper.

A slightly sweet cream sauce to serve with hot-smoked or fresh salmon, chicken or lamb. For a Scottish theme, serve alongside roast venison and mashed swede, plus some crisp steamed green beans or broccoli.

Curry Cream Sauce

SERVES 4

50g/1¾oz unsalted butter
1 shallot, chopped
1 small carrot, chopped
1 stalk celery, chopped
1 clove garlic, chopped
¼ teaspoon chilli powder
¼ teaspoon ground coriander
¼ teaspoon ground cumin
¼ teaspoon ground ginger
¼ teaspoon turmeric
seeds of 1 cardamom pod
300ml/½ pint chicken or vegetable stock
150ml/5fl oz double cream
salt and black pepper

Heat the butter in a small saucepan, add the chopped shallot, carrot, celery and garlic and cook them gently for 5 minutes until the vegetables have softened slightly. Stir in the spices, including a pinch of black pepper, and continue cooking over a low heat for a further 5 minutes.

Pour the stock into the saucepan, raise the heat to a moderate temperature and simmer the mixture until it has reduced in volume by half. Stir in the cream, lower the heat and cook the sauce for 10 minutes, stirring frequently.

Strain the sauce through a sieve, pressing down on the vegetables to extract as much flavour as possible, then taste and season as required with some salt and extra black pepper. Reheat if necessary before serving.

Best with chicken, egg, fish and rice dishes. Use the sauce to cover a mixture of hard-boiled eggs, smoked fish and rice to make a kedgeree, or use to coat hard-boiled or poached eggs and serve with toast and salad. The sauce can also be used to bind canned salmon or tuna: place the mixture in an ovenproof dish, top it with breadcrumbs and grated cheese then grill until browned.

Brown Sauce

This glossy, concentrated sauce was traditionally thickened with a nut-brown roux and simmered for many hours. These days, most chefs prefer to use arrowroot or *fecule* as a thickener after the stock has been reduced by rapid boiling. If you are using this sauce to make another, use *fecule*, not arrowroot, and omit the seasoning.

MAKES 300ML/½ PINT

300ml/½ pint brown beef stock (see page 8)
1 tablespoon potato flour *(fecule)* or arrowroot
2 tablespoons madeira or cold water
salt and pepper

Reheat the stock if necessary, bringing it to a simmer; it should already have been reduced to a good flavour and thoroughly skimmed. Mix the potato flour or arrowroot with the Madeira to make a smooth, pourable paste, then whisk this mixture into the simmering stock. The sauce will instantly thicken; it should just coat the back of a spoon. As soon as the sauce boils, remove it from the heat and season to taste.

Brown sauce can be cooled then stored in the refrigerator for up to 2 days, or frozen.

Serve with meats and poultry.

Above: freshly chopped herbs add a final flourish to this hearty dish of Steak Chasseur, made with button mushrooms, wine and tomato passata.

Sauce Chasseur

MAKES 450ML/16FL OZ

50g/1¾oz unsalted butter, chilled and diced
1 medium shallot, finely chopped
100g/3½oz button mushrooms, finely sliced
150ml/5fl oz dry white wine
300ml/½ pint Brown Sauce (see above) or
  brown beef stock (see page 8)
4 tablespoons tomato passata
salt and pepper
1 tablespoon chopped mixed herbs

Melt 20g/¾oz of the butter in a medium-sized heavy saucepan. Stir in the shallot and cook gently for 3-4 minutes until it is very soft but not browned. Add the mushrooms, stir well then cook gently, stirring frequently, for 5-7 minutes or until soft.

Using a large-holed conical sieve or a fine colander, drain the vegetable mixture then return it to the rinsed-out saucepan. Add the wine to the vegetables and boil vigorously

until the liquid has reduced to a volume of about 4-5 tablespoons.

Stir in the brown sauce or stock and the passata, bring the sauce back to a boil and simmer for 1 minute. When it is ready, the sauce should very lightly coat the back of a spoon. Season to taste with salt and pepper.

Remove the pan from the heat and whisk in the diced butter, 2 pieces at a time. Stir in the herbs and serve immediately. Once the butter has been added the sauce will separate if boiled or reheated.

Variation: choose dark-coloured mushrooms instead of the white button variety if you are making a sauce for dark meats. Vary your choice of stock and herbs to suit the meat.

Sauce Chasseur made with beef stock can be served with fried, grilled or roast beef. When made with chicken stock and flavoured with chives, parsley and tarragon, it is also an ideal sauce for roast or grilled poultry.

Sauce Bordelaise

Red wine and shallots are the essential added ingredients to this sauce, but as the marrow scooped from a beef bone used to be *de rigueur* for true Sauce Bordelaise, I have included some optional instructions. The sauce can be made using brown sauce or a really well-flavoured stock – this gives a different taste and consistency, but ultimately the quality of any sauce will depend on the quality of the stock. Choose a value for money red wine that you think is worth drinking rather than something top-notch and expensive or one akin to paint stripper.

MAKES 350ML/12FL OZ

2 medium shallots, finely diced
¼ teaspoon peppercorns, crushed
150ml/5fl oz red wine, plus 1 tablespoon extra
1 bouquet garni
300ml/½ pint Brown Sauce (see left) or brown beef stock (see page 8)
salt and pepper
25g/1oz unsalted butter, chilled and diced

Put the shallots, crushed peppercorns and 150ml/5fl oz of red wine into a small, heavy-based saucepan. Bring it to a boil and boil vigorously over a medium heat until the wine has reduced in volume to 3 tablespoons.

Add the bouquet garni and the brown sauce or beef stock to the reduction and simmer the mixture gently for 5 minutes. Strain it through a fine-meshed conical sieve into a clean pan, pressing down lightly on the shallots in the sieve with the back of a ladle to extract all the flavour.

When ready to serve, reheat the sauce then taste and add salt and pepper as required; you may need to add a little extra red wine to lift the flavour. Remove the hot sauce from the heat and gradually whisk in the diced butter to thicken the sauce. Serve immediately; the sauce will separate if reheated or allowed to boil.

Variation: to add bone marrow, ask your butcher to chop a large marrow bone into pieces about 4cm/1½in long. Blanch them in boiling water for 1 minute then scoop out the marrow and slice it thinly. Put the marrow into a small pan with a little stock or cold water to cover. Bring it to a boil, simmer for 1 minute, then drain. Add the marrow to the sauce after the butter.

This is perfect for an entrecôte of beef, or indeed any grilled steak or roast beef. Slices of pan-fried liver, slightly pink in the centre, are also a good match for this sauce.

Sauce Robert

This is a piquant, opaque sauce flavoured with onions and mustard and has been served with pork for several centuries, since the late Middle Ages. Dijon mustard is the best choice for this sauce as it is pale and pungent yet does not overwhelm the flavour

of the meat. You should not use the brilliant-yellow English style of mustard for this sauce as it is too fiery. Once the mustard is added the sauce should not be allowed to boil or it will turn unpleasantly bitter.

MAKES 350ML/12FL OZ

20g/¾oz unsalted butter
1 small onion, finely chopped
¼ teaspoon peppercorns, crushed
100ml/3½fl oz dry white wine
3 tablespoons white wine vinegar
300ml/½ pint Brown Sauce (see left) or brown beef stock (see page 8)
2-3 teaspoons Dijon mustard
salt and pepper

Gently heat the butter in a small, heavy-based saucepan. Add the onion, stir well then cover with a circle of dampened greaseproof paper and the pan lid. Cook the onion very gently, stirring frequently, for 20 minutes or until it is really soft but not coloured.

Stir in the peppercorns, wine and vinegar and boil until the liquid has reduced to 3 tablespoons. Stir in the brown sauce or stock and simmer gently for 5 minutes. Strain the sauce through a fine-meshed conical sieve into a clean pan, pressing down lightly on the onions in the sieve to extract all the flavour.

Reheat the sauce and add the mustard, salt and pepper to taste, whisking well to make a smooth sauce. Serve immediately.

Variation: add 4 small cocktail gherkins, cut into julienne or matchsticks, before serving.

Serve Sauce Robert with a traditional pork roast, or with grilled or pan-fried pork, or try it with a mixed grill including bacon, lamb chops, liver, sausages and mushrooms.

BROWN SAUCES AND WINE SAUCES

Sauce Bigarade

This is the sauce for duck *à l'orange* which nobody seems to serve in the good old classic way anymore. Properly made, it was a *tour de force* and part of a chef's final exams. The bitter orange sauce should be made from bigarade or Seville oranges to complement the richness of the meat. When they are out of season, the sauce needs to be sharpened with lemon juice; it should not be sweet or reminiscent of marmalade. If you are using stock, make sure that it is thoroughly skimmed of fat.

SERVES 4-6

1 Seville or bitter orange
15g/½oz unsalted butter
1 medium shallot, finely chopped
100ml/3½fl oz white wine
300ml/½ pint Brown Sauce or brown chicken
   or duck stock (see pages 8-9)
salt and pepper
sugar or lemon juice, to taste

Pare the rind from the orange then cut the strips into fine julienne or needle-like shreds. Blanch the rind for 1 minute in a small pan of boiling water then drain and set aside.

Paring an orange: use a vegetable peeler to remove the rind in strips. Pare only the thin layer of zest, leaving the white pith on the fruit.

Squeeze the juice from the orange, discarding the pips. Heat the butter in a small, heavy-based saucepan and gently cook the shallot until soft but not coloured.

Add the wine and the orange juice, bring to a boil and simmer until the mixture has reduced to about 4 tablespoons. Add the brown sauce or stock, simmer for 2 minutes then strain the liquid through a fine-meshed sieve into a clean pan, pressing down lightly on the shallots to extract all the flavour.

Reheat the sauce, then taste and season as necessary with salt and pepper. Add a little sugar if the sauce is very bitter, lemon juice if the sauce lacks acidity. Just before serving, stir in the reserved orange zest.

This sauce can be served with chicken as well as duck and goes well with pork.

Sauce Diable

SERVES 4-6

2 medium shallots, finely chopped
½ teaspoon peppercorns, crushed
1 small bouquet garni
100ml/3½fl oz dry white wine
4 tablespoons white wine vinegar
300ml/½ pint Brown Sauce or brown
   chicken stock (see page 8)
3 tablespoons tomato passata
few drops of Tabasco sauce
few drops of Worcestershire sauce
25g/1oz unsalted butter, chilled and diced
salt and pepper

Put the shallots, peppercorns, bouquet garni, wine and vinegar into a small, heavy pan and boil the mixture until it has reduced to about 4 tablespoons. Stir in the brown sauce or stock and the passata, return to a boil and simmer for 5 minutes.

Strain the sauce through a fine-meshed sieve into a clean pan. Reheat and season to

taste, adding just enough of the Tabasco and Worcestershire sauces to give the sauce a kick. Remove the pan from the heat and gradually whisk in the pieces of butter.

Serve immediately; the sauce will separate if boiled or reheated.

Variation: add 2 tomatoes, peeled, seeded and cut into thin strips, plus 1 tablespoon of finely chopped flat-leafed parsley to the sauce after adding the butter.

Sauce Diable can be served with grilled chicken or turkey.

Tarragon and Sherry Sauce

SERVES 4

1 tablespoon olive oil
2 medium shallots, finely chopped
125ml/4fl oz chicken stock
125ml/4fl oz Amontillado sherry
1 sprig thyme
125ml/4fl oz double cream
1½-2 tablespoons finely chopped tarragon
salt and pepper

Heat the olive oil in a small, heavy-based saucepan and cook the shallots until they are soft but not coloured. Add the stock, sherry and thyme and simmer until the mixture has reduced by half.

Stir in the cream and seasoning then simmer until the sauce is thick enough to coat the back of a spoon. Strain it into a clean pan, add the tarragon then taste and adjust the seasoning before serving.

An excellent sauce with good quality chicken breasts that have been quickly browned in olive oil and then baked until tender.

Quick White Wine Sauce

Because this simple, quick, low-fat sauce contains few ingredients, it is absolutely essential that they are of good quality.

MAKES 300ML/½ PINT

**150ml/5fl oz sweet white wine such as
   Sauternes or Muscat
2 teaspoons cornflour
150ml/5fl oz chicken stock
1 bouquet garni
salt and pepper**

In a small bowl, blend 1 tablespoon of the wine with the cornflour to give a smooth paste. Put the remaining wine, stock and the bouquet garni into a small, non-aluminium saucepan and bring the mixture to a boil.

   Remove the pan from the heat and whisk in the cornflour paste. Return to the heat and simmer the sauce for 2 minutes, stirring constantly, until smooth and thick. Discard the bouquet garni, season to taste and serve.

Serve this strongly-flavoured sauce in small quantities with chicken or white fish.

Sauce Meurette

An oft-quoted rule is that one should not serve red wine sauces with light-coloured ingredients, but this shows it can be done.

SERVES 6

**25g/1oz unsalted butter
1 tablespoon finely chopped onion
1 tablespoon finely chopped carrot
1 tablespoon finely chopped celery
1 teaspoon thyme leaves
750ml/1⅓ pints red Burgundy wine
500ml/18fl oz stock
1 tablespoon butter extra, softened
1 tablespoon plain flour**

Melt the butter in a large, heavy saucepan, add all the vegetables and thyme and sweat them gently until they are softened but not browned. Pour in the wine and stock then bring the mixture to a boil and simmer until the liquid has reduced in volume by half.

   Meanwhile, blend the extra butter with the flour on a small plate to make a beurre manié. Use it to thicken the reduced sauce by gradually whisking small pieces of the paste into the liquid. Serve the sauce hot.

Above: Sauce Meurette is easy to make yet boasts a complex flavour, achieved by simmering good red wine with vegetables, herbs and stock.

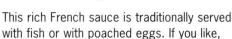

This rich French sauce is traditionally served with fish or with poached eggs. If you like, the eggs and sauce can be accompanied by fried lardons of bacon and some mushrooms to make a sophisticated brunch dish.

COOKING SAUCES

In casseroles, the sauce is a vital, integral part of the dish, used as a cooking medium rather than simply to accompany the main ingredient. The sauce can be a simple gravy based on stock or a richly fragrant wine and herb mixture. As the sauce infuses the fish, meat, poultry or vegetables with flavour, it helps to tenderize and moisten.

The leanest, most tender joints and pieces of meat and poultry can be quickly cooked at high temperature, but we must not forget the dishes our grandparents swooned over, those less expensive ingredients cooked long and slow. The aroma of a well-simmered daube, redolent of red wine and orange, is long remembered.

Most of these recipes are one-pot dishes – all you need for a warm, comforting, hearty main dish – and they usually benefit from reheating. Timing is not vital, another few minutes in the oven will not be a problem, but a good oven thermometer will prevent disasters.

Left: Seafood Stew.

Beef in Wine and Port

Ask the butcher to wrap the joint in a strip of barding fat, tied with string, to keep the meat moist during cooking.

SERVES 6

1.3kg/3lb beef joint
3 tablespoons olive oil
2 onions, finely chopped
150ml/5fl oz beef or game stock
salt and pepper
15g/½oz plain flour
15g/½oz unsalted butter, softened
FOR THE MARINADE:
300ml/½ pint full-bodied red wine
150ml/5fl oz port
1 large onion, cut in wedges
2 large carrots, thickly sliced
½ teaspoon peppercorns
1 bouquet garni

Put the meat into a deep china or glass bowl and add all the marinade ingredients. Cover and leave it to marinate for 3 days in the refrigerator, turning the meat every half day.

When you are ready to cook the meat, preheat the oven to 170°C/325°F/Gas 3. Lift the meat from the marinade, drain it thoroughly then pat dry with kitchen paper. Strain the marinade, reserving the liquid.

Heat the oil in a large flameproof casserole and cook the onions very gently for about 20 minutes or until very soft. Raise the heat and add the meat, cooking it briskly until it is browned on all sides and the onions are crispy but not burnt.

Add the reserved marinade liquid and the stock to the casserole, plus a little salt and pepper and bring the mixture to a boil. Cover with a tight-fitting lid and cook gently in the oven for about 3 hours, stirring occasionally, until the meat is tender.

When cooked, lift out the meat and keep it warm. Bring the sauce to a boil on top of the stove. Mash the flour and butter together then whisk the paste into the bubbling sauce

until it thickens. Taste the sauce and adjust the seasoning as necessary. Thickly slice the meat and serve it with the sauce.

Variation: replace the beef with venison.

———— 🥄 ————

Mashed or boiled potatoes and a green vegetable or salad are best with this dish.

Aromatic Braised Steak

The combination of flavours in this casserole dates back centuries.

SERVES 6

1kg/2lb 4oz braising steak, thickly sliced
3 tablespoons plain flour
3 tablespoons olive oil
2 sticks celery, finely chopped
2 medium onions, finely chopped
2 medium carrots, finely chopped
2 cloves garlic, finely chopped
6 cloves
1 stick cinnamon
400ml/14fl oz port
100ml/3½fl oz water or vegetable stock
salt and pepper

Preheat the oven to 170°C/325°F/Gas 3. Season the flour with a little salt and pepper and use the mixture to lightly coat the meat, shaking off any excess.

In a large, flameproof casserole, heat the oil over a fairly high heat and quickly brown the meat on each side, a couple of pieces at a time. Set the steak aside.

Add the chopped vegetables and garlic to the fat left in the pan then lower the heat and cook gently, stirring frequently, until golden and softened. Stir in the cloves and cinnamon and cook for 2-3 minutes.

Add the port and water or stock then return the meat to the casserole and bring the mixture to a boil. Season with a little salt

and plenty of pepper then cover and cook very slowly in the oven for 1½-2 hours or until tender. Check the casserole and stir it frequently: if it is cooking too fast, reduce the oven temperature; if the sauce is drying out, add more water.

Taste the sauce and adjust the seasoning as necessary, then remove the whole spices from the casserole and serve.

———— 🥄 ————

Mashed potatoes or celeriac make a creamy accompaniment to this rich casserole.

Beef Carbonade

SERVES 4

700g/1lb 9oz braising steak, cubed
25g/1oz plain flour
25g/1oz butter
225g/8oz onions, chopped
300ml/½ pint beer
300ml/½ pint beef stock
3 tablespoons chopped parsley
salt and pepper

Preheat the oven to 150°C/300°F/Gas 2. Lightly season the flour with salt and pepper then toss the meat in it, shaking off any excess. Heat the butter in a flameproof casserole and brown the meat all over, then remove it from the pan and set aside.

Add the onions to the hot fat and cook, stirring frequently, until transparent. Return the meat to the casserole and add the beer and stock. Cover and cook in the oven for 2½ hours or until the meat is tender.

Before serving, adjust the seasoning to taste and sprinkle with parsley.

Variation: use venison instead of beef.

———— 🥄 ————

Creamy mashed potatoes are the best partner to this Flemish speciality.

BEEF SAUCES

Boeuf en Daube Provençale

This dish is named after the pot-bellied casserole or *daubière* designed for long, slow cooking. Start well ahead: the meat needs to marinate overnight, cooking takes several hours, and the dish tastes best if it is then chilled, skimmed of fat and reheated.

SERVES 6

1kg/2lb 4oz chuck or braising steak, cubed
3 tablespoons virgin olive oil
150g/5½oz unsmoked bacon, cut in strips
4 large plum tomatoes, roughly chopped
250g/9oz button mushrooms
100g/3½oz black olives, stoned and roughly chopped or 15g/½oz can anchovies, drained and roughly chopped
FOR THE MARINADE:
750ml/1 pint 7fl oz full-bodied red wine
1 large bouquet garni
pared rind of 1 orange, preferably Seville
2 medium onions, cut in wedges
2 medium carrots, thickly sliced
3 cloves garlic, sliced
8 peppercorns
1 tablespoon virgin olive oil

Place the meat in a large china or glass bowl. Pour in the wine and add the remaining marinade ingredients. Mix well then cover and leave the beef to marinate in the refrigerator for 12-24 hours.

When ready to cook, preheat the oven to 170°C/325°F/Gas 3. Remove the meat from the marinade and pat it dry with kitchen paper. Strain the marinade and discard the peppercorns. Reserve the strained liquid and vegetables separately.

In a large, heavy, lidded casserole, heat the oil and cook the bacon over a moderate heat. Remove the bacon, draining the fat back into the casserole, and set it aside. Brown the meat in batches in the hot fat then remove and set aside with the bacon.

Add the reserved marinade vegetables and orange rind to the casserole and stir well before adding the beef and bacon. Gently stir in the tomatoes, mushrooms, olives or anchovies and the marinade liquid.

Bring the mixture to a boil then cover and gently cook the casserole in the oven for 3½ hours or until the meat is very tender. Stir the mixture occasionally and top up with hot water if the daube is looking dry. If the daube is bubbling vigorously, lower the oven temperature so the liquid only just simmers.

Above: Mediterranean flavourings of orange and black olives or anchovies make Boeuf en Daube Provençale a casserole out of the ordinary.

When cooked, stir the daube gently then taste and season as necessary. Discard the orange rind and bouquet garni. The sauce should just coat the back of a spoon.

Serve the daube with noodles or macaroni.

Irish Stew

SERVES 4

900g/2lb boneless lamb shoulder, cubed
900g/2lb potatoes, cubed
2 large onions, sliced
1 tablespoon pearl barley
300ml/1/2 pint water or stock
2 tablespoons chopped parsley
salt and pepper

Preheat the oven to 120°C/250°F/Gas ½. In a flameproof casserole, layer the meat and potatoes with the onion, sprinkling each layer with a little pearl barley and finishing with a layer of potatoes. Season lightly then add enough cold water to come halfway up the sides of the casserole. Cover and cook in the oven for 3 hours. Serve sprinkled with the chopped parsley.

Best accompanied by braised red cabbage.

Gigot Brayaude

SERVES 8

1 leg lamb, about 2kg/4½lb, tied with string
2 onions, sliced
2 carrots, sliced
1 sprig thyme
1 bay leaf
500ml/18fl oz water or stock
125ml/4fl oz brandy
salt and pepper

Preheat the oven to 120°C/250°F/Gas ½. Put the lamb in a large flameproof casserole with the vegetables, herbs, salt and pepper. Add the water or stock then cover and cook in the oven for 5 hours. Turn the meat 3-4 times during cooking. Add a little more water if the casserole seems to be drying out. If the liquid starts to simmer, reduce the heat so that it bubbles very gently.

After braising for 5 hours, add the brandy and continue cooking for a further hour. The meat should be meltingly tender.

Remove the string from the lamb and carve the meat thickly. Strain the sauce from the casserole, discarding the vegetables, then skim off any fat and serve.

Serve the gigot with potatoes and carrots.

Lamb and Broad Bean Tagine

SERVES 4

500g/1lb 2oz trimmed lean lamb, cubed
3 cloves garlic, finely chopped
1 large onion, finely chopped
¼ teaspoon sea salt
½ teaspoon ground black pepper
½ teaspoon ground ginger
large pinch of saffron threads, crumbled
500g/1lb 2oz shelled broad beans
1 preserved lemon, rinsed and quartered
small bunch of coriander, finely chopped

Put the lamb, garlic, onion, salt, pepper, ginger and saffron in a tagine or flameproof casserole and mix well. Add just enough cold water to cover the meat then bring to a boil. Cover, reduce the heat so that the tagine just simmers and cook for 1 hour or until the meat is tender, stirring occasionally and adding more water if it becomes dry.

Add the broad beans and lemon and mix thoroughly. Cover again and cook until the beans are tender: 10 minutes for young beans, 20 minutes for older ones. Stir in the coriander, then taste and add more pepper if necessary. If the sauce is watery, reduce it before adding the coriander.

Offer couscous alongside the tagine.

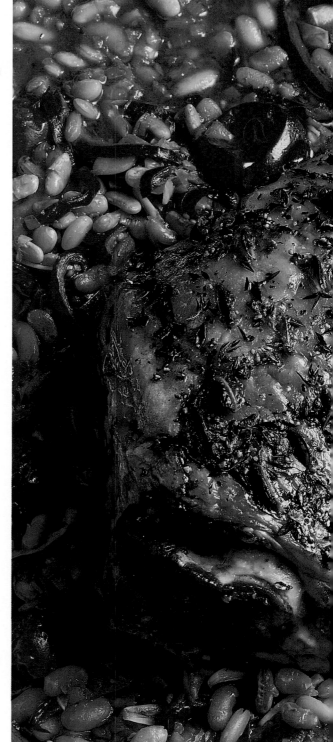

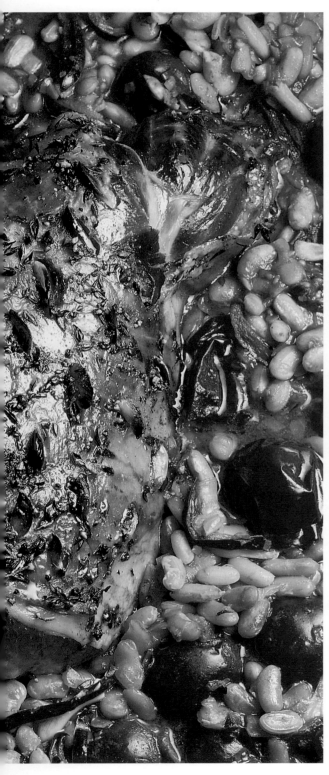

Leg of Lamb with Flageolet Beans

Here's another great combination of beans and lamb. In Brittany, roast lamb is often served with white beans. For a richer taste, I like to cook green flageolet beans around the meat in a tomato and red pepper sauce. This makes an excellent winter Sunday lunch, as all the preparation can be done in advance and the meat can be left to cook while you chat with your guests.

SERVES 8

FOR THE BEANS:
500g/1lb 2oz dried flageolet beans
2 bay leaves
1 large sprig thyme
1 carrot, quartered
1 medium onion, peeled but left whole
FOR THE SAUCE:
3 tablespoons olive oil
2 medium onions, finely chopped
4-6 cloves garlic, to taste, finely sliced
1 tablespoon thyme leaves
2 medium red peppers, cored and sliced
800g/28oz canned cherry tomatoes in juice
salt and pepper
FOR THE LAMB:
1 leg lamb, about 2.25kg/5lb
3 cloves garlic
1 tablespoon olive oil
1 tablespoon thyme leaves
sea salt and coarsely ground black pepper

Soak the beans overnight, or for at least 12 hours, in plenty of cold water. Drain and pick them over, then rinse thoroughly. In a large pan, cover the beans with fresh water and bring them to a boil. Skim off any scum, then boil hard for 10 minutes. Add the herbs

Left: a sauce of red peppers and tomatoes makes a spectacular base for this juicy Leg of Lamb with Flageolet Beans. The meat is studded with fresh thyme and slivers of garlic for extra flavour.

and vegetables, but no salt at this stage, then cover and simmer for 45 minutes or until the beans are tender (the exact time will depend on the age of the beans). Drain the cooked beans, saving the liquid but discarding the flavourings.

Meanwhile, prepare the tomato and pepper sauce. Heat the olive oil in a large, heavy pan. Add the onions, garlic and thyme. Cover and cook very slowly for about 20 minutes or until the onions are soft and golden. Add the peppers and cook for another 5 minutes. Add the tomatoes with their juice and remove the pan from the heat. (This sauce can be made up to this point 1 day in advance and kept tightly covered in the refrigerator.)

To cook the meat, preheat the oven to 220°C/425°F/Gas 7. Trim the lamb to remove all but a thin covering of fat. Slice the garlic into slivers, then make small, deep slits in the meat with a sharp knife. Insert the garlic so the lamb is liberally and evenly studded. Rub with the olive oil then sprinkle with the thyme leaves and season with salt and pepper. Place the leg of lamb in a large casserole, baking dish or deep roasting tin and roast uncovered for 30 minutes.

Add the drained beans to the tomato and pepper sauce and season to taste. Reheat if necessary. The mixture should be soupy, so, if necessary, add some of the reserved bean cooking liquid. Reduce the oven temperature to 200°C/400°F/Gas 6. Spoon the sauce into the casserole around the lamb and cook uncovered for another 45 minutes, stirring the beans occasionally. If the mixture becomes dry, add more bean liquor.

Variations: plum tomatoes can be used in place of tinned cherry tomatoes. In season, you can use 1kg/2lb 4oz of fresh Gardener's Delight cherry tomatoes.

Present the lamb and sauce on a large platter, then carve the meat into thick slices.

Pork Braised with Dried Fruits

I first ate this hearty, really warming winter dish one freezing day in northern France, and I have since enjoyed similar versions in Germany and in Lancaster County, Pennsylvania as part of a large Mennonite meal. The Pennsylvanian Dutch (or Deutsch) originally came from Germany and have maintained their traditional dishes. Funnily enough, my husband has a student from Tunisia who cooks this with chicken in a tagine, but uses a tablespoon of honey to finish it rather than lemon juice.

SERVES 4

4 large loin pork chops, about 900g/2lb in total
1 tablespoon plain flour
salt and pepper
1 tablespoon vegetable oil
400ml/14fl oz chicken or vegetable stock
½ lemon
100g/3½oz ready-to-eat dried prunes
100g/3½oz ready-to-eat dried apricots
1 large tart eating apple, peeled, cored and cut into eighths

Preheat the oven to 180°C/350°F/Gas 4. Dust the chops in the flour seasoned with a little salt and pepper. Heat the oil in a large flameproof casserole and brown the chops, 1 or 2 at a time, until they are a good golden brown on each side. Remove the chops and pour out the fat, leaving the cooking juices and brown sediment in the bottom of the casserole.

Add the stock to the casserole and bring it to a boil, stirring and scraping to dissolve all the sediment and caramelized cooking juices. Using a vegetable peeler, pare the rind from the lemon half and add the rind to the casserole with the prunes, apricots and apples. Bring the mixture to a boil then add a little seasoning and stir well. Replace the chops then cover the casserole with the lid

and cook it in the oven until the meat is very tender, about 40 minutes. If the casserole is cooking too fast, turn down the oven to 170°C/325°F/Gas 3.

Stir before serving: the apples should have partially broken down to slightly thicken the sauce. Taste, adding salt, pepper and lemon juice to suit your taste.

Above: plump apricots, prunes and fresh apple add delicious natural sweetness to Pork Braised with Dried Fruits, a warming family supper.

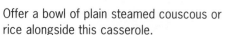

Offer a bowl of plain steamed couscous or rice alongside this casserole.

Country Red Wine Casserole

This is a robust, dark and richly flavoured red wine casserole, but deceptively easy and quick for such an impressive result. Reducing the wine before adding the other ingredients drives off the harsh alcohol flavours, making the sauce taste as though it has been simmered for several hours.

SERVES 4-6

**4 tablespoons plain flour
salt and pepper
700g/1lb 9oz thick pork chops
4 tablespoons virgin olive oil
4 rashers thick-cut back bacon, diced
100g/3½oz brown cap mushrooms
200g/7oz small shallots, peeled but left whole
750ml/1 pint 7fl oz red wine
600-700ml/1-1¼ pints beef stock
4 large cloves garlic, chopped
1 large bouquet garni**

Mix the flour with enough salt and freshly ground black pepper to lightly season the pork then toss it with the meat until it is well covered, dusting off any excess.

Heat the oil in a large, heavy flameproof casserole or saucepan and fry the meat in batches until it is thoroughly browned on all sides. Remove it with a slotted spoon and reserve. When all the meat has been browned and removed, add the bacon to the pan and cook, stirring frequently, until it is lightly browned. Remove the bacon, draining the fat back into the pan, and reserve it in a separate bowl to the meat.

Add the whole mushrooms and the shallots to the fat in the pan and toss them for a few minutes until lightly browned. Lift out the vegetables and add them to the bacon. Add all but 2 tablespoons of the wine to the pan and deglaze it over a fairly high heat, stirring well to dislodge and dissolve all the caramelized meat juices.

Boil the wine fairly rapidly until it has reduced by half. Stir in 600ml/1 pint of the stock and boil the liquid again until it has reduced by a third, stirring frequently.

Add the garlic and bouquet garni to the pan with the reserved pork and stir well. Return the casserole to a boil then cover and leave it to simmer very gently for 1½ hours or until the pork is almost tender. Stir from time to time, adding a little more stock if the sauce is reducing too quickly and leaving the meat exposed.

When the meat is almost cooked, add the reserved bacon, mushrooms and shallots. Stir well, adding a little of the extra stock if needed. Cover the pan and cook for another 20 minutes or until the meat is really tender.

Remove the bouquet garni and stir well. The sauce should be really dark and syrupy. If it is far too thin and runny, boil it uncovered for a few minutes until it coats the back of a spoon; if it is well flavoured but a little thin, add some beurre manié (see page 14) to the boiling liquid; if the sauce is too thick, add some more stock, then bring the casserole back to the boil.

When the sauce has reached the correct consistency, taste it and add salt and pepper as necessary. Add the remaining wine – this livens up the sauce, giving it a fresh taste, cutting any excess richness – then serve. The casserole freezes well and is better if made a day or so in advance, well chilled then thoroughly reheated.

Variations: replace the pork with cubed braising steak, venison chunks, large portions of chicken on the bone, pheasant or grouse and select the flavour of the stock to suit the meat you have chosen. The length of time the casserole should be simmered before the bacon and vegetables are added depends on the size and quality of the meat chosen. Chicken pieces need only be simmered for around 40 minutes, however tough game meats will require 1 hour or more in the oven.

Buttered noodles and a robust green salad are best with this dish.

Filet de Porc Normande

SERVES 4

**25g/1oz butter
750g/1½lb pork tenderloin
1 medium onion, finely sliced
1 dessert apple, peeled, cored and sliced
1 tablespoon flour
110ml/3¾fl oz dry cider
150ml/5fl oz stock
2 tablespoons double cream or crème fraîche
salt and pepper**

Preheat the oven to 180°C/350°F/Gas 4. Gently heat the butter in a flameproof lidded casserole, then add the whole pork fillet and brown it all over. Remove it from the casserole and set aside. Add the onion to the pan and fry it for 2-3 minutes, then add the apple and continue cooking until both are golden brown.

Add the flour to the pan, then stir in the cider and stock and bring the mixture to the boil. Return the pork fillet to the casserole, burying it within the sauce, then cover and bake in the oven for 30-35 minutes.

When the meat is thoroughly cooked and tender, remove the casserole from the oven and slice the pork fillet. Keep it warm while you finish the sauce.

Purée the sauce mixture until smooth, then return it to the heat and reduce by boiling a little if necessary. Add the cream or crème fraîche, allow it to heat through then taste and season as needed with salt and pepper. Pour the sauce over the meat and serve.

Serve with steamed green vegetables and, if you like, boiled new potatoes or some very lightly buttered noodles.

Chicken with Chanterelles Sauce

These delicate, delightful golden wild mushrooms add a superb flavour to chicken.

SERVES 4-6

1 medium chicken, about 1.5kg/3lb 5oz
40g/1½oz unsalted butter
2 tablespoons vegetable oil
250g/9oz chanterelles, trimmed
4 large shallots, cut into wedges
2 cloves garlic, finely sliced
300ml/½ pint chicken stock
juice of ½ lemon
100ml/3½fl oz crème fraîche
2 egg yolks
salt and pepper
sprigs of flat-leafed parsley

Preheat the oven to 180°C/350°F/Gas 4. Wipe the chicken inside and out with kitchen paper and trim off any large lumps of fat at the opening to the body cavity.

Heat half the butter with the oil in a heavy casserole and brown the chicken on all sides. Remove it from the casserole and set aside, then wipe out the pan with kitchen paper.

Heat half the remaining butter in the casserole and quickly cook the mushrooms until they are lightly coloured. Remove with a slotted spoon and reserve. Heat the remaining butter, add the shallots and garlic and cook, stirring frequently, until golden. Replace the chicken, pour in the stock and bring the mixture to a boil.

Cover the casserole and cook in the oven for 1 hour or until a skewer inserted in the thickest part of the thigh releases clear juices. After the chicken has been cooking for about 45 minutes, add the mushrooms to the casserole and continue cooking.

To finish, remove the chicken and keep it warm. Bring the sauce to a boil and simmer, uncovered, for 5 minutes until slightly reduced. Stir in the lemon juice.

Above: the pretty shapes of the wild mushrooms make Chicken with Chanterelles Sauce a feast for the eyes as well as the tastebuds.

Mix the crème fraîche and egg yolks together in a small bowl then stir in a ladle of the cooking liquid. Remove the casserole from the heat and pour in the egg mixture, stirring continuously until the sauce thickens. Do not let it boil. Taste and add salt, pepper and more lemon juice as necessary. Spoon the sauce over the chicken, garnish with the parsley sprigs and serve jointed or carved.

Variation: add a handful of bacon lardons to the sauce before putting it in the oven.

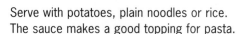

Serve with potatoes, plain noodles or rice. The sauce makes a good topping for pasta.

*C*HICKEN *S*AUCES

Coq au Vin

A classic French dish and one that is always appreciated by guests and family.

SERVES 4-6

1 medium chicken, about 1.5kg/3lb 5oz
1 tablespoon olive oil
85g/3oz unsalted butter
120g/4oz green streaky bacon or pickled belly pork, diced
2 tablespoons brandy
600ml/1 pint red wine
120g/4oz button onions, peeled but left whole
120g/4oz mushrooms, sliced
1 large clove garlic, crushed
300ml/½ pint chicken stock
25g/1oz flour
2 tablespoons freshly chopped parsley

Preheat the oven to 150°C/300°F/Gas 2. Wipe the chicken inside and out with kitchen paper and trim off any large lumps of fat at the opening to the body cavity.

Heat the oil and 60g/2oz of the butter in a flameproof lidded casserole, then add the bacon or pork and fry until the pieces are lightly browned and the fat is translucent. Remove the bacon or pork, then brown the chicken in the casserole.

Meanwhile, heat the brandy in a small pan. When the chicken is browned all over, spoon off any excess fat from the casserole. Set the brandy alight in the small pan then pour it flaming over the bird. When the flames have subsided, return the bacon or pork to the casserole and add the wine, onions, mushrooms and garlic. Pour in enough stock to come halfway up the sides of the bird.

Cover the casserole and cook it in the oven for 1 hour, or until the chicken is tender and the juices run clear when a skewer is inserted in the thickest part of the thigh. Turn the bird twice during cooking.

When the chicken is cooked, remove it from the oven and carve it into joints. Lift the onions, bacon and mushrooms from the casserole and place them on a serving platter with the chicken. Keep them warm in the oven while you finish the sauce.

Bring the casserole juices to a boil on the stovetop. Work the remaining 25g/1oz of butter and the flour together to make a beurre manié and, when the liquid has reduced by about a third, gradually whisk in small pieces of the paste until the sauce thickens. Season to taste with salt and pepper, pour the sauce over the chicken and vegetables and garnish with the parsley.

Variation: you can substitute a joint of pork or beef for the chicken, replacing the chicken stock with beef stock if preferred.

Chicken in Paprika Sauce

SERVES 4

25g/1oz unsalted butter
1 tablespoon virgin olive oil
4 boneless chicken breasts, unskinned
2 shallots, thinly sliced
1 medium carrot, thickly sliced
3 stalks celery, thickly sliced
125ml/4fl oz dry white wine
salt and pepper
1 bouquet garni
250ml/9fl oz crème fraîche
1 tablespoon paprika

Heat the butter and oil in a large sauté pan, add the chicken and brown it thoroughly before removing it to a plate. Lower the heat and stir in the vegetables. Cook them gently, stirring frequently, for 15 minutes or until softened and lightly coloured.

Return the chicken to the pan and pour in the wine. Bring the mixture to a boil, season lightly and add the bouquet garni. Cover the pan and simmer gently for 25-30 minutes or until the chicken is thoroughly cooked.

Lift the chicken from the pan, draining it thoroughly, and keep it warm in a serving dish. Skim the sauce if necessary then stir in the crème fraîche and paprika and simmer until the sauce just coats the back of a spoon. Taste and adjust the seasoning as necessary. Strain the sauce through a fine-meshed sieve onto the chicken and serve.

Variations: this lovely dish can also be made with pheasant and guinea fowl.

———————— ☞ ————————

The paprika sauce is well-matched by noodles and a side dish of courgettes.

Chicken with Lemon and Rosemary Sauce

SERVES 4

20g/¾oz unsalted butter
1 tablespoon olive oil
4 large boneless chicken breasts, trimmed
1 large sprig fresh rosemary
4 cloves garlic, peeled but left whole
juice of 1 lemon
2 strips lemon rind
salt and black pepper

Heat the butter and oil in a heavy sauté pan. Add the chicken pieces, skin side down, and cook on both sides until golden brown.

Reduce the heat and add the rest of the ingredients. Stir well, then bring the sauce to a simmer. Cover the pan and cook slowly for 20 minutes or until tender, turning the chicken occasionally. Add salt, pepper or some more lemon juice to taste, then remove the lemon rind and serve.

———————— ☞ ————————

Boiled or steamed new potatoes and green beans or salad are the best accompaniments to this aromatic dish.

Saffron Fish Casserole

A good looking one-pot recipe that makes a fine summer supper. The tiniest ingredient makes the most impact – a good pinch of saffron threads between thumb and forefinger are briefly toasted then soaked to give a glorious golden stock. This is poured over thinly sliced potatoes layered with thick fish fillets (choose well-flavoured fish like haddock or John Dory) and ripe tomatoes.

SERVES 4

large pinch of saffron threads
300ml/½ pint fish stock
2 tablespoons virgin olive oil
4 shallots, finely chopped
2 cloves garlic, crushed
2 teaspoons very finely chopped thyme leaves
4 medium-large potatoes (not too waxy), peeled and very thinly sliced
4 fish fillets, about 900g/2lb in total, skinned if desired
4 medium tomatoes, thinly sliced
salt and pepper
25g/1oz unsalted butter, diced

Preheat the oven to 200°C/400°F/Gas 6. Roast the saffron in a small ramekin or other ovenproof dish for 10-12 minutes until it is darker in colour but not scorched. Crumble the threads then mix with 4 tablespoons of the stock. Cover and leave the saffron to soak for 15 minutes or overnight if possible.

Thoroughly butter a large earthenware dish that will take the fish in a single layer. Heat the oil in a medium saucepan and gently cook the shallots, garlic and thyme for 10-12 minutes until very soft and golden.

Put a layer of sliced potatoes, overlapping them slightly, in the bottom of the dish. Season lightly then scatter over half the shallot mixture. Arrange the fish fillets on top then season lightly again. Cover this with the tomatoes, then the rest of the shallots. Season again, then top with two layers of potatoes, seasoning as you go.

Combine the saffron liquid with the rest of the stock and carefully pour the mixture over the casserole so that it seeps down between the layers evenly rather than hovering around the edges of the dish. When you have finished the stock should come about halfway up the side of the dish.

Dot the top of the casserole with the diced butter and bake it uncovered for 40-50 minutes until the top is golden and crispy and the potatoes are tender.

Seafood Stew

Choose your favourite fish, but for maximum flavour add a couple of handfuls of mussels, clams, unshelled large raw prawns, red mullet, John Dory, sea bass, or hake: a good selection need not be expensive.

SERVES 4

100g/3½oz dried butter beans
about 1.25kg/2lb 12oz seafood, including shells
3 shallots, finely chopped
2-4 cloves garlic, finely chopped
3 tablespoons virgin olive oil
350g/12oz potatoes (not too waxy), finely diced
4 ripe tomatoes, peeled and roughly chopped
200ml/7fl oz fish stock
100ml/3½fl oz dry white wine
1 large bouquet garni, including 1 sprig of rosemary
squeeze of lemon juice (optional)
salt and pepper

Soak the beans overnight, or for 12 hours, in plenty of cold water. Drain, then put them into a medium-sized pan with plenty of fresh cold water to cover. Bring the beans to a boil, skim well then boil hard for 10 minutes. Reduce the heat and simmer the beans for 25-30 minutes or until tender. Drain the beans and set them aside.

Preheat the oven to 170°C/325°F/Gas 3. Cut the fish into medium-sized chunks. Scrub

the mussels, remove any hairy beards and discard any that do not close when tapped sharply. Scrub the clams and discard any that do not close in the same way.

Put the beans, seafood and all the remaining ingredients into a large flameproof casserole with a tight-fitting lid and stir gently. Bring the casserole to a boil on the stovetop then cover and cook in the oven for 30-40 minutes until the fish and potatoes are tender. Discard any unopened shellfish.

Stir gently then taste the sauce and adjust the seasonings as necessary: you may need a squeeze of lemon juice. The sauce should be soupy but thickened with the potatoes and beans. Discard the bouquet garni and serve as soon as possible.

Variations: add 1 sliced bulb of fennel to the vegetables. You can replace some of the fresh tomatoes with sun-dried tomatoes preserved in oil and use the flavoured oil in place of the olive oil. Replace the wine with vermouth and finish the dish with 2 tablespoons of chopped fresh herbs.

Mussels in Coriander, Chilli and Lemongrass

My favourite way of cooking mussels reminds me of the restaurant where I met my husband – it is their most popular dish.

SERVES 2-4

1kg/2lb 4oz mussels
25g/1oz unsalted butter
4 medium spring onions, finely chopped
2 cloves garlic, finely chopped
1 stalk lemongrass, very finely chopped
1 small red bird's eye chilli, seeded and finely chopped
150ml/5fl oz dry white wine
small bunch of coriander, leaves and stems chopped
freshly ground black pepper

𝒮eafood 𝒮auces

To prepare the mussels, put them into a large bowl or a sink of cold water and stir gently. Leave them for 5 minutes then lift the mussels out of the water so the grit and sand is left at the bottom. Scrub the mussels under cold running water and scrape off any barnacles and dirt with a small knife. Pull away the hairy black beards. Put the cleaned mussels into another bowl of clean, cold water. Discard any mussels with broken or damaged shells and any open mussels that do not close when tapped.

Melt the butter in a large pan then add the spring onions and garlic and cook very gently for 1 minute until softened. Add the lemongrass and chillies and cook a further minute. Pour in the wine and boil rapidly to reduce the liquid by about a third. Add the mussels to the pan and stir well. Cover with a lid and cook over a medium-high heat for about 2 minutes until the mussels have opened, shaking the pan frequently. Discard any mussels that will not open.

Using a slotted spoon, lift the mussels out of the pan and into warmed serving bowls. Add freshly ground black pepper to taste to the sauce left in the pan then stir in the chopped coriander. Spoon the sauce over the mussels and serve immediately.

Serve the mussels as a starter for 4 people with plenty of fresh white bread to mop up the sauce. Alternatively, this dish makes a delicious main course for two. You can pick the mussels from their shells using a fork or use an empty shell as a pincer.

Left: the fresh taste of the sea is highlighted in this simple yet beautiful dish of Mussels in Coriander, Chilli and Lemongrass.

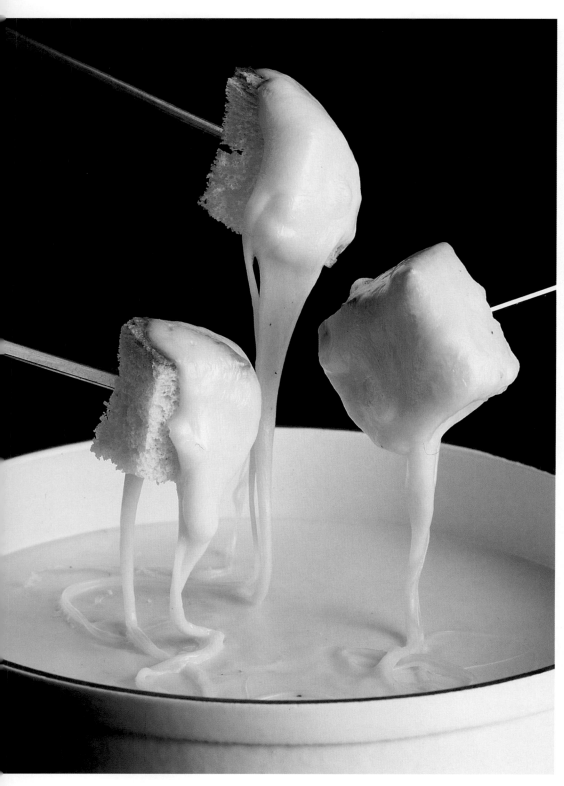

Cheese Fondue

Fondue Savoyarde, from the mountainous, dairying Savoie region of France, is properly made in a small earthenware pan with two local cheeses. They are traditionally finely sliced, not grated, and melted in the local dry white wine flavoured with a shot of kirsch. Fondue is eaten by putting a cube of *pain de campagne*, French rustic white bread, on the end of a long-handled fork and swirling it in the molten mixture.

SERVES 4

250g/9oz Emmental cheese
250g/9oz Beaufort cheese
1 clove garlic, thickly sliced
250ml/9fl oz dry white wine, preferably from
  the Savoie
ground black pepper
2 tablespoons kirsch, or to taste

Finely slice the cheeses. Rub the inside of the fondue pan all over with the garlic slices, then discard them.

Bring the wine to a boil in the pan then stir in the cheeses. Continue stirring (traditionally in a figure-of-eight motion) until the cheese melts. Set the pan over a table burner, and gently stir in the ground black pepper and kirsch to taste. The burner should keep the fondue warm and liquid without allowing it to boil. Eat immediately.

Variation: Gruyère and Comté cheeses can also be used to make the fondue.

———————⌐∘⌐———————

Serve with a loaf of *pain de campagne*, cubed, or with small, freshly boiled new potatoes in their jackets and lightly blanched green vegetables such as broccoli florets.

Right: a table burner keeps Cheese Fondue warm and creamy while you enjoy it. Give the mixture a stir each time you dip in the bread.

Cheese and Vegetable Sauces

Boston Baked Beans

This old-fashioned recipe is traditionally flavoured with a piece of salt pork, cooked overnight in a slow oven then served with Boston brown bread, a moist, steamed loaf made with molasses. It makes a hearty meal. Each area of the United States has its own version, made with locally grown beans (black-eyed, green, pea-beans), and some maple syrup, sugar or molasses to keep out the winter chill, plus as much smoked pork or ham as is economically viable.

SERVES 4

250g/9oz dried haricot beans
1 onion, studded with 1 clove
1 bouquet garni
FOR THE SAUCE:
2 tablespoons virgin olive oil
1 small onion, finely chopped
2 cloves garlic, finely chopped (optional)
2 tablespoons tomato purée or sun-dried tomato purée
2 tablespoons maple syrup
salt and pepper

Soak the beans overnight, or for 12 hours, in plenty of cold water. Next day, drain and rinse the beans then put them into a large pan with enough fresh cold water to cover. Add the onion and bouquet garni; do not add salt to the beans at this stage as it will prevent them softening as they cook. Bring the beans to a boil, skimming frequently, and boil them hard for 10 minutes, then lower the heat and simmer for 45-50 minutes until completely tender. Drain, reserving the cooking liquid but discarding the flavourings.

Preheat the oven to 170°C/325°F/Gas 3. Heat the oil in a heavy flameproof casserole and cook the onion gently for 20 minutes until very soft and slightly golden. Stir in the garlic, tomato purée and maple syrup, cook for 1 minute then add the beans. Stir well, adding enough of the bean cooking liquid (about 400ml/14fl oz) to make a soupy sauce. Season the mixture lightly then bring it to the boil. Cover and cook slowly in the oven for 45 minutes, stirring occasionally. If the mixture seems to be getting a bit too dry, stir in a little more of the cooking liquid.

Remove the casserole from the oven and stir well before serving. If the sauce is too runny, gently reduce it by simmering the casserole on the stovetop. Taste and adjust the seasonings as necessary before serving.

Variations: for a simpler dish, omit the onion and garlic. For a more elaborate meal, fry 150g/5½oz of diced smoked bacon or ham in the oil before adding the onion and arrange 8 lightly browned sausages on top of the beans before placing the casserole in the oven. Alternatively, before serving, you can stir in 2 tablespoons of chopped herbs or, for a spicy flavour, add ¼ teaspoon cayenne pepper or chilli powder to the onion just before adding the garlic.

Gnocchi-Topped Vegetable Casserole

Choose a really colourful combination of vegetables for this substantial winter dish. I think celeriac is a must for its flavour and texture, plus a few Jerusalem artichokes, carrots, parsnips, leeks – even a little cauliflower or broccoli. Don't worry if the quantity of each vegetable is not exact as it won't make a difference to the end result.

SERVES 6

FOR THE TOPPING:
600ml/1 pint milk
85g/3oz semolina
freshly grated nutmeg
salt and pepper
1 large egg, beaten
20g/¾oz unsalted butter, diced
50g/2oz Parmesan cheese, grated
25g/1oz Gruyère or Emmental cheese, grated

FOR THE CASSEROLE:
1 medium onion, finely chopped
3 cloves garlic, finely chopped
2 tablespoons virgin olive oil
½ teaspoon ground coriander
¼ teaspoon ground cumin
250g/9oz celeriac, cut into thick strips
250g/9oz mixed Jerusalem artichokes and carrots, chopped
100g/3½oz parsnips, diced
100g/3½oz leeks, cut into chunks
400g/14oz canned chopped tomatoes
75ml/2½fl oz vegetable stock
100g/3½oz broccoli or cauliflower florets
extra grated cheese, for sprinkling

To make the gnocchi topping, bring the milk to the boil in a large pan, stirring frequently, then stir in the semolina, nutmeg and a little salt and pepper. Cook the mixture gently, stirring constantly, until it has thickened then remove it from the heat and beat in the egg, butter and cheeses. Return the pan to the heat and cook gently, stirring constantly, for 2-3 minutes. Taste and adjust the seasoning as necessary then leave the mixture to cool.

To make the casserole, gently cook the onion and garlic in the oil for 15-20 minutes or until very soft and slightly golden. Add the spices and cook, stirring, for 2-3 minutes. Stir in the celeriac, artichokes, carrots, parsnips, leeks, tomatoes and their juices. Add the stock, bring the mixture to a boil and simmer gently for 10 minutes.

Preheat the oven to 200°C/400°F/Gas 6. Stir the cauliflower or broccoli, if using, into the casserole then adjust the seasoning and remove it from the heat. Transfer the mixture to a large, shallow, greased baking dish and spread the gnocchi over the vegetables in an even layer. Sprinkle with the extra cheese. Bake for 20-25 minutes until the top is golden and the sauce is bubbling.

Variation: replace the gnocchi with a topping of mashed potatoes flavoured with plenty of chopped parsley.

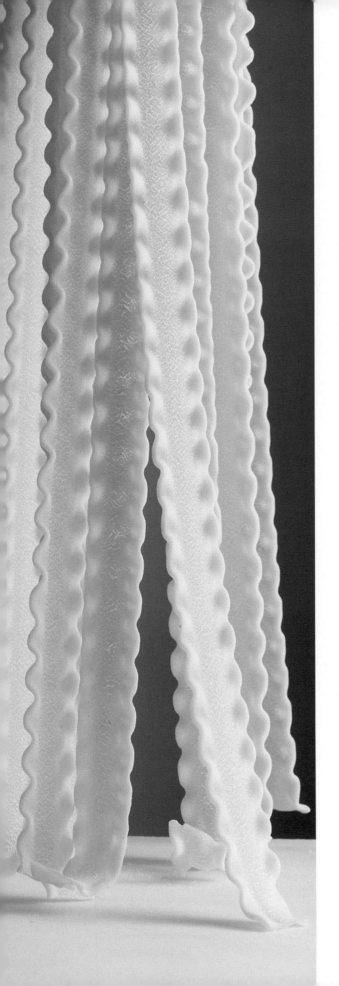

PASTA SAUCES

Pasta has lost its trattoria image and become the ultimate international good fast food. It has also shed its stodgy reputation. Silky-fine tagliatelle combined with luxurious olive oil and white truffle shavings, or quick-cooking Chinese egg noodles tossed with a few piquant flavourings, have a place on every classy restaurant menu.

Sauces for pasta can be quick and simply prepared: crumbled goat's cheese melted with lemon, or a classic carbonara. They can also be slowly cooked, richly flavoured tomato or bolognese mixtures that taste even better when reheated the next day.

The great advantage of these sauces is there is something for every occasion, every weather, every appetite. There are cold spicy noodle salads for hot days and picnics, a hearty baked cannelloni for a warm comforting meal, light low-fat vegetable sauces and powerful pestos of every hue. Many need not be restricted to pasta and noodles but work just as well as an accompaniment to couscous, polenta or rice.

Left (from top to bottom): Confetti Sauce, Pesto Genovese, Red Pepper and Tomato Sauce.

𝒯 O M A T O 𝒮 A U C E S

Fresh Tomato and Basil Sauce

SERVES 4-6

**5 plum tomatoes, about 400g/14oz, peeled,
 seeded and finely diced**
1 small shallot, finely chopped
1 clove garlic, crushed
large bunch of basil, torn into small pieces
150ml/5fl oz extra virgin olive oil
squeeze of lemon juice, or to taste
salt and black pepper

Mix the diced tomatoes with the other
ingredients in a bowl. Cover and leave the
sauce for at least 1 hour to allow the
flavours to develop. If the sauce is to be
kept any longer, refrigerate it straightaway in
a sealed container and use within 24 hours.

A versatile sauce for all kinds of pasta.

Confetti Sauce

SERVES 4

100ml/3½fl oz virgin olive oil
1 teaspoon finely chopped garlic
1 teaspoon grated ginger
1 teaspoon finely chopped mild green chilli
6 anchovy fillets, finely chopped
2 red peppers, cored and finely diced
2 yellow peppers, cored and finely diced
100ml/3½fl oz dry white wine or vegetable stock
2 tablespoons chopped flat-leafed parsley
salt and pepper

Heat the oil in a medium pan then gently fry
the garlic, ginger and chilli for 30 seconds,
just until the garlic releases its aroma.

*Left: this uncooked Fresh Tomato and Basil
Sauce, with its torn basil leaves and juicy plum
tomatoes, gives pasta a bright summery flavour.*

Stir in the anchovy fillets and cook, stirring frequently, for about 2 minutes until they dissolve into the oil. Add the peppers and stir over a medium heat until they are soft.

Pour in the wine, bring the sauce to a boil then cover and simmer for about 20 minutes until the sauce is cooked and thickened. Add the parsley and salt and pepper to taste when you toss the sauce with the pasta.

Variation: for a more powerful sauce use fresh hot chilli pepper to taste.

———— 🥄 ————

Farfalle pasta is best for this sauce, which can also be served with steamed couscous or slices of grilled polenta.

Celery and Tomato Sauce

This sauce has plenty of flavour even though it is low in fat. Use a food processor to make light work of preparing the vegetables.

SERVES 4-6

3 tablespoons virgin olive oil
2 medium onions, finely chopped
2 medium carrots, finely chopped
4 large stalks celery, or 1 large celery heart, finely chopped and any leaves reserved
4 cloves garlic, or to taste, finely chopped
680g/1lb 8oz canned chopped tomatoes
1 tablespoon tomato purée or sun-dried tomato paste
salt and pepper

Heat the oil in a large, heavy pan and stir in the onions, carrots and celery. Cover and cook very gently for about 15 minutes or until soft and lightly golden. Stir in the garlic, tomatoes and their juice, tomato purée and a little seasoning. Bring the mixture to a boil, stir well then cover and simmer for 30-45 minutes or until the sauce is thick

and well-flavoured. Taste the sauce and adjust the seasonings as necessary. Serve it garnished with celery leaves.

The sauce can be cooled then chilled overnight, or frozen for up to 1 month.

———— 🥄 ————

Suitable for pasta, rice, couscous or polenta.

Red Pepper and Tomato Sauce

MAKES 800ML/1⅓ PINTS

3 tablespoons extra virgin olive oil
1 medium onion, roughly chopped
4 large cloves garlic, roughly chopped
2 large red peppers, cored, seeded and roughly chopped
750g/1lb 10oz tomatoes, roughly chopped
1 large bouquet garni
2-3 drops Tabasco sauce, or to taste
pinch of sugar, or to taste
squeeze of lemon juice, or to taste
salt and pepper

Heat the oil in a large, heavy pan, add the onion and stir well. Cover the pan with the lid or a disc of greaseproof paper dampened with cold water and cook very slowly for about 20 minutes or until soft but not coloured. Add the garlic and peppers and stir well. Cook over a medium heat for a couple of minutes, stirring frequently.

Add the chopped tomatoes to the pan with the bouquet garni and a little seasoning. Stir well then bring the mixture to the boil. Cover and simmer gently, stirring occasionally, for 35 minutes or until the vegetables are really tender. You should not have to add any extra liquid if the tomatoes are ripe, the pan is covered, and the sauce is gently simmered.

Remove the bouquet garni then transfer the sauce to a food processor or a blender and process it to make a thick purée.

The sauce can be poured back into the rinsed-out pan, reheated then seasoned to taste using salt, pepper, a few drops of Tabasco sauce if wished and a little sugar or lemon juice, depending on the flavour – it could be a little acidic or a bit too sweet.

Variations: to make a smoother sauce, pour the purée back into the pan through a coarse conical sieve, pushing down well on the vegetables in the sieve with the back of a ladle so only the skin and seeds remain.

For a thin, glossy, elegant sauce, pour the purée back into the pan through a fine conical sieve, pushing down lightly with the back of a small ladle so that the sauce drains through, but all the skin, seeds and thick pulpy flesh is left in the sieve. Reheat and season to taste. The sauce can be slightly thickened, made more glossy and enriched by mounting it with 50g/1¾oz of unsalted butter just before serving.

If you like, you can add more Tabasco, or some cayenne pepper or Worcestershire sauce to give the mixture a spicy kick.

For a herb sauce, add shredded basil or snipped chives just before serving, or you can add 2 teaspoons of dried oregano to the sauce when you add the tomatoes.

To make a heavier, richer sauce, add 1 tablespoon of sun-dried tomato paste when you add the red peppers.

You can add 2 tablespoons of chopped black olives and/or 1 very finely shredded red pepper just before serving. Alternatively, stir 3 tablespoons of double cream or crème fraîche into the finished sauce.

———— 🥄 ————

Good with strands of pasta such as spaghetti and fettuccini, but this sauce is extraordinarily versatile. You can use the smooth, slightly thickened version for lasagne, cannelloni and similar pasta dishes. The thin, glossy version mounted with butter can be served with roast cod or monkfish, with grilled chicken or with liver.

Pesto Genovese

This bright, pungent basil sauce comes from Genoa in Italy where it is invariably matched with long, thin pasta. Pesto however has many more uses and you will have great fun coming up with your own ideas. The cheeses traditionally used in making pesto are well-matured Parmesan or the hard ewes' milk cheese Pecorino, both of which contribute a sharpening flavour to the sauce and give a texture that is more grainy than creamy.

MAKES 350G/12OZ

100g/3½oz fresh basil leaves
5 cloves garlic
75g/2¾oz pine kernels
100g/3½oz Parmesan or Pecorino cheese, grated
100ml/3½fl oz extra virgin olive oil
salt and black pepper

Put the basil, garlic, pine kernels and grated cheese into a food processor and process just until the mixture becomes a rough paste, scraping the sides down frequently. With the machine still running, add the oil in a slow, steady stream until the mixture emulsifies and becomes a smooth purée. Season to taste with salt and pepper.

Store in a jar in the refrigerator for no more than 1 week, making sure that a thin layer of oil covers the surface (this can simply be stirred in prior to use). If you want to freeze pesto, make it without the garlic. Then, when the pesto has defrosted, crush some garlic and stir it through the sauce.

———— 🥄 ————

Use pesto in hot pasta dishes, cold pasta salads, or with grilled robust fish, lamb or chicken. You can spread it on crostini and bruschetta, or use it as a topping for stuffed tomatoes, peppers or onions. Pesto is an excellent accompaniment to minestrone, or any tomato or red pepper soup, and makes a tasty topping for baked potatoes.

Coriander and Almond Pesto

MAKES 350G/12OZ

100g/3½oz coriander leaves
5 cloves garlic
75g/2¾oz blanched almonds, roughly chopped
100g/3½oz Parmesan or Pecorino cheese, grated
100ml/3½fl oz extra virgin olive oil
salt and black pepper

Put the coriander, garlic, chopped almonds and grated cheese into a food processor and process just until the mixture becomes a rough paste, scraping the sides down frequently. With the machine still running, add the oil in a slow, steady stream until the mixture emulsifies into a smooth purée. Taste and add salt and pepper as necessary. Store the sauce in a jar in the refrigerator for no more than 1 week.

———— 🥄 ————

This pesto goes particularly well with grilled or baked chicken and fresh seafood such as tuna, scallops and mussels.

Sage Pesto

MAKES 250G/9OZ

6 large sage leaves
3 cloves garlic
1 red chilli, seeded and chopped
25g/1oz pine kernels
100g/3½oz Parmesan or Pecorino cheese, grated
75ml/2½fl oz virgin olive oil
salt and black pepper

Put the sage, garlic, chilli, pine kernels and grated cheese into a food processor and process just until the mixture becomes a rough paste, scraping the sides down

Pesto Sauces

frequently. With the machine still running, add the oil in a slow, steady stream until the mixture emulsifies into a smooth purée. Taste and add salt and pepper as necessary. Store the sauce in a jar in the refrigerator for no more than 1 week.

A particularly good sauce for chicken, polenta and tomatoes as well as pasta.

Rocket and Goats' Cheese Pesto

This sauce is mild and creamy but has the peppery, slightly bitter taste of rocket.

MAKES 450G/1LB

100g/3½oz rocket leaves
5 cloves garlic
75g/2¾oz pine kernels
200g/7oz soft fresh goats' cheese
100ml/3½fl oz extra virgin olive oil
salt and pepper

Put the rocket, garlic, pine kernels and goats' cheese into a food processor and process the mixture to a rough paste, scraping the sides down frequently. With the machine still running, add the oil in a slow, steady stream until the mixture emulsifies into a purée, then season to taste. Store in a jar in the refrigerator for up to 1 week.

A marvellous and unusual topping for baked potatoes, grilled lamb or pan-fried fillet steak. You can also stir this pesto through warm white beans such as cannellini, use it as a topping for char-grilled vegetables or simply spread it on bread.

Left: fruity olive oil and sharp-flavoured Italian cheese are blended with aromatic basil leaves to produce a traditional Pesto Genovese.

Red Pesto

MAKES 350G/12OZ

100g/3½oz sun-dried tomatoes preserved
 in oil, drained
5 cloves garlic
75g/2¾oz pine kernels
100g/3½oz Parmesan or Pecorino cheese,
 grated
100ml/3½fl oz extra virgin olive oil
salt and pepper

Put the sun-dried tomatoes, garlic, pine kernels and cheese into a food processor and process the mixture to a rough paste, scraping the sides down frequently. With the machine still running, add the oil in a slow, steady stream until the mixture emulsifies into a purée. Season to taste with salt and pepper. Store in a jar in the refrigerator for no more than 1 week.

Red pesto can be stirred successfully into couscous as well as pasta. It is an excellent base for pizzas, bruschetta and crostini, or can be layered with soft cheese and salad to make a flavour-packed sandwich filling.

Black Olive Pesto

MAKES 225G/8OZ

200g/7oz stoned black olives
1 teaspoon thyme leaves
3 tablespoons extra virgin olive oil

Place the olives in a blender with the thyme leaves and process to a purée. Slowly blend in the olive oil until the mixture emulsifies.

Use as the base of a pasta sauce, adding tomatoes or roasted peppers for freshness. It can also be served as a dip or spread, or drizzled over pizzas or roasted vegetables.

Nut and Cheese Sauces

Green Pepper and Pine Kernel Sauce

SERVES 2-4

25g/1oz pine kernels
1 clove garlic, unpeeled
1 large green pepper
grated rind of 1 lemon plus half its juice
1 rounded tablespoon coriander leaves
½ teaspoon chopped green chilli, or to taste
100ml/3½fl oz extra virgin olive oil
salt and pepper

Set the oven to 190°C/375°F/Gas 5. Toast the pine kernels in the heating oven for 7 minutes or until they turn light golden brown. At the same time, roast the unpeeled garlic for about 10 minutes or until soft. Leave the pine kernels and garlic to cool.

Char the green pepper under a hot grill, turning frequently, until its skin is black all over. Cool and peel it under cold running water then quarter the pepper and discard its core and seeds. Peel the roasted garlic.

Place the lemon rind and juice in a food processor with the green pepper, pine kernels, garlic, coriander and chilli and process until smooth. With the machine running slowly, pour in the oil through the feed tube. Season to taste.

The sauce can be stored, tightly covered, in the refrigerator for up to 48 hours. Bring it to room temperature and stir before use.

───────⋯───────

Serve with short pasta or steamed rice. This sauce also goes well with seafood such as grilled halibut, swordfish or tuna steaks, or alongside green prawns that have been fried in garlic-flavoured oil.

Above (left to right): Green Pepper and Pine Kernel Sauce, Walnut and Gorgonzola Sauce and Romesco Sauce add a nutty taste to pasta.

Romesco Sauce

MAKES ABOUT 500ML/18FL OZ

2 red peppers
3 plum tomatoes
4 cloves garlic, unpeeled
50g/1¾oz pine kernels
1 large dried romesco pepper
1-2 tablespoons white wine vinegar
4 tablespoons extra virgin olive oil
salt and pepper

Set the oven to 220°C/425°F/Gas 7. Put the fresh peppers, tomatoes and garlic into a non-stick roasting pan. Spread the pine kernels in a single layer in another baking

Nut and Cheese Sauces

tin. Place both tins in the oven: remove the pine kernels when golden (after 5 minutes), the tomatoes and garlic when soft (about 10 minutes), and the peppers when dark brown (about 35 minutes). Leave them to cool. Meanwhile, cover the dried pepper with hot water and leave to soak for 30 minutes.

Peel, quarter and core the fresh peppers and peel the tomatoes and garlic. Drain and chop the dried pepper, discarding the seeds and stem. Blend them with the pine kernels and vinegar in a food processor. With the machine running slowly, pour in the oil through the feed tube. Season to taste, adding extra oil or vinegar as needed.

Store covered in the refrigerator for 48 hours and use at room temperature.

Variation: add two finely chopped anchovy fillets to the sauce. Replace the romesco pepper with a mild, seeded, fresh red chilli pepper or a few drops of Tabasco sauce.

Can be used with seafood as well as pasta.

Zucchini Walnut Sauce

Make this with very fresh baby courgettes.

SERVES 4-6

500g/1lb 2oz dried pasta
Parmesan cheese, for sprinkling
FOR THE SAUCE:
4 tablespoons extra virgin olive oil
500g/1lb 2oz small courgettes, finely sliced
1 large clove garlic, finely chopped
3 heaped tablespoons finely chopped parsley
3 large eggs, beaten
75g/2¾oz walnut pieces
salt and pepper

Cook the pasta according to the packet instructions. Meanwhile, heat the olive oil in a large, heavy-based frying pan and cook the courgettes and garlic until golden brown and soft, stirring frequently. Stir in the parsley.

Drain the cooked pasta then return it to the hot, empty pasta pan. Immediately add the beaten egg and stir and toss the pasta quite vigorously to thoroughly cook the eggs and mix them with the pasta. Add the walnuts and the contents of the frying pan to the pasta and mix well. Taste and add salt and pepper as necessary. Serve immediately with Parmesan cheese.

Variation: omit the walnuts if desired. For a stronger flavour, simply add more garlic, and vary the herbs as you like.

Walnut and Gorgonzola Sauce

A very rich sauce. Use the finest, freshest walnuts or the sauce will taste bitter.

SERVES 4-6

75g/2¾oz walnut halves, finely chopped
1-2 cloves garlic, to taste, crushed
150ml/5fl oz extra virgin olive oil
100g/3½oz Gorgonzola cheese
1 tablespoon finely chopped flat-leafed parsley
salt and black pepper

Stir the walnuts and garlic into the oil. Mix thoroughly, then crumble in the Gorgonzola. If using the sauce immediately, add the parsley; if not, add it just before serving. Season to taste using salt only if necessary.

Without the parsley, the sauce can be stored covered overnight in the refrigerator.

Instant Cheese Sauce

This recipe could not be quicker or simpler. The heat of the pan and the pasta melt the cheese to a smooth sauce.

SERVES 4

350g/12oz pasta such as farfalle or fusilli
FOR THE SAUCE:
150g/5½oz soft goats' or cows' milk cheese
small bunch of chives, snipped
grated rind and juice of 1 small lemon
salt and pepper

Cook the pasta according to the packet directions, then drain. While the pasta is draining, crumble the cheese into the hot, empty pasta pan. Stir in the steaming pasta, followed by the chives, lemon rind and juice. Toss gently so the cheese melts to smoothly coat the pasta. Season to taste and serve.

Sauce Miffi

SERVES 4-6

500g/1lb 2oz uncooked rigatoni
FOR THE SAUCE:
2 tablespoons extra virgin olive oil
1 clove garlic, or to taste, finely chopped
500g/1lb 2oz young spinach leaves
115g/4oz ricotta cheese
salt and pepper
freshly grated nutmeg

Cook the pasta according to the packet instructions. Meanwhile, heat the oil in a large, heavy pan, add the garlic and cook gently for a few seconds. Add the spinach, raise the heat and cook, stirring, until wilted.

Put the spinach mixture into a food processor with the ricotta and pulse to a rough sauce. Alternatively, add the ricotta to the spinach in the pan and beat them well.

Drain the pasta then add the sauce to the hot, empty pasta pan. Add the steaming pasta, toss until thoroughly combined then season with salt, pepper and a little grated nutmeg to taste. Serve immediately.

Variation: add 100g/3½oz of shredded Parma ham or cooked bacon before serving.

Tagliatelle with Smoked Salmon

Very quick and very smart. For even faster preparation, buy a packet of smoked salmon trimmings: they are already cut up and have the added benefit of being inexpensive.

SERVES 4

250g/9oz uncooked tagliatelle
FOR THE SAUCE:
425ml/¾ pint soured cream
175g/6oz smoked salmon, cut in strips
black pepper
1 tablespoon chopped fresh dill

Cook the pasta according to the packet directions then drain. Pour the cream into the hot, empty pasta pan and bring it to the boil. Remove the pan from the heat and stir in the smoked salmon. Season the sauce with plenty of black pepper.

Tip the pasta into a warmed serving bowl then pour over the hot sauce. Sprinkle with the dill, then toss to thoroughly combine and serve immediately.

———— ✦ ————

Accompany with a watercress salad. For a treat, garnish the pasta with salmon eggs.

Marco's Anchovy Sauce

SERVES 4-6

500g/1lb 2oz uncooked penne
Parmesan cheese, for sprinkling
FOR THE SAUCE:
3 tablespoons extra virgin olive oil
3 large cloves garlic, thinly sliced
1 large tomato, peeled and thinly sliced
4 anchovies, drained and roughly chopped
115g/4oz Caprino or cottage cheese
3 tablespoons black olive paste or tapenade
salt and pepper

Cook the penne according to the packet directions. Meanwhile, heat the olive oil in a small pan, add the garlic and tomato and cook them very gently for 5 minutes, stirring frequently. Stir in the anchovies and continue cooking over the lowest possible heat for 15 minutes, stirring frequently.

Tip the contents of the pan into a food processor and add the cheese and black olive paste or tapenade. Process until the mixture is thoroughly combined; if you prefer a rough texture, stir the ingredients together.

Drain the pasta. Pour the sauce into the hot, empty pasta pan, add the steaming pasta and toss until thoroughly mixed. Season to taste and serve immediately with grated Parmesan cheese.

Rigatoni Niçoise

A colourful, well-flavoured sauce made with canned tuna, anchovies and olives (those marinated in herbs would be very good).

SERVES 4

1 large onion, finely chopped
3 large cloves garlic, or to taste, finely chopped
3 tablespoons virgin olive oil
50g/1¾oz canned anchovies, drained
425g/15oz canned tomatoes
425g/15oz canned tuna in olive oil, drained
50g/1¾oz black olives
2 tablespoons chopped basil
salt and pepper

Cook the onion and garlic very gently in the heated oil for 10-15 minutes or until really soft but not coloured. Purée the anchovies with the tomatoes and their juice in a food processor or blender then add the mixture to the pan. Stir well then simmer gently for 10 minutes, stirring frequently.

Flake the tuna and stir it into the sauce. When it is thoroughly heated, stir in the olives and basil then season to taste.

Variation: omit the anchovies, olives and basil. Add a 3cm/1¼in piece of fresh root ginger, peeled and grated, with the onions and 1 finely diced medium-hot chilli pepper with the puréed tomatoes. Finish with 1 tablespoon of finely chopped coriander.

———— ✦ ————

Serve with rigatoni pasta or polenta.

Fish and Four Cheese Macaroni

While this is no more difficult to make than a standard macaroni cheese, it tastes classy.

SERVES 4

700g/1lb 9oz firm white fish fillets
300g/10½oz elbow macaroni or cellentani
FOR THE SAUCE:
40g/1½oz unsalted butter
40g/1½oz plain flour
600ml/1 pint milk
100g/3½oz Gorgonzola cheese, crumbled
100g/3½oz buffalo Mozzarella cheese, diced
100g/3½oz Gruyère or Emmental cheese, grated
salt and pepper
50g/1¾oz Parmesan, grated

Poach the fish then leave it to cool. Flake the flesh, removing the skin and bones.

Cook the pasta according to the directions on the packet. Meanwhile, make the sauce. Melt the butter in a heavy-based pan and stir in the flour. Cook the roux over a low heat, stirring constantly, for 1 minute then whisk in the milk. Stir until smooth, then set the pan over a medium heat and stir constantly until the sauce boils and thickens. Simmer gently for 3 minutes, stirring frequently to prevent the sauce catching on the base of the pan.

Remove the pan from the heat and stir in the Gorgonzola, Mozzarella and Gruyère. When the cheeses have melted completely, add salt and pepper to taste.

Seafood Sauces

Drain the cooked pasta and return it to the hot, empty pasta pan then stir in the cheese sauce. Pour half the macaroni mixture into a large buttered baking dish, cover it with the flaked fish then the remaining macaroni. Sprinkle with Parmesan cheese.

If serving immediately, put the dish under a hot grill until the top is browned and bubbling. If you are making it in advance, cool the macaroni quickly then cover and chill for up to 24 hours. Reheat the dish for about 25-35 minutes, or until bubbling, in an oven set to 190°C/375°F/Gas 5, then finish it off by browning it under the grill.

Below: a curly pasta such as cresti di gallo or fusilli is best for Tuna and Artichoke Sauce. This recipe uses larder ingredients, so you can rely on it to rescue you from unexpected guests.

Tuna and Artichoke Sauce

This sauce, with its mixture of Italian and Chinese ingredients, is typical of my husband's cooking style. It is quick, easy, delicious and the children ask for it regularly.

SERVES 4

400g/14oz canned artichoke hearts, chopped
4 tablespoons olive oil
1 clove garlic, finely chopped
200g/7oz canned tuna in olive oil
2 tablespoons sun-dried tomato paste
1 tablespoon sweet chilli sauce
4 tablespoons rice wine or dry white wine
2 tablespoons finely chopped fresh coriander
salt and black pepper

Lightly crush the artichoke hearts with a pestle and mortar and set aside.

Heat the olive oil in a medium-sized saucepan. Add the garlic and cook just until golden. Add the tuna, with the oil from the tin, and break it into small pieces. Stir in the artichokes, tomato paste and chilli sauce and simmer for 2-3 minutes. Add the wine, stir, cover and simmer for 15 minutes more.

Just before serving, stir the coriander into the sauce and season with black pepper.

Variation: cook 1 teaspoon of finely grated fresh ginger in the olive oil with the garlic.

———

Choose a curly pasta such as fusilli or cresti di gallo for this sauce.

Sauce Vongole

SERVES 2

1 tablespoon olive oil
1 clove garlic, chopped
8 plum tomatoes, chopped
200g/7oz canned clams, drained
3-4 basil leaves
salt and black pepper

Gently heat the olive oil in a small saucepan or frying pan. Add the chopped garlic and cook for just 30 seconds, making sure it does not turn brown.

Add the tomatoes to the pan and leave them to cook over a low heat for about 10-15 minutes or until the mixture is thick and pulpy. Carefully stir in the drained clams and heat through for just 2-3 minutes.

Tear the basil leaves into small strips and add them to the sauce. Season to taste with salt and pepper, then serve.

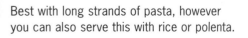

Best with long strands of pasta, however you can also serve this with rice or polenta.

Beef and Mushroom Sauce

SERVES 4

15g/½oz dried cep or porcini mushrooms
200ml/7fl oz hot water
2 tablespoons olive oil
1 medium onion, finely chopped
500g/1lb 2oz lean minced beef
1 clove garlic, finely chopped
1 tablespoon tomato purée
salt and black pepper

Soak the mushrooms in the hot water for 20 minutes. Heat the oil in a large frying pan and fry the onion until soft. Add the meat and cook, stirring frequently, until browned.

Drain the mushrooms, saving the soaking liquid, then chop them roughly and add to the meat with the garlic. Fry for 1-2 minutes then add the strained mushroom liquid and tomato purée. Season lightly, cover and simmer gently, stirring occasionally, for 20 minutes. Taste and adjust the seasoning.

The cooled sauce can be stored in the refrigerator for up to 4 days, or frozen.

Toss the sauce with pasta, use it to make lasagne or fill crêpes. You can also use it to stuff vegetables then bake them with or without a tomato sauce poured over the top.

Cannelloni

For a lighter touch, I make cannelloni with a smooth, well-flavoured tomato sauce instead of the usual rich and creamy béchamel.

SERVES 4-6

250g/9oz dried cannelloni tubes
Beef and Mushroom Sauce (see above)
butter or oil, for greasing
75g/3oz Parmesan cheese, grated

FOR THE TOMATO SAUCE:
2 tablespoons olive oil
1 large onion, chopped
2 cloves garlic, chopped
1 stick celery, chopped
1 medium carrot, peeled and thinly sliced
800g/1lb 12oz canned chopped plum tomatoes,
**   or 1kg/2lb 4oz passata**
salt and black pepper

To make the tomato sauce, heat the oil in a heavy pan. Add the onion, cover and cook

Above: a satisfying meal of Cannelloni. Tubes of pasta are stuffed with a hearty meat sauce then baked with tomato sauce and grated cheese.

very slowly for 15 minutes or until soft and golden. Stir in the garlic, celery, and carrot then cover and continue cooking for another 5 minutes. Add the tomatoes or passata and seasoning, then cook gently for a further 20 minutes. Process the mixture until smooth in a food processor then taste and

Meat Sauces

adjust the seasoning. The cooled sauce can be stored in the refrigerator for 5 days.

To make the cannelloni, preheat the oven to 190°C/375°F/Gas 5. Stuff the cannelloni tubes with the meat sauce.

Grease a large baking dish and put a layer of tomato sauce in the bottom. Arrange the filled pasta on top, in a single layer if possible. Spoon over the rest of the tomato sauce, then sprinkle with the Parmesan cheese. Bake for 25 minutes or until the pasta is tender and the sauce is bubbling. Be careful not to overcook the cannelloni as it will become tough and dry. Serve hot.

Variations: cannelloni can be made with any minced meat – beef is most common, but lamb, pork and venison are also excellent, as are chicken or turkey.

Bolognese Sauce

There are more recipes for this sauce from Bologna than there are types of spaghetti, so I am giving my favourite. Bolognese should be made from a combination of meats, slowly simmered to taste really rich.

SERVES 6

2 tablespoons virgin olive oil
400g/14oz Italian-style cured meat sausages
600g/1lb 5oz lean minced beef
1 large onion, finely chopped
1 stalk celery, finely diced
1 tablespoon tomato purée
800g/1lb 12oz canned plum tomatoes
3 cloves garlic, or to taste, finely chopped
1 rounded tablespoon dried oregano
150ml/5fl oz red wine
1 large bouquet garni
salt and pepper

Heat the oil in a large, heavy-based saucepan. Slit the sausages lengthways, peel off their skins and slice the meat.

Quickly brown the sausage meat in the oil then remove it from the pan and leave to drain. Add the beef to the pan and brown it thoroughly, removing it with a slotted spoon so the fat drains back into the pan.

Lower the heat, add the onion and celery and cook slowly, stirring frequently, until they are soft and golden. Stir in the tomato purée, cook for 1 minute, then add the tomatoes and roughly break them up.

Return the sausages and beef to the pan and add the remaining ingredients. Add a little pepper but no salt at this stage as the sausages will season the sauce. Bring the mixture to a boil, stirring well, then cover and simmer very gently for 2 hours either on top of the stove or in a low oven. Stir occasionally to break up the sausages.

The finished sauce should be thick and rich. Discard the bouquet garni and add more seasoning as needed before serving. This sauce tastes best when quickly cooled, chilled overnight and reheated before serving. It can be frozen for up to 1 month.

———— 🥄 ————

Serve with thick spaghetti and freshly grated Parmesan, or with polenta or brown rice.

Pasta alla Carbonara

This classic combination of bacon, eggs and cheese should be seasoned with care. Use good quality dry-cured bacon.

SERVES 4

250g/9oz linguine
FOR THE SAUCE:
1 tablespoon virgin olive oil
175g/6oz unsmoked back bacon, cut in strips
2 large cloves garlic, crushed
2 large eggs
4 tablespoons grated Parmesan cheese
4 tablespoons single or double cream
salt and black pepper

Cook the pasta according to the directions on the packet. Meanwhile, heat the oil in a frying pan and cook the bacon until crispy and golden. Add the garlic and cook for another minute, stirring.

In a medium bowl, beat the eggs with the cheese, cream, pepper and a little salt.

Drain the pasta and return it to the hot, empty pan. Add the bacon, garlic and the egg mixture and toss them gently until thoroughly combined. Taste, season as necessary, then serve immediately.

Pasta with Mortadella, Cream and Peas

SERVES 6

25g/1oz butter
1 shallot, chopped
100ml/3½fl oz dry white wine
125ml/4fl oz double cream
100g/3½oz petit pois
450g/1lb dried pasta
225g/8oz mortadella sausage, diced
grated rind of 1 lemon and half its juice
50g/2oz Parmesan cheese, grated
salt and black pepper

In a medium-sized saucepan, melt the butter then add the shallot and cook over a low heat until softened. Add the white wine to the pan, raise the heat and simmer the liquid until it has almost evaporated.

Add half the cream to the pan, lower the heat and simmer gently for 5 minutes. Stir in the petit pois and continue cooking for another 5 minutes.

Cook the pasta in a large pan according to the packet instructions. Drain the pasta well then return it to the pan and place it over a low heat. Toss the cream sauce into the pasta. Add the mortadella, lemon rind and juice, the remaining cream and Parmesan. Toss again, season to taste and serve.

Teriyaki Salmon and Japanese Noodles

The unusual ingredients for this recipe are generally available from Oriental grocers, in many health food shops and even in some supermarkets nowadays. By the way, you'll need large, deep soup bowls to serve this.

SERVES 4

500g/1lb 2oz salmon fillet, skinned
250g/9oz udon noodles
250g/9oz soba noodles
1 litre/1¾ pints dashi (see page 10)
large bunch of watercress, trimmed
FOR THE TERIYAKI MARINADE:
1½ tablespoons soy sauce
1½ tablespoons mirin
1½ tablespoons sake
TO GARNISH:
4 spring onions, sliced into long slivers
sliced pickled ginger, finely chopped

Heat a cast-iron griddle or frying pan until very hot. Mix the marinade ingredients in a small bowl and brush onto the salmon. Sear the fish for 1-2 minutes on each side then remove the griddle from the heat but leave the fish on it to cook through. When the salmon is pale pink and moist on the inside, break it into bite-sized pieces.

Bring a large pot of water to a rolling boil. Add the udon noodles then, after 3 minutes, add the soba noodles. When they are both cooked al dente, drain them thoroughly.

Meanwhile, heat the dashi in a large saucepan until steam rises from the surface of the stock. For each serving, put a layer of mixed noodles in the centre of a large soup bowl, cover it with a layer of watercress, then a layer of salmon pieces. Finally, drench them with a generous ladle or two of the dashi broth.

Before serving, garnish each bowl with 1 tablespoon of slivered spring onions and sprinkle with the chopped pickled ginger.

Soba with Ginger and Soy Glaze

Soba noodles are made from buckwheat flour and can taste a little strong but here they are enlivened with a sauce of fresh ginger juice and vegetables.

SERVES 2

7.5cm/3in piece root ginger, peeled
175g/6oz soba noodles
2 tablespoons vegetable oil
1 small leek, halved and finely sliced
½ red pepper, seeded and finely diced
1 large carrot, halved and finely sliced
100g/3½oz fine green beans, cut into
    2.5cm/1in lengths
2 teaspoons soy sauce, plus extra to taste
60g/2oz roasted unsalted cashew nuts
100g/3½oz fresh tofu, diced
sesame oil

Make the ginger juice by finely grating the ginger onto a board, then collecting all the pulp in your hand and squeezing it tightly so that the juice runs into a small bowl. Add any excess juice from the board to the bowl and then set it aside.

Cook the soba noodles according to the packet instructions, then drain them.

Meanwhile, heat the vegetable oil in a large saucepan and cook the leeks and pepper gently until they are softened but not coloured. Add the carrot, beans and soy sauce and stir-fry the vegetables over a moderate heat for 5-6 minutes.

Add the cashews, tofu and cooked noodles to the pan and toss carefully so that the vegetables and noodles are thoroughly combined but the tofu does not break up. Stir in the ginger juice and a few drops of sesame oil. Taste and add extra sesame oil and soy sauce as needed. The starch from the noodles will form a light glaze when combined with the ginger juice, sesame oil and soy sauce.

Variation: if you cannot find roasted unsalted cashews, buy unroasted cashews and quickly dry-fry them before use.

Tahini Chicken Noodles

SERVES 6

400g/14oz dried Chinese egg noodles
1 teaspoon sesame oil
FOR THE CHICKEN:
4 boneless chicken breasts
2cm/¾in piece root ginger, finely sliced
1 small onion, sliced
6 peppercorns
FOR THE SAUCE:
4 tablespoons tahini
3cm/1¼in piece root ginger, thinly sliced
3 cloves garlic, peeled
2 tablespoons soy sauce
1 tablespoon sesame oil
1 small red medium-hot chilli, or to taste,
    seeded and quartered
¾ teaspoon roasted ground Sichuan peppercorns
1 teaspoon golden caster sugar
2 tablespoons chopped coriander leaves
1 tablespoon toasted sesame seeds

Cook the noodles according to the packet instructions, then drain, rinse with cold water and drain again thoroughly. Toss the noodles with the teaspoon of oil and set aside.

Put the chicken into a large pan with the ginger, onions and peppercorns and water to cover. Bring to a boil then cover and simmer for 20 minutes or until the chicken is cooked through. Leave the chicken to cool in the liquid, then shred the flesh. Strain and reserve the poaching liquid.

To make the sauce, put the tahini, ginger, garlic, soy sauce, sesame oil, chilli, Sichuan peppercorns and sugar in a food processor and process until smooth. Add enough of the reserved poaching liquid to make a sauce the consistency of double cream. Taste and adjust the flavourings as needed.

*N*OODLE *S*AUCES

Mix the noodles with the chicken and the sauce then garnish the dish with coriander leaves and toasted sesame seeds. Cover and chill until ready to serve, up to 12 hours.

Chilli Citrus Dressing

This sauce is the basis of my favourite Chinese noodle dish, a salad which I make for warm weather meals, indoors and out, as well as for parties.

MAKES 300ML/½ PINT

1 lemon
1 orange
4 tablespoons tahini
4 tablespoons vegetable oil
2 tablespoons sweet chilli sauce, or to taste
2 cloves garlic
4 medium spring onions, trimmed and sliced
2 tablespoons soy sauce
2 tablespoons sugar
½ teaspoon roasted ground Sichuan peppercorns
1 tablespoon sesame oil
Chinese white rice vinegar, to taste (optional)

Grate the rind from the lemon and orange and squeeze out their juices. Place them in a food processor along with the remaining ingredients and process to a slightly textured sauce. Add more soy sauce, chilli sauce, or white rice vinegar to taste; as noodles are very bland, the sauce should be spicy and a balance between sweet, sour, and salty flavours. It can be stored, tightly covered, in the refrigerator for up to 3 days.

Toss the dressing with hot egg noodles. Or make a salad by tossing it with cold noodles then cover and chill for up to 12 hours: the longer you wait, the stronger the flavours and the drier the noodles. Serve alone or with Tahini Chicken Noodles, cold meats or fish.

Quick Curried Coconut Sauce

Coconut cream, sold in Tetra-paks, has a fresher flavour than canned coconut milk, although both are suitable for this recipe.

SERVES 4

300ml/½ pint coconut cream
175g/6oz mild Malaysian curry paste
150g/5½oz mangetout, halved crossways
150g/5½oz baby carrots, halved crossways
4 tablespoons chopped coriander

In a medium-sized saucepan, stir the coconut cream and curry paste together over a moderate heat until smooth. Add the mangetout and carrots and simmer gently for 5 minutes. Stir the chopped coriander into the sauce and serve hot.

Variation: if Malaysian curry paste is unavailable substitute a mild or moderately flavoured Indian curry paste.

Pour the sauce over cooked egg noodles and serve as a meal on its own or as part of a selection of South-east Asian dishes.

Below: lemon and orange add zest to Chinese egg noodles in Chilli Citrus Dressing, a spicy blend of sweet, sour and salty flavours.

HOT AND SPICY

The heat in these hot, spicy and aromatic sauces comes from adding a pungent, fiery ingredient. Peppers and chillies are the first to spring to mind, but other heat sources are garlic, root ginger and mustard.

In this broad selection of recipes from all around the world you will find the nutty satay of Indonesia, fragrant Thai curry pastes, harissa from Tunisia and the most aromatic blends of Indian spices. There are creamy sauces from Kashmir, a black bean stir-fry from China and a stunning chilli jam from the fusion cooking style of the Pacific Rim area. Western or Oriental, sweet and mild, fiery hot, fragrant and appetising, the range of sauces in this chapter will appeal to all palates.

Left (clockwise from top): Thai Red Curry Paste, Fresh Mango Salsa, Plum Sauce.

Fennel and Orange Salsa

This is best described as a sweet and sour salsa, with the sweetness of the orange enhancing the aniseed bite of the fennel.

SERVES 4

½ bulb fennel, finely chopped
1 medium green chilli, finely chopped
1 medium red chilli, finely chopped
grated rind and juice of 1 orange
pinch of sugar, or to taste
salt and pepper

Place the chopped fennel and chillies in a bowl and add just enough orange juice to give a sauce. Stir in the grated orange rind then add sugar to taste – the amount you need will depend on the sweetness of the orange. Season with salt and pepper and chill for at least 1 hour before use. Taste and adjust the seasoning as necessary before serving.

An unusual salsa to serve with all kinds of seafood as well as chicken.

The Simplest Salsa

For the best texture, prepare the vegetables by hand rather than in a food processor.

SERVES 4

2 large tomatoes
1-2 hot green peppers
½ teaspoon salt

Peel, seed and roughly chop the tomatoes to make a lumpy purée. Seed and core the peppers, chop them very finely then stir into the tomatoes along with the salt. Chill.

Variations: for a deeper flavour, roast the peppers until the skin is blackened, let them cool, then peel off the skins and core, seed and chop the peppers finely. You can add 2 tablespoons of finely chopped fresh coriander to the salsa when you add the salt, plus some canned corn kernels if you like. Alternatively, add a large, finely diced sweet yellow pepper, a diced avocado, or a large, ripe, peeled peach with 2 teaspoons of freshly squeezed lemon juice.

Above: add a diced peach and some lemon juice to The Simplest Salsa for a lively, fresh fruit flavour. The pretty colours and juicy texture of the sauce enhance grilled or barbecued fish steaks.

Serve your salsa icy-cold with tortilla chips, grilled meats, barbecued chicken or fish.

Tropical Salsa Picante

SERVES 6

75g/3oz honeydew melon, finely chopped
75g/3oz mango, finely chopped
75g/3oz pineapple, finely chopped
½ medium red pepper, finely chopped
1 small-medium red chilli, finely chopped
3 tablespoons finely chopped coriander
¼ teaspoon salt
2-3 tablespoons balsamic vinegar

Carefully stir all the ingredients together, adding any juice exuded from the fruit to the bowl and just enough balsamic vinegar to

*S*ALSAS

give a thick sauce. Refrigerate the salsa for 8-24 hours before use. Adjust the seasoning as necessary before serving.

Variation: add some finely chopped spring onion or celery to the salsa, if you like.

Grilled or barbecued fish, meats and poultry are all suitable for this salsa.

Fresh Mango Salsa

For this fast, fresh tasting salsa you need really ripe and juicy mangoes. Add chilli to suit your palate.

SERVES 4

2 large mangoes, peeled
juice of 1 lime, or to taste
¼ teaspoon sea salt
1 green chilli, seeded
2cm/¾in piece root ginger, peeled

Cut the mango flesh away from the stone then dice it fairly finely. Mix with the lime juice and salt. Finely chop the chilli, grate

Dicing a mango: cut each half of the fruit into squares without cutting through the skin. Then bend it backwards and cut away the dice.

the ginger and stir them into the mango. Taste the salsa and add more salt as needed. Cover and chill the mixture for up to 4 hours. Stir well before serving.

Wonderful with char-grilled chicken and fish.

Black Bean Salsa

There's no chilli in this salsa, but the spring onions and coriander still pack a punch.

SERVES 4

200g/7oz dried black beans
3 spring onions, sliced
3 plum tomatoes, chopped
large bunch of coriander, chopped
1 tablespoon olive oil
juice of 1 lime
salt and pepper

Rinse and pick over the black beans then put them in a bowl and cover with a generous quantity of cold water. Leave the beans to soak for 8 hours or overnight.

Drain the beans thoroughly and put them in a medium-sized saucepan with plenty of fresh water to cover. Cook the beans for 30-45 minutes or until tender, then drain. Refresh them under cold running water, drain again thoroughly and leave the beans to cool while you prepare the other ingredients.

In a medium-sized bowl, gently combine the spring onions, tomatoes, coriander, olive oil and lime juice with the beans. Taste and season with salt and pepper as necessary.

The meaty flavour of the beans make this a good match for hot-smoked salmon, or fresh salmon that you have grilled or barbecued. Serve the fish and salsa with guacamole, soured cream and tortillas for a real feast. You can also serve this salsa with chicken.

Avocado Sultana Salsa

SERVES 4

50g/1¾oz sultanas
grated rind and juice of 1 lime
1 avocado, finely chopped
½ mango, finely chopped
1 small red onion, finely chopped
1 green chilli, seeded and finely chopped
3 tablespoons finely chopped coriander

In a medium-sized bowl, combine the sultanas with the lime rind and juice. Cover and chill for 8 hours or overnight.

To finish the salsa, add the remaining ingredients to the bowl of sultanas and stir well. Serve at room temperature.

Chicken, grilled or barbecued, is best with this colourful, rich-tasting salsa.

Sun-Dried Tomato Salsa

SERVES 4

200g/7oz sun-dried tomatoes packed in olive oil
2 teaspoons garam masala
½ teaspoon chilli powder
1 small red onion, finely chopped
50ml/2fl oz red wine vinegar
salt and pepper

Drain the oil from the sun-dried tomatoes into a small saucepan and stir in the garam masala and chilli powder. Heat the mixture gently for 5 minutes to allow the flavours to infuse then remove from the heat and cool.

Finely chop the sun-dried tomatoes then stir them into the cooled oil with the onion and vinegar. Season the salsa to taste with salt and pepper. Serve at room temperature.

A versatile salsa to serve with grilled meats, firm white fish or poultry.

ℒOY-BASED ℒAUCES

Japanese Lemon Sauce

SERVES 4

2 tablespoons lemon juice
1 tablespoon soy sauce
1 tablespoon rice wine or dry sherry
2 teaspoons sugar
1 spring onion, finely chopped

In a small saucepan, gently heat the lemon juice, soy sauce, wine or sherry and sugar until the sugar dissolves. When the mixture is quite hot but not boiling, stir in the chopped spring onion and remove the sauce from the heat. Serve warm or leave to cool.

An excellent sauce to serve with vegetables such as grilled mushrooms and steamed broccoli. It can also be tossed with noodles.

Black Vinegar Sauce

Chinese black vinegar is available from Oriental supermarkets.

SERVES 4

1 tablespoon vegetable oil
3-4 drops sesame oil
2 teaspoons finely grated root ginger
4 spring onions, chopped
60ml/2floz Chinese black vinegar
4 tablespoons soy sauce
300ml/½ pint fish stock
2 tablespoons demerara sugar
1 tablespoon cornflour
2 tablespoons cold water

Heat the oil in a medium-sized saucepan and flavour it with the sesame oil. Add the ginger and spring onions and cook them gently for 1-2 minutes until softened.

Stir in the vinegar, soy sauce, fish stock and sugar, bring the mixture to a boil and simmer for 10 minutes.

Teriyaki Sauce

The name of this simple sauce comes from the Japanese *teri* meaning glossy and *yaki* meaning grill. This recipe features naturally brewed Japanese soy sauce, sake (an alcohol made or brewed from fermented rice) and mirin (sweet cooking sake), all of which are now often sold in supermarkets.

MAKES 90ML/3FL OZ

2 tablespoons soy sauce
2 tablespoons sake
2 tablespoons mirin
½ teaspoon caster sugar

Mix all the ingredients together in a small bowl or screw-topped jar. The sauce can be

Above: versatile Teriyaki Sauce from Japan makes an excellent marinade for tender cubes of meat which can then be placed on skewers and quickly barbecued or grilled.

kept, tightly covered, in the refrigerator for an indefinite period.

Variation: add a crushed clove of garlic and a 2cm/¾in piece of fresh root ginger, peeled and grated just before use.

Marinate beef, chicken or fish in the sauce, using the remainder to baste the ingredients during cooking. It can also be used as an alternative to plain soy sauce in stir-fries.

In a small cup, blend the cornflour with the water to give a smooth paste then slowly pour it into the sauce. Cook for 1-2 minutes until the sauce is of a coating consistency.

_____ 🥄 _____

Best with white fish, whole or fillets, and vegetables steamed in the Chinese style.

Beef in Black Bean Sauce

The black beans used in this sauce are soy beans that have been salted and fermented. They are sold in cans from Oriental grocers.

SERVES 2-4

350g/12oz lean beef steak
3 tablespoons vegetable or peanut oil
1 teaspoon sesame oil
FOR THE MARINADE:
2 tablespoons soy sauce
1 teaspoon sesame oil
2 teaspoons rice wine
2 teaspoons cornflour
FOR THE BLACK BEAN SAUCE:
3 tablespoons fermented black beans, rinsed
1 teaspoon caster sugar
2 tablespoons chicken or beef stock or water
1 tablespoon soy sauce
1 tablespoon rice wine
4cm/1½in piece root ginger, finely grated
4 medium spring onions, sliced
2 cloves garlic, chopped
½ large red pepper, cored, seeded and sliced

Chill the steak in the freezer for 5 minutes, then slice it into the thinnest possible strips. Mix all the marinade ingredients together in a large bowl, add the beef strips, then leave to marinate for 1 hour, if possible.

Sprinkle the rinsed and drained black beans with the sugar, then chop coarsely and set aside. Mix the stock, soy sauce and rice wine together in a small bowl.

Heat the vegetable or peanut oil in a wok until smoking. Drain the meat, discarding any excess marinade and stir-fry for 3-4 minutes until evenly browned. Remove the meat with a slotted spoon and drain it in a colander.

Stir-fry the ginger, onions, garlic and pepper for 1 minute, then add the stock mixture and beans and bring to a boil. Stir in the beef and allow it to reheat. Remove from the heat, add the sesame oil and serve.

Variation: replace the beef with strips of chicken, lamb or venison.

_____ 🥄 _____

Serve with rice, plus some leaves of bok choy that you have quickly stir-fried in another pan with a little sliced garlic.

Below: fermented soy beans add a rich flavour to the Chinese favourite Beef in Black Bean Sauce.

Sweet and Sour Sauces

Plum Sauce

MAKES 450ML/16FL OZ

500g/1lb 2oz damsons or tart plums, stoned
125ml/4fl oz rice wine
50g/1¾oz light muscovado sugar
1 teaspoon sea salt
3 tablespoons vegetable oil
5cm/2in piece root ginger, grated
4 cloves garlic, crushed

¼-½ teaspoon finely chopped green chilli

Put the fruit and rice wine into a stainless steel pan. Cover and cook for 5-10 minutes or until soft. Liquidize the mixture until smooth then return it to the pan. Stir in the sugar and salt and cook until thick.

Heat the oil in a small, heavy pan. Add the ginger, garlic and chilli and stir-fry for 30 seconds. Stir this mixture into the fruit purée and cook for 1 minute or until the sauce is very thick and shiny.

———————— ⟞ ————————

Serve with chops, as a dipping sauce or add it to meat casseroles for a fruity flavour.

Sweet and Sour Sauce

Fresh fruit juice makes this sauce better than that served in most Chinese restaurants.

SERVES 4

1 tablespoon vegetable oil
3 medium shallots, finely chopped
2 tablespoons golden caster sugar
3 large tangerines
2 tablespoons white rice vinegar, or to taste
salt and pepper
1 teaspoon cornflour
1 tablespoon water

Heat the oil in a medium-sized saucepan and cook the shallots gently until softened. Sprinkle over the sugar and cook over a

medium heat, stirring frequently, until the shallots are golden and slightly caramelized.

Meanwhile, pare the rind from one of the tangerines and cut the strips into needle-like shreds. Squeeze the juice from all the fruit and add it to the pan with the shredded rind and vinegar. Simmer gently for 5 minutes.

Taste and season well with salt and pepper, then adjust the sweet-sour balance as necessary: you may need to add a little more vinegar. In a small bowl, mix the cornflour to a paste with the water and stir into the sauce. Bring the mixture to a boil, stirring constantly, to make a thick sauce.

Above: this Sweet and Sour Sauce takes its citrus flavour from fresh tangerines. Deep-fried pork and steamed rice turn it into a meal.

———————— ⟞ ————————

Best hot with large cubes of deep-fried lean meat such as chicken or pork. Marinate the meat for 30 minutes in 1 tablespoon of soy sauce, 1 teaspoon of sesame oil, 1 beaten egg, 1 tablespoon of cornflour and some salt and black pepper. Toss the drained, marinated meat in some more cornflour then deep-fry and serve it with the sauce.

Chilli Sauces

Chinese Chilli Sauce

MAKES 250ML/9FL OZ

1 small red pepper
2 cloves garlic, chopped
100ml/3½fl oz rice vinegar
4 tablespoons caster sugar
2 large dried red chillies, seeded and chopped
50ml/2fl oz cold water, plus 1 tablespoon extra
1 teaspoon cornflour

Put the red pepper, garlic, vinegar, sugar, chillies and the 50ml/2fl oz of water into a food processor and blend until smooth.

Transfer the sauce to a non-aluminium saucepan and set it over a low heat. Cook for 10 minutes, skimming as necessary.

Meanwhile, in a small cup, blend the cornflour with the extra tablespoon of water. Slowly pour this paste into the chilli sauce, stirring constantly until the sauce thickens. Leave to cool then pour into a clean bottle or jar. The sauce can be stored in the refrigerator for up to 2 weeks.

Variation: add 1 teaspoon of chopped root ginger to the mixture in the food processor.

Toss with cold cooked prawns, noodles and Chinese leaves to make a stylish salad, or serve it with deep-fried fish, shellfish, pork or poultry. Can be used as a dipping sauce.

Harissa

MAKES 350G/12OZ

250g/9oz red chillies, seeded and chopped
1 head garlic, peeled
1 tablespoon ground coriander
1 tablespoon caraway seeds
1 tablespoon dried mint
3 tablespoons chopped coriander leaves
1 tablespoon salt
2 tablespoons olive oil

Place all the ingredients in the bowl of a food processor or blender and process them to a smooth, thick paste. Add a little more oil if the mixture is too dry. Store the sauce, covered with a thin film of olive oil, in a jar in the refrigerator for up to 3 months.

A powerful sauce to serve in tiny quantities with barbecued meats and poultry or tagines.

Chilli Jam

MAKES 700ML/1¼ PINTS

1kg/2lb 4oz tomatoes
75ml/2½fl oz olive oil
5 cloves garlic, peeled
15g/½oz root ginger, peeled
4 small red chillies, stems removed
15g/½oz cumin seeds
15g/½oz black mustard seeds
100ml/3½fl oz cider vinegar
30ml/1fl oz fish sauce
150g/5½oz demerara sugar
2 teaspoons turmeric
25g/1oz coriander, chopped

Preheat the oven to 180°C/350°F/Gas 4. Place the tomatoes in a roasting tin and pour over the oil. Roast the tomatoes for 20 minutes until soft but not browned.

In a food processor or blender, combine the garlic, ginger, chillies, cumin, mustard seeds and vinegar and process until smooth.

Transfer the mixture to a large heavy pan then add the tomatoes, fish sauce, sugar and turmeric. Bring to a boil and simmer gently for 1½-2 hours until very thick.

Lightly purée the mixture then stir in the coriander. Pour into a warm jar and seal. Store in the refrigerator for up to 1 month.

Offer the jam with pan-fried fish or pork, accompanied by Asian-style salads.

Salsa Chipotle

This cooked sauce from Mexico has a delicious smoky flavour provided by the dried chipotle chillies.

SERVES 4

6 dried chipotle chillies
125ml/4fl oz boiling water
4 cloves garlic, unpeeled
1 tablespoon olive oil
1 small onion, chopped
200g/7oz tomatoes, chopped
300ml/½ pint vegetable stock
salt and pepper

Preheat the oven to 200°C/400°F/Gas 6. Place the dried chillies in a small bowl and pour the boiling water over them. Leave to soak for at least 30 minutes.

Meanwhile, put the garlic cloves on a baking tray and roast them in the oven for 10-15 minutes until tender. Leave to cool, then peel and chop the cloves.

When the chillies have rehydrated, line a sieve with a piece of kitchen paper and strain the soaking water from the chillies into a jug. Halve, core and seed the chillies, chop the flesh roughly and add it to the soaking water. Purée the chillies with a hand blender until a smooth liquid is formed.

Heat the oil in a small saucepan and add the onion. Cook over a low to moderate heat for 5 minutes or until the onion is softened but not browned. Stir in the chopped garlic and tomatoes and continue cooking for another 3 minutes.

Pour the vegetable stock and the puréed chilli liquid into the pan, bring to the boil and simmer for 15-20 minutes until the sauce is thick and reduced to the consistency you desire. Taste and season as necessary with salt and pepper. Serve hot.

Choose beef, chicken, lamb, or meaty fish steaks for this sauce.

Satay Sauce

MAKES 400ML/14FL OZ

4 shallots, quartered
2 cloves garlic
1cm/about ½in cube shrimp paste
¼ teaspoon sea salt
1 teaspoon tamarind paste
1 tablespoon cold water
1 tablespoon vegetable oil
½ teaspoon chilli powder
1 teaspoon dark muscovado sugar
1 tablespoon soy sauce
300g/10½oz crunchy peanut butter
about 300ml/½ pint water

If you have a spice blender, process the shallots, garlic, shrimp paste, and salt until smooth; if not, chop them finely, then crush them in a mortar.

Mash the tamarind paste with the water then strain the mixture, reserving the liquid.

Heat the oil in a medium-sized, heavy pan and fry the spice mixture for 20 seconds. Add the chilli powder, sugar and soy sauce and stir-fry for another 30 seconds.

Add the peanut butter and the water to the pan and bring the mixture to a boil. Simmer for 10 minutes or until thick: if the sauce becomes too thick for dipping, add some more water. Stir in the tamarind water, then taste and adjust the flavouring, adding more salt or soy sauce as necessary.

This sauce can be stored in a jar in the refrigerator for up to 5 days then gently reheated before serving.

———————⟨spoon⟩———————

Use to accompany marinated grilled meats or plainly cooked chicken strips, lamb steaks, prawns or crudités.

Right: Gado-Gado, an Indonesian dish in which a variety of cold vegetables, cooked separately, are served with nutty Satay Sauce and garnished with crisply fried onion rings.

Gado-Gado

SERVES 6

100g/3½oz beansprouts
100g/3½oz green beans, topped and tailed
100g/3½oz carrots, sliced
100g/3½oz cauliflower florets
50g/1¾oz cabbage, shredded
1 large potato
100g/3½oz cucumber, peeled and sliced
4 tablespoons vegetable oil
2 shallots, thinly sliced
400ml/14fl oz Satay Sauce (see left), warmed

Steam the beansprouts for 1 minute or blanch them in boiling water. Drain, refresh them with cold water, drain again, and set aside. Steam or blanch the green beans for 3 minutes. Drain, refresh with cold water, drain again, and reserve.

Steam or blanch the carrots and the cauliflower separately for 2 minutes each, and the cabbage for 1 minute. Drain, refresh with cold water, drain again, and reserve.

Boil the potato in its skin until tender. Leave the potato to cool then peel and dice it. Arrange all the vegetables with the sliced cucumber on a big platter.

To make the garnish, heat the oil in a frying pan and cook the shallots until crisp, then drain them on kitchen paper. Spoon the warm sauce over the vegetables, then garnish with the fried shallots. Serve with rice or on its own as a starter.

C URRIES

Murgh Korma

Kormas should be aromatic rather than hot.

SERVES 4-6

6 pieces chicken, skinned and halved
2 tablespoons clarified butter, ghee or
    vegetable oil
2 medium onions, chopped
1 cinnamon stick
1 mild green chilli, sliced into thin rings, seeded
FOR THE MARINADE:
225g/8oz plain set wholemilk yogurt
½ teaspoon sea salt
4 large cloves garlic, crushed
3cm/1¼in piece root ginger, grated
FOR THE DRY MIXTURE:
1 rounded tablespoon whole blanched almonds
2 tablespoons desiccated coconut
½ teaspoon cardamom seeds
½ teaspoon cumin seeds
1 small dried chilli (optional)
½ teaspoon ground turmeric

Put the chicken into a large non-metallic dish. Combine the marinade ingredients and pour them over the chicken. Mix well, cover and marinate in the refrigerator for 1-12 hours.

Preheat the oven to 190°C/375°F/Gas 5. Put the almonds and coconut into a baking dish and toast them in the oven for about 10 minutes or until golden. Leave to cool.

Put the cardamom, cumin and dried chilli, if using, into a mortar and crush them to a fine powder. Mix in the turmeric and the almond mixture and set aside.

Heat the butter, ghee or oil in a large heavy pan or flameproof casserole. Fry the onions, stirring frequently, until golden brown. Remove them from the pan with a slotted spoon and turn off the heat.

Process the onions and dry spice mixture in a food processor or blender until smooth.

Reheat the pan with the fat left from cooking the onions. Add the chicken and marinade and cook, stirring gently, over a medium-high heat for 2-3 minutes. Add the onion paste and the cinnamon stick and stir until thoroughly combined. Bring the sauce to a boil then cover the pan and simmer over a very low heat, stirring frequently, for about 30 minutes or until the chicken is very tender. Taste and adjust the seasonings then remove the cinnamon stick. Garnish with the sliced green chilli and serve.

Variations: replace the chicken with pieces of turkey or lamb.

Chicken Vindaloo

This Goan recipe is less fiery than the staple of most neighbourhood Indian restaurants.

SERVES 4

4 pieces chicken, skinned and trimmed
FOR THE SAUCE:
2 tablespoons cumin seeds
1 tablespoon black mustard seeds
½ teaspoon chilli powder, or to taste
5cm/2in piece root ginger, grated
5 cloves garlic, chopped
100ml/3½fl oz cider vinegar
1 teaspoon ground cinnamon
black seeds of 10 cardamom pods
1 teaspoon sea salt
½ teaspoon ground black pepper
3 tablespoons vegetable oil

Thoroughly process all the sauce ingredients except the oil in a food processor or blender.

In a large, heavy pan or flameproof casserole, heat the oil, add the sauce and stir-fry, off the heat, for a few seconds. Add the chicken and stir to coat it with the sauce. Bring the mixture to a boil then cover and simmer for 40 minutes or until the chicken is tender, stirring frequently. Adjust the seasoning of the sauce to taste, adding salt, pepper or vinegar as necessary, then serve.

Variation: use lamb instead of chicken.

Green Chilli and Apricot Sauce

SERVES 4

100g/3½oz Hunza apricots
125ml/4fl oz cold water
3 mild green chillies, seeded and chopped
2cm/¾in piece root ginger, sliced
3 cloves garlic, chopped
2 medium onions, chopped
black seeds of 3 cardamom pods
3 tablespoons clarified butter, ghee or
    vegetable oil
1 cinnamon stick
4 pieces chicken, on the bone, trimmed
2 medium tomatoes, roughly chopped
salt and pepper

Soak the apricots overnight in the water. Process the chillies, ginger, garlic, onions and cardamom seeds in a food processor or blender until finely chopped.

Heat the butter, ghee or oil in a large, heavy pan or flameproof casserole, add the spice paste and cinnamon stick and stir over a medium heat for 3 minutes until lightly coloured. Push this mixture to one side of the pan then add the chicken and cook until lightly browned on each side, adding a little more fat if necessary. Stir in the tomatoes, the soaking water from the apricots, some salt and pepper then bring to a boil.

Cover the pan, lower the heat and simmer gently for 25 minutes or until the chicken is almost tender, stirring occasionally.

Stir in the apricots and cook for another 10 minutes or until the chicken is thoroughly cooked and the apricots are soft but still whole. Taste and adjust the seasoning: the sauce should have a good balance of sweet, savoury and spicy, so add more salt, pepper or a squeeze of lemon juice as necessary. Remove the cinnamon stick before serving.

Variations: replace the chicken with 800g/1lb 12oz of diced turkey or lamb.

Crab and Coriander Sauce

A creamy medium-hot curry sauce requiring the white roots of coriander as well as the stems and leaves.

SERVES 2-4

1 rounded teaspoon tamarind paste
1 tablespoon hot water
small bunch of coriander, stems and leaves chopped, white roots chopped and reserved separately
2 tablespoons vegetable oil
400ml/14fl oz coconut milk
200g/7oz cooked fresh crab meat, flaked
1-2 tablespoons fish sauce
FOR THE SPICE PASTE:
1 red onion, chopped
3 large cloves garlic, chopped
1.5cm/½in piece root ginger, sliced
½-1 large medium-hot chilli, seeded and chopped
5cm/2in piece lemongrass, chopped
1 teaspoon ground coriander
½ teaspoon ground turmeric
¼ teaspoon shrimp paste
1 tablespoon vegetable oil

Soak the tamarind paste in the hot water. Put the ingredients for the spice paste plus the white roots of the fresh coriander into the bowl of a food processor. Process, scraping down the sides of the bowl every 20 seconds or so, until the mixture has formed a thick, smooth paste. This will take several minutes. If the paste is difficult to process, add 1 tablespoon of the coconut milk. The spice paste can be made in advance and kept, tightly covered, in the refrigerator for up to 24 hours.

Heat the oil in a large, heavy pan, add the spice paste and fry over a medium heat, stirring constantly, for about 5 minutes. Add the coconut milk and the strained tamarind water and stir until the mixture comes to a boil. Reduce the heat and simmer gently for

10-15 minutes until the sauce thickens and lightly coats the back of a spoon. Stir in the crab meat and 1 tablespoon of fish sauce and cook gently for 5 minutes. Taste and add more fish sauce as needed. Stir in the coriander leaves and stems then serve.

Variations: add 1kg/2lb 4oz of large uncooked prawns, shelled, deveined and gently flattened, to the sauce along with the crab, or 500g/1lb 2oz of generously diced white fish such as halibut or monkfish. Alternatively, cut 3 skinned chicken breasts into generous cubes and add them to the sauce with the crab, allowing it to simmer for 7-10 minutes until the chicken is cooked.

Beef in Black Sauce

Very thick, dark and gently spiced, this is an Indonesian sauce. Choose braising beef or venison for the best taste and texture – very lean meat will become too dry during the long cooking time needed for the sauce.

SERVES 4

500g/1lb 2oz braising beef or venison steak
2 rounded teaspoons tamarind paste
3 tablespoons hot water
2 medium red onions, chopped
4 cloves garlic, chopped
2cm/¾in piece root ginger, sliced
3 tablespoons vegetable oil
¼ teaspoon coarsely ground black pepper
¼ teaspoon freshly grated nutmeg
¼ teaspoon ground black cardamom seeds
2 whole cloves
1 cinnamon stick
3 tablespoons soy sauce
1 tablespoon palm sugar (jaggery) or dark muscovado sugar
250ml/9fl oz unsalted beef or vegetable stock

Trim the excess fat from the meat then cut it into generous cubes. Soak the tamarind

paste in the hot water for about 10 minutes. Meanwhile, put the onions, garlic and ginger into the bowl of a food processor and process until finely chopped.

Heat the oil in a medium-sized heavy pan or flameproof casserole then fry the onion mixture over a moderate heat, stirring constantly, for about 3 minutes until it starts to colour. Push it to one side of the pan. Fry the meat until it is browned on all sides, then stir in the onion mixture. Add the ground and whole spices and cook, stirring constantly for 1 minute. Stir the soy sauce, sugar and stock into the pan.

Mash the softened tamarind flesh and liquid together then strain the mixture through a coarse sieve. Add it to the pan, stir then bring the mixture to a boil. Cover and simmer very gently for 1½-2 hours or until the meat is very tender and the sauce very thick. If necessary, remove the lid and simmer the sauce until it thickens. Taste and adjust the seasoning as necessary. Remove the cinnamon stick before serving.

Thai Red Curry Paste

MAKES 225G/8OZ

1 tablespoon coriander seeds
1 tablespoon cumin seeds
2cm/¾in piece root ginger, finely chopped
10 medium dried chillies, seeded and chopped
2 teaspoons chopped lemongrass
2 teaspoons ground nutmeg
pared rind of 1 lime, roughly chopped
6 cloves garlic, chopped
5 shallots, quartered
½ teaspoon shrimp paste
2 teaspoons salt
4 tablespoons vegetable oil

Using a spice grinder or a pestle and mortar, grind the coriander and cumin seeds to a fine powder. Transfer the mixture to a blender or the small goblet of a food

Curries

processor and process with the remaining ingredients to make a smooth paste.

Store the curry paste in the refrigerator in a covered jar for up to 1 month.

———————— ⟶ ————————

Combine the curry paste with coconut milk to make poultry, seafood and vegetable curries. Duck is particularly good.

Green Curry Paste

This recipe is the basis for many Thai curries and in devising it I was helped by our local Thai grocers, who sell all these ingredients much cheaper and fresher than a large supermarket. They insist that galangal is vital and fresh root ginger should only be substituted as a last resort. The chillies are the tiny Thai or bird's eye variety and extremely hot so handle them with care. It is a good idea to wear rubber gloves for protection while preparing chillies.

MAKES 225G/8OZ

4 cloves garlic
4 green chillies, cored and roughly chopped
3 shallots, roughly chopped
1 teaspoon shrimp paste
1 teaspoon sea salt
3cm/1¼in piece galangal, peeled and
  roughly chopped
1 teaspoon ground cumin
2 teaspoons ground coriander
1 stalk lemongrass, roughly chopped
pared rind of 1 lime, roughly chopped
25g/1oz coriander, including the white
  roots, roughly chopped
2 tablespoons vegetable oil

Put all the ingredients into a food processor and blend until smooth, scraping the mixture down from the sides from time to time. Store the curry paste tightly covered in the refrigerator for up to 1 week.

Green Prawn Curry

SERVES 2-4

16 large raw prawns, defrosted if necessary
3-4 tablespoons green curry paste, to taste
2 tablespoons vegetable oil
400ml/14fl oz coconut milk
4 kaffir lime leaves, central stem discarded,
  very finely shredded
small bunch fresh Thai basil
2 teaspoons fish sauce, or to taste

Remove the shells from the prawns then slit them along the back and remove the black, thread-like intestinal tract. Open the prawns out like a book and gently flatten them.

Above: once you have acquired the authentic Thai ingredients for this spicy, aromatic Green Prawn Curry, it is very quick to prepare.

In a medium-sized saucepan, cook the curry paste in the oil for 3-4 minutes. Add the coconut milk and lime leaves and simmer for 20 minutes, stirring frequently. Add a little water if the sauce becomes too thick.

Add the prawns to the pan and cook gently for 3 minutes or until just firm to the touch. Pick the basil leaves from their stems and add the leaves to the curry with the fish sauce. Stir briefly to combine, then remove the pan from the heat and adjust the sauce seasonings as necessary. Serve the curry immediately with steamed Thai rice.

*D*IPS AND *C*HUTNEYS

Vietnamese Dipping Sauce (Nuoc Mam)

SERVES 6

1 red chilli, chopped
1 clove garlic, chopped
1 teaspoon sugar
1 tablespoon rice vinegar
3 tablespoons water
3 tablespoons fish sauce
2 teaspoons shredded carrot
2 teaspoons shredded mouli

Put the chilli, garlic and sugar in a mortar and pound them to a paste. Stir in the vinegar, water and fish sauce, then the shredded carrot and mouli. Serve in a bowl.

Variation: for a different type of acidity, replace the rice vinegar with lime juice.

Rice paper rolls and other Oriental appetisers and snacks are great with this sauce.

Nutty Hoisin Sauce

SERVES 4-6

1 teaspoon shredded carrot
1 teaspoon sugar
1 tablespoon rice vinegar
4 tablespoons hoisin sauce
2 tablespoons water
1 tablespoon peanut butter
1 red chilli, seeded and finely diced

Mix the carrot, sugar and rice vinegar together in a small bowl and set aside to marinate for 15 minutes.

Meanwhile, in a small saucepan, bring the hoisin sauce and the water to a boil and simmer until you have a thick pouring sauce. Stir in the peanut butter, then remove from the heat and allow the mixture to cool.

Strain the carrot mixture through a fine-meshed sieve, pressing down on the carrot pulp to extract as much liquid as possible. Discard the liquid and add the carrot pulp to the cooled hoisin sauce mixture. Stir in the diced chilli and serve.

A thick, rich, slightly sweet sauce that tastes best with unfried snacks. Try it in Chinese pancakes with cucumber and spring onions.

Dark Soy Dipping Sauce

SERVES 8

4 tablespoons soy sauce
2 tablespoons sugar
2 tablespoons finely chopped spring onions
1 tablespoon finely grated root ginger
1 teaspoon finely chopped lemongrass
sesame oil, to taste

Mix the soy sauce, sugar, spring onions, ginger and lemongrass together in a small bowl. Add the sesame oil a few drops at a time, tasting until you are happy with the balance of flavours.

This dipping sauce is excellent with seafood such as raw or cooked tuna and grilled prawns. It can also be used in small amounts as a salad dressing.

Date Sauce

SERVES 4

150g/5½oz fresh dates, stoned
juice of 1 lemon
225ml/8fl oz water
1 teaspoon ground cumin
½ teaspoon chilli powder
½ teaspoon salt

Chop the dates and place them in a small saucepan with the remaining ingredients. Bring to a boil then lower the heat and simmer gently for 10-15 minutes or until the dates are very tender.

Liquidize the mixture using a hand blender or food processor, then strain it through a fine-meshed sieve to remove the tougher bits of date skin. Serve in a small bowl.

An unusual sweet sauce for poppadoms, onion bhajias and pakora.

Coriander and Mint Chutney

SERVES 8

100g/3½oz coriander, stalks included, roughly chopped
25g/1oz mint leaves
1 tablespoon chopped onion
2 tablespoons chopped green pepper
1 teaspoon grated root ginger
2 cloves garlic
2 medium green chillies
6 tablespoons yogurt
3 tablespoons water
1 teaspoon sugar
1 teaspoon salt

Place all the ingredients in a food processor or blender and process to a smooth sauce, scraping down the sides of the bowl from time to time. Taste and adjust the flavours to your liking, then chill before serving.

Variation: omit the yogurt to give a fresh-tasting curry paste that will last for weeks in the refrigerator if covered with a little oil.

Drizzle the chutney over fried Indian snacks such as bhajias, pakora and poppadoms.

Gujarati-style Vegetable Pickle

This is an attractive, easy pickle, especially if you use a food processor to shred the carrot and pepper.

SERVES 6-8

2 tablespoons ground mustard seeds
¾ teaspoon turmeric
1½ teaspoons chilli powder
1½ teaspoons salt
3 tablespoons lemon juice
1 tablespoon vegetable oil
1 large carrot, coarsely shredded
1 small red or yellow pepper, cored, seeded
   and coarsely shredded
100g/3½oz fine green beans, sliced lengthways

Place the spices, lemon juice and vegetable oil in a medium-sized bowl and whisk until combined. Carefully stir in the prepared vegetables and chill for several hours. Bring to room temperature before serving.

——————— ⤚ ———————

Offer this chutney as part of an Indian dip selection to serve with fried snacks or starters, or serve alongside curries.

Fresh Mint Raita

Raitas are not hot in themselves. Rather, they are a cooling accompaniment to spicy foods. Add a good pinch of sugar to the mint leaves as you chop them: this will help to release the oils.

SERVES 4

150ml/5fl oz plain yogurt
¼ teaspoon sea salt
ground black pepper
1 tablespoon finely chopped mint leaves
1 medium red onion, finely chopped
1 medium carrot, finely grated

In a small bowl, mix all the ingredients together then taste and add more salt and pepper as necessary. Cover and chill for at least 30 minutes. Stir before serving.

——————— ⤚ ———————

Serve with Indian curries and snacks.

Above: not hot itself, Fresh Mint Raita is a refreshing chilled mixture of yogurt, red onion, carrot and mint to serve alongside spicy foods.

SIDE SAUCES

A tablespoon or two of these quirky condiments added at the table bring a contrast of flavour – and usually temperature – to the main dish. Most of these recipes are traditional favourites. They include cooling, fruity jellies to go with sharp hard cheeses or cold meats, juicy citrus-sharp cranberry sauce for roast turkey, creamy smooth bread sauce for game and chicken, and cold, piquant horseradish.

The fresh sauces can be quickly made and served hot or cold. The preserves – relishes, jellies, ketchup – are made when the ingredients are in season, then carefully cooked and potted ready to bring out whenever appropriate.

Left (from left to right): Warm Mustard Sauce, Minted Apple Jelly, Apple Sauce.

Cranberry and Orange Sauce

MAKES 600ML/1 PINT

500g/1lb 2oz cranberries, fresh or frozen
175g/6oz golden caster sugar, or to taste
finely grated rind and juice of 1 large orange

Pick over the cranberries (there is no need to thaw frozen fruit). Wash and thoroughly drain the fresh fruit, if using. Put it into a preserving pan or large non-aluminium saucepan with the sugar, orange rind and juice and cook over a low heat until the sugar has dissolved.

Bring the mixture to a boil then simmer it gently until the berries start to pop. Cover the pan, remove from the heat and leave to stand for 15 minutes. Stir well, then cool before storing in a tightly covered jar in the refrigerator. Use the sauce within 1 week.

A tangy sauce, traditionally served cold with the Christmas turkey, but also good when served hot with game or duck, and at room temperature with cold sliced meats.

Cranberry and Port Sauce

SERVES 8

350g/12oz cranberries, fresh or frozen
175g/6oz light brown muscovado sugar
grated rind and juice of 1 orange
150ml/5fl oz port
¼ teaspoon ground mixed spice
black pepper

Put all of the ingredients into a large, non-aluminium pan and heat them gently, stirring, until the sugar has dissolved. Bring the mixture to the boil then reduce the heat and

simmer the mixture, stirring frequently, for 25 minutes or until the cranberries are really soft. The cooled sauce can be stored in the refrigerator for 3 days.

Cranberry and Port Sauce is best served hot with roast turkey or baked ham.

Cumberland Sauce

MAKES 350ML/12FL OZ

pared rind and juice of 1 lemon
pared rind and juice of 1 orange
250g/9oz redcurrant jelly
100ml/3½fl oz port
1 tablespoon Grand Marnier

Above: England's Cumberland Sauce adds fruity sweetness to traditional roast turkey.

Cut the pared lemon and orange rinds into very fine julienne strips and put them into a small pan with cold water to cover. Bring to the boil then remove the pan from the heat and strain, reserving the strips of rind.

Put the redcurrant jelly into a medium-sized, non-aluminium pan with the fruit juice. Heat gently, stirring to break down the jelly, until the mixture has melted to a smooth sauce. Add the port and simmer gently for 3 minutes. Remove the pan from the heat and stir in the blanched rind and the Grand Marnier. Leave the sauce until cold before serving. It can be kept tightly covered in the refrigerator for up to 1 week.

Fruit Sauces

Spoon onto roast turkey or serve with cold meats (my grandmother used it with pressed tongue), pork pies and cold game.

Apple Sauce

Use tart Bramley cooking apples for this recipe as the sauce should not be sweet.

SERVES 4-6

1 large Bramley apple, about 350g/12oz
3 tablespoons water
25g/1oz butter, chilled and diced
sugar to taste

Wash the apple then quarter and roughly chop it: there is no need to remove the peel and core. Put it into a medium-sized, heavy-based, non-aluminium pan with the water. Cover and cook gently until the fruit is soft and pulpy. Cool the pulp slightly then press it through a fine sieve.

Reheat the sauce then beat in the butter. Add a little sugar only if necessary: the sauce should taste quite tart to counteract the rich meat it accompanies. Serve warm.

The classic sauce for roast pork.

Gooseberry Sauce

Another tart sauce: this time the flavour of the fruit is enhanced with the aniseed bite of some diced fresh fennel.

SERVES 4

250g/9oz tart (not dessert) gooseberries
6 tablespoons water
1 tablespoon finely chopped fennel bulb
50g/1¾oz golden caster sugar, or to taste
25g/1oz unsalted butter, chilled and diced

Rinse then top and tail the gooseberries. Put them into a heavy-based, non-aluminium pan with the water and chopped fennel. Cover and simmer gently until the fruit and fennel are very tender, stirring frequently.

Remove the pan from the heat and beat the mixture until smooth, or purée it in a processor or using a hand blender. Stir in the sugar to taste, then whisk in the butter at the last minute and serve.

To make this sauce in advance, prepare the recipe up to the point where the sugar is stirred in and keep it warm. Add the butter only just before serving.

Use this pale green sauce to accompany rich fish and roast pork.

Quince and Apricot Sauce

This pretty, utterly delicious sauce is simple to make, once you have the quince jelly.

MAKES 450ML/16FL OZ

225g/8oz dried apricots
300ml/½ pint dry white wine
40g/1½oz unsalted butter
4 tablespoons quince jelly (see page 118)
salt and pepper

Put the apricots in a bowl and pour over the wine. Cover and leave to soak overnight.

Next day, transfer the apricots and wine to a small non-aluminium pan, then cover and simmer the fruit gently until very soft.

Tip the contents of the pan into a food processor or blender. Add the butter and quince jelly then process the mixture until smooth, scraping down the sides of the bowl from time to time. Taste and season the sauce as required with salt and pepper.

The cooled sauce can be kept tightly covered in the refrigerator for up to 4 days.

Serve the sauce warm with lamb, either a roasted joint or grilled chops, or serve it cold with cold meats such as duck, ham and pork, or with bread and cheese.

Pumpkin Sauce

SERVES 6-8

450g/1lb pumpkin flesh, diced
1 tablespoon olive oil
2 medium onions, chopped
small bunch thyme
125ml/4fl oz white wine
600ml/1 pint chicken stock
15g/½oz butter
salt and pepper

Put the diced pumpkin in a large saucepan. Cover it with water, bring it to a boil and simmer for 15-20 minutes or until tender. Drain and refresh under cold running water then leave to cool. Purée the pumpkin using a hand blender or a food processor. Alternatively, mash it thoroughly and then push it through a sieve.

Heat the olive oil in a large saucepan and add the chopped onions. Cover and cook over a gentle heat until softened but not browned, stirring occasionally. Raise the heat and add the thyme, white wine and 125ml/4fl oz of the stock. Bring the mixture to a boil and simmer until the liquid has almost evaporated. Add the remaining stock, return to a boil and simmer until the volume has reduced by a third, skimming as needed. Strain the liquid, discarding the solids. Stir in the puréed pumpkin, then the butter to give a sauce the consistency of gravy. Reheat if necessary, adding a little water if the mixture is too thick. Season to taste and serve.

Roast turkey is the natural partner to this velvety orange sauce.

Minted Apple Jelly

MAKES 1.35KG/3LB 2OZ

1kg/2lb 4oz cooking apples, roughly chopped
juice of 1 large lemon
golden granulated sugar (see recipe)
40g/1½oz fresh mint leaves

Put the apples into a large, non-aluminium preserving pan with 1.2 litres/2 pints of water and the lemon juice. Bring to a boil, stirring frequently, then lower the heat and simmer for 20-25 minutes until the apples are soft. Stir frequently to prevent sticking.

Suspend a jelly bag or conical sieve lined with muslin over a large basin. Transfer the apple mixture to the jelly bag or sieve and leave it to drip overnight or until all the liquid has drained through into the bowl. Do not squeeze the bag or the jelly will be cloudy.

Measure the liquid then put it into the cleaned pan, adding 450g/1lb of sugar per 570ml/1 pint of liquid. Heat the mixture gently, stirring frequently, until the sugar has dissolved. Bring to a boil, without stirring, and cook the mixture rapidly for 5 minutes.

Meanwhile chop 30g/1oz of the mint and tie it in a muslin bag. Add the bag to the pan and stir gently. Continue cooking until setting point is reached. To test for setting point, draw the pan off the heat and have several saucers chilling in the refrigerator. Drop a spoonful of the mixture onto a cold saucer so that it quickly cools. Draw a finger through the mixture: if the surface wrinkles the mixture will set; if not, continue boiling for 2-3 minutes then test again. Alternatively, test the mixture using a sugar thermometer: setting point is 105°C/220°F.

Remove the pan from the heat and cool for 5 minutes. Finely chop the rest of the mint, put it into a heatproof bowl and cover with boiling water. Infuse for 2 minutes then drain the mint through a fine sieve, squeezing out all the water. Remove the muslin bag from the pan, squeeze it between 2 small plates to extract all the juices, then discard.

Stir the mint leaves into the jelly then pot in warmed sterilized jars. Cover and label.

This jelly is ideal for grilled or roast lamb.

Crab-Apple Cranberry Jelly

MAKES 3.2KG/7LB

2.25kg/5lb crab-apples, quartered
500g/1lb 2oz cranberries
golden granulated sugar (see recipe)

Put the fruit into a non-aluminium preserving pan with 3.5 litres/6 pints 3fl oz of water. Bring the mixture to a boil and simmer for 30 minutes until the fruit is soft and pulpy. Tip the mixture into a jelly bag or conical sieve lined with muslin and set over a large basin. Leave to drain overnight.

Measure the liquid from the basin and put it into the cleaned preserving pan, adding 450g/1lb of sugar per 570ml/1 pint of liquid. Set the pan over a low heat and cook, stirring frequently, until all the sugar has dissolved. Raise the heat and boil rapidly for 20-30 minutes until the jelly has reached setting point (see previous recipe). Pour the jelly into warmed jars, then cover and label.

Best with roast game, lamb, pork or turkey.

Rowan Jelly

MAKES 1.6KG/3LB 8OZ

1kg/2lb 4oz rowan berries, picked over
golden granulated sugar (see recipe)

Put the fruit into a non-aluminium preserving pan with 700ml/1¼ pints of cold water. Bring to a boil then simmer gently for 30 minutes until the fruit is soft, squashing out the juice occasionally with a potato masher.

Tip the contents of the pan into a jelly bag or conical sieve lined with muslin and set it over a clean basin. Leave to drain overnight.

Measure the liquid then put it into the cleaned pan with 450g/1lb of sugar for each 570ml/1 pint of liquid. Stir over a low heat until the sugar has dissolved, then raise the heat and boil rapidly until setting point is reached (see previous recipe). Skim the jelly, pour it into warmed jars, cover and label.

A particularly good, traditional jelly for venison, game and cold meats.

Quince Jelly

MAKES 500G/1LB 2OZ

1kg/2lb 4oz quinces, roughly chopped
finely grated rind and juice of 1 large lemon
golden granulated sugar (see recipe)

Put the quinces into a preserving pan or large non-aluminium pan with the lemon rind and just enough cold water to cover the fruit. Bring to a boil, cover and simmer for 1 hour, stirring occasionally, until the fruit is very soft. Pour the mixture into a jelly bag or conical sieve lined with muslin, set it over a large bowl and leave to strain.

Measure the liquid and put it into the clean preserving pan with 450g/1lb of sugar for each 570ml/1 pint of liquid. Add the lemon juice and stir over a low heat until the sugar has completely dissolved. Raise the heat and boil rapidly for 10-15 minutes until setting point is reached (see previous recipe). Skim then pot into warm, dry jars. Cover and label.

Serve cold with roast lamb or game or stir a spoonful into gravy just before serving.

*B*read *S*auce

Old-Fashioned Bread Sauce

A creamy, richly flavoured sauce that should be light, smooth and free from lumps.

SERVES 6

300ml/½ pint creamy milk
1 medium onion, peeled and studded with
   2 cloves
1 bayleaf
6 black peppercorns
1 blade mace
50g/1¾oz white breadcrumbs
25g/1oz unsalted butter, diced
salt and pepper
1 tablespoon double cream

Place the milk in a small saucepan with the studded onion, bayleaf, peppercorns and mace and heat until scalding hot but not boiling. Remove from the heat, cover and leave to infuse for 30 minutes.

   Strain the milk into a clean pan, discarding the flavourings. Reheat then stir in the breadcrumbs and cook, stirring constantly, for 2-3 minutes or until the sauce thickens. Remove the pan from the heat and stir in the butter. Season to taste (the sauce should not be bland) then stir in the cream and serve. The sauce will thicken as it stands. Do not be tempted to reheat bread sauce: that way lies disaster.

Traditionally served with roast turkey at Christmas as well as with roast chicken, or roast grouse and other game birds.

Below: rich milk is essential for a superior Bread Sauce, traditionally flavoured with bay, mace, peppercorns and a clove-studded onion.

Crunchy Mustard

MAKES 325G/11½OZ

60g/2¼oz white mustard seeds
60g/2¼oz black mustard seeds
150ml/5fl oz white wine vinegar
3 tablespoons clear honey
1 teaspoon sea salt
¼ teaspoon ground cinnamon

Put the mustard seeds and vinegar into a glass or china bowl, cover with plastic film and leave for 36 hours.

Put the seed mixture into a blender with the honey, salt and cinnamon and process at maximum speed until the mixture is thick; if the paste is too dry, add a little more vinegar. Put the mustard into a sterilized preserving jar and seal tightly. Once opened, store it in the refrigerator. The mixture will rapidly dry out if not well sealed.

Serve with cold meats or use in vinaigrettes, dressings and when making pan sauces.

Mustard Pickle

This is a pickle that requires a fair amount of preparation but little cooking time. The vegetables are brined to remove some of the water and keep the pickle crunchy.

MAKES 3KG/6LB 8OZ

450g/1lb cucumber, diced
700g/1lb 9oz marrow, diced
375g/13½oz salt
2.25 litres/4 pints water
450g/1lb pickling onions or shallots, peeled
450g/1lb cauliflower florets
50g/1¾oz red pepper, shredded
50g/1¾oz green pepper, shredded
200g/7oz cabbage heart, shredded
450g/1lb French or bobby beans, cut into
   3cm/1¼in pieces

FOR THE MUSTARD SAUCE:
15g/½oz root ginger, bruised with a rolling pin
½ teaspoon peppercorns
25g/1oz plain flour
20g/¾oz curry powder
40g/1½oz turmeric
25g/1oz mustard powder
1.2 litres/2 pints distilled white vinegar
115g/4oz demerara sugar

Layer the cucumber and marrow in a large dish with a total of 150g/5½oz of the salt. Put the rest of the vegetables in a wet brine made from the remaining salt and the water: dissolve the salt in the water in a non-metallic bowl then add the vegetables and cover with a plate so they remain below the surface. Cover the bowl and the plate and leave to stand overnight at room temperature.

To make the mustard sauce, tie the ginger and peppercorns in a piece of muslin. In a small bowl, blend the flour, curry powder, turmeric and mustard powder with a little of the vinegar. Put the rest of the vinegar into a large preserving pan with the mustard paste and the bag of spices. Stir the mixture over a moderate heat until it boils, then lower the heat and simmer for 15 minutes until smooth and creamy. Stir in the sugar.

Brining the vegetables: sit a plate on top of the vegetables to keep them weighted down so that they are fully immersed in the brine mixture.

Drain the vegetables thoroughly and add them to the sauce. Simmer for 5 minutes then remove the spice bag. Pack the pickle into warm preserving jars, ensuring that the vegetables are well covered with sauce.

Particularly good with cold pork and beef.

Warm Mustard Sauce

MAKES 400ML/14FL OZ

2 teaspoons black or brown mustard seeds,
   coarsely crushed
2 teaspoons white mustard seeds, coarsely
   crushed
1½ tablespoons white wine vinegar
300ml/10fl oz chicken stock
1 tablespoon lemon juice
1 tablespoon English mustard powder
2½ tablespoons cream
1 tablespoon cornflour
1 tablespoon water
salt and pepper

In a small bowl, place the crushed mustard seeds and the vinegar, stir and leave them to soak for 2-3 hours.

In a medium-sized saucepan, combine the stock, lemon juice, English mustard and cream and slowly bring to a boil.

In a small bowl, blend the water into the cornflour to give a smooth paste then slowly pour it into the boiling sauce, stirring constantly. Lower the heat and simmer the sauce for 3 minutes.

Remove the pan from the heat, stir in the crushed mustard seeds and vinegar and season to taste with salt and pepper. Serve hot or warm. The sauce will keep in the refrigerator for up to 3 days.

Roast chicken, fish and pork are best with this mild, creamy sauce.

Left: Horseradish Sauce adds creamy piquancy to smoked trout and salad.

Drain the anchovy fillets and soak them in the milk for 10 minutes. Drain off the milk then process the anchovies in a food processor or blender with the butter and seasonings until a smooth purée is formed.

Store the paste in a covered container in the refrigerator for up to 3 weeks.

————— 🥄 —————

Good with baked potatoes, pasta and spread on toast and crumpets.

Red Onion Relish

Adjust the sharpness of this relish to taste: some onions are sweeter than others.

MAKES 500G/1LB 2OZ

500g/1lb 2oz red onions, thinly sliced in rounds
50ml/2fl oz red wine vinegar
3 tablespoons virgin olive oil
40g/1½oz dark brown muscovado sugar
3 tablespoons sun-dried tomato paste
1 large bouquet garni
3 cloves garlic, crushed
75g/2¾oz large raisins
300ml/½ pint water
salt and pepper

Place all the ingredients in a large non-aluminium pan. Bring the mixture to a boil, stirring frequently, until the sugar completely dissolves, then simmer gently, uncovered, for 45 minutes until very soft and moist.

Taste and adjust the flavourings as needed. Remove the bouquet garni then spoon the mixture into a warmed jar and seal. Store in the refrigerator and use within 2 weeks.

————— 🥄 —————

Cold meats, pies and sharp cheeses are ideal for this relish.

Horseradish Sauce

MAKES 150ML/¼ PINT

125ml/4fl oz double cream, chilled
1 tablespoon finely grated fresh horseradish, or to taste
juice of ½ lemon
pinch of English mustard powder
pinch of caster sugar
salt and pepper

Whip the cream until it forms soft peaks. Stir in the grated horseradish, lemon juice, mustard and sugar then mix well.

Taste the sauce, adding a little salt and pepper and adjusting the other flavourings as necessary. Cover and chill the sauce for up to 4 hours until ready to serve. Stir gently before serving.

Variation: use soured cream instead of double cream. In this case you may only need a couple of drops of lemon juice.

————— 🥄 —————

Horseradish sauce is most often served chilled with beef, however it is also good with smoked fish, particularly trout and eel.

Anchovy Relish

MAKES 225G/8OZ

150g/5½oz tinned anchovy fillets
6 tablespoons milk
140g/5oz unsalted butter, softened
pinch of cayenne pepper, or to taste
ground black pepper

Tomato Ketchup

This is only worth making if you have plenty of good, ripe, well-flavoured tomatoes. Sun-ripened plum tomatoes usually have a more concentrated taste than watery early greenhouse varieties.

MAKES 1.2 LITRES/2 PINTS

1kg/2lb 4oz tomatoes, quartered
250g/9oz onions, finely chopped
450g/1lb cooking apples, cored and finely
chopped
1.2 litres/2 pints distilled white vinegar
25g/1oz mustard seeds, roughly crushed
1 dried chilli
1 cinnamon stick
3 blades mace
1 teaspoon peppercorns
½ teaspoon grated nutmeg
60g/2¼oz sea salt
225g/8oz golden granulated sugar

Put the tomatoes, onions and apples in a preserving pan with half the vinegar, the crushed mustard seeds, chilli, cinnamon, mace, peppercorns, nutmeg and salt. Bring the mixture slowly to a boil and simmer it for 1-1½ hours or until it has reduced by a third. Stir frequently to avoid the mixture sticking on the base of the pan.

Strain the hot mixture through a coarse-meshed conical sieve, discarding the solids. Put the pulp into the clean preserving pan with the remaining vinegar and the sugar and stir the mixture over a low heat until the sugar has completely dissolved.

Bring the pan to a boil and simmer for 30-45 minutes or until the mixture is very thick. Pour the ketchup into clean, warm bottles and seal. Store it in a very cool spot and use within 6 months. Once opened, store the ketchup bottles in the refrigerator.

Serve with sausages, burgers and other grilled or fried meats.

Barbecue Ketchup

MAKES 850ML/1½ PINTS

90g/3¼oz unsalted butter
5 cloves garlic, finely chopped
3 medium onions, finely chopped
3 tablespoons dark brown muscovado sugar
3 tablespoons naturally brewed soy sauce
3 tablespoons cider vinegar
3 tablespoons Worcestershire sauce
450ml/16fl oz tomato ketchup
2-3 drops Tabasco sauce

Above (from left): Oyster Ketchup is flavoured with mace and cayenne while Barbecue Ketchup takes its heat from garlic and hot pepper sauce.

Heat the butter in a medium-sized pan, add the garlic and onions, stir well then cover and cook gently, stirring occasionally, for about 20 minutes or until very soft but not browned. Add the rest of the ingredients and cook for another 5 minutes. Taste and adjust the flavourings to suit your palate.

$\mathscr{K}$ETCHUPS

The cooled sauce can be kept, tightly covered, in the refrigerator for up to 1 week.

Offer the ketchup at room temperature or hot with plainly grilled meats and sausages. When cold, this sauce can also be used as a baste to brush over ribs, chops or chicken pieces towards the end of cooking.

Oyster Ketchup

An old English recipe. You can use dry or sweet sherry for this sauce, depending on which flavour you prefer.

MAKES 700ML/1¼ PINTS

**8 live oysters
600ml/1 pint sherry
1 tablespoon salt
4 blades mace
pinch of cayenne pepper or paprika
1 tablespoon brandy**

Shuck each oyster by holding the rounded side down on a board and inserting an oyster knife into the hinged end to prise it open. Cut out the oyster, being careful to reserve the liquor, and put it into a mortar. Pour the liquor into a bowl and set aside.

Pound the oysters to a smooth paste with a pestle: this is vital otherwise the sauce will be lumpy. Place the pounded oysters in a large saucepan with the reserved liquor and sherry and bring the mixture to a boil.

Add the salt, mace and cayenne pepper or paprika and allow to boil for another minute. Skim the mixture then strain it through a fine-meshed sieve and leave to cool. Stir in the brandy then bottle the ketchup. It can be stored in the refrigerator for up to 6 weeks.

Beef is best with this ketchup. You can add a few drops to stews and pasta sauces.

Tamarind Sauce

The flavour of this versatile sauce is spicy and aromatic rather than hot. You can buy tamarind paste in blocks from Oriental and Indian supermarkets. Soak it overnight in hot water and remove the stones before use.

MAKES 500ML/18FL OZ

**250g/9oz tamarind paste
300ml/½ pint hot water
100g/3½oz raisins
20g/¾oz root ginger, peeled and chopped
20g/¾oz black mustard seeds
3 medium dried red chillies
6 cloves garlic
350ml/12fl oz brown malt vinegar
350g/12oz dark muscovado sugar
1 tablespoon sea salt**

In a non-metallic bowl, place the tamarind and pour over 200ml/7fl oz of the hot water. Put the raisins in another bowl and cover them with the remaining hot water. Leave both to soak overnight.

Next day, drain the raisins and put them into the bowl of a food processor with the ginger, mustard seeds, chillies and garlic. Add 50ml/2fl oz of the vinegar and process them to make a smooth paste.

In a large, non-aluminium saucepan, mix the rest of the vinegar with the sugar and salt. Heat gently until the sugar dissolves.

Meanwhile, using your fingers, squeeze and break up the pieces of tamarind in the soaking liquid to give a thick, pulpy slurry. Remove the stones and any fibrous pieces of tamarind then add the tamarind mixture and the spice paste to the pan of vinegar. Bring to a boil then lower the heat and simmer for 15-20 minutes until the sauce is very thick and dark.

Push the sauce through a coarse sieve into a jug then pot it into clean, dry, warm bottles or jars. Seal the containers then store the sauce for 1 month before using. Once opened, store in the refrigerator.

Richly spiced, dark and thick, this sauce can be served as a ketchup with hot or cold cooked meats and poultry. It can also be used as a marinade or baste. You can add a little to mayonnaise to make a quick sauce in the style of Coronation Chicken, or add it to gravies and casseroles for extra flavour.

Roasted Garlic Sauce

MAKES 500ML/18FL OZ

**250g/9oz garlic cloves, unpeeled
150g/5½oz root ginger, peeled and chopped
2 medium-hot red chillies, cored, seeded and chopped
50g/1¾oz black mustard seeds
400ml/14fl oz cider vinegar
300g/10½oz light muscovado sugar
2 teaspoons sea salt**

Preheat the oven to 190°C/375°F/Gas 5. Put the garlic into a baking dish and roast it in the hot oven for 10 minutes or until aromatic, golden and soft. Leave to cool then squeeze the cloves out of the skins.

Put the garlic cloves into a food processor with the ginger, chillies and mustard seeds. Process to a smooth purée, adding a little of the vinegar if necessary.

In a non-aluminium saucepan, slowly heat the rest of the vinegar and the sugar without boiling until the sugar has dissolved. Raise the heat, add the garlic purée and stir as the mixture comes to a boil. Simmer very gently, stirring frequently, for 20 minutes or until the sauce is very thick, then add the salt.

Leave the mixture to cool and pour it into clean bottles or jars. Seal and store for 1 month before use. Once opened, store the sauce in the refrigerator.

Use as a sauce with hot or cold cooked meats, or as a marinade and baste.

DESSERT SAUCES

For those with a sweet tooth, a meal is incomplete without dessert. This chapter offers ways to turn simple ice-cream into a mid-week treat, or to make weekend brunch pancakes extra special. For grand occasions, there are alcoholic fruit sauces that can be spectacularly flamed at the table and classic dinner party favourites like crêpes Suzette, zabaglione and profiteroles. Old-fashioned creamy custards and even a pudding baked in its own sauce are perfect for Sunday lunch and family get-togethers.

All your favourite flavours are here: autumnal berries, tropical and citrus fruits, chocolate of all descriptions, coffee, toffee, brandy and rum, coconut and pecan nuts. There's plenty of butter, eggs and sugar too, but also a variety of low-fat recipes so that everyone can enjoy a sweet treat.

Left (from left to right): Chocolate Cream Sauce, Passion Fruit Syrup, Red Fruit Slump.

Raspberry Coulis (Melba Sauce)

This attractive, useful and very easy sauce was named by Escoffier, the famous chef of the Savoy Hotel, after the soprano Dame Nellie Melba, a regular guest when she sang at Covent Garden. He used it to accompany whole ripe peaches and vanilla ice-cream.

MAKES 400ML/14FL OZ

**400g/14oz fresh raspberries, or thawed frozen
  raspberries
icing sugar, to taste**

Purée the raspberries in a food processor. Add icing sugar to taste: the amount you will need depends on the tartness of the fruit (thawed frozen raspberries usually demand more than fresh) and on how the sauce is to be used. Process again for 1 minute to thicken the mixture.

Strain the sauce through a nylon sieve into a bowl or jug. Taste and adjust the flavour if necessary: if the sauce is too sweet, add a few drops of fresh lemon juice; if it is too tart, add a little more sieved icing sugar, beating well to avoid lumps.

Cover the sauce tightly and chill until required. The sauce can be stored in the refrigerator for up to 2 days. If fresh fruit is used, the sauce can be frozen for up to 1 month; do not freeze a sauce made from thawed frozen raspberries.

Variation: add 1-2 tablespoons of kirsch, framboise or eau-de-vie just before serving.

———— ✑ ————

Use as a sauce for fresh fruit, ice-cream, or rich patisserie-style desserts such as chocolate mousse cake and profiteroles. An effective presentation is to drizzle a little crème anglaise on the plate, then some raspberry coulis, place the cake or pastry on top and dust with icing sugar or cocoa.

Hunza Apricot Purée

When cooked, the small, hard, dried Hunza apricots have a rich, slightly caramelized flavour reminiscent of warm spices such as nutmeg and cinnamon.

SERVES 4

**150g/5½oz Hunza apricots
icing sugar, to taste (optional)**

Place the dried apricots in a bowl and cover them with a generous quantity of water. Leave to soak for 8 hours or overnight.

When they have reconstituted, drain the apricots, put them in a small saucepan and cover them with fresh cold water. Bring to a boil and simmer the apricots until tender. At the end of the cooking time the water should only just cover the apricots, so add more if necessary, or reduce by boiling vigorously.

Squeeze the stones from the apricots and return the flesh to the cooking liquid. Purée the apricots with their liquor using a hand

Below: one of the simplest sauces, Raspberry Coulis provides a red silky finish to this dish of tender fresh peaches and vanilla ice-cream.

F*RUIT* S*AUCES*

blender or food processor. Sweeten to taste if desired. Return the sauce to the pan and reheat if necessary, or leave it to cool.

Delicious as a sauce for Greek yogurt or ice-cream, particularly apricot, caramel or vanilla-flavoured. It also works well with pastries made from wholemeal flour.

Kiwi Coconut Sauce

SERVES 4

2 kiwi fruit, halved
150ml/¼ pint coconut milk
2 tablespoons caster sugar, or to taste

Using a teaspoon, scoop the flesh from the kiwi fruit and place it in the bowl of a food processor or blender. Pour in the coconut milk and purée until the mixture is smooth.

Stir in the sugar then taste and add a little more if necessary – this will depend on the sweetness of the fruit and coconut milk. Serve at room temperature or lightly chilled.

A spoonful of this mixture on top of a tropical fruit salad is delicious. Alternatively, use it to fill warm rolled crêpes and top with some lightly toasted shredded coconut.

Rhubarb and Fig Jam

MAKES 1.75KG/3LB 10OZ

1.3kg/3lb rhubarb
500g/1lb 2oz ready-to-eat dried figs
1.3kg/3lb preserving sugar or golden granulated
  sugar
juice of 2 large lemons

Wash the rhubarb and chop it into pieces about 2cm/¾in long. Chop the figs as

coarsely or finely as you wish. Put both fruits into a large china or glass bowl with the sugar and stir well. Cover and leave for 24 hours – the sugar should have almost completely dissolved.

Transfer the mixture to a preserving pan and add the lemon juice. Slowly bring the mixture to a boil, stirring frequently. Raise the heat a little then simmer until the mixture has thickened and setting point is reached. Pour into warmed sterilized jars then seal.

Variation: *Rhubarb and Orange Preserve*
Replace the figs and lemon juice with the chopped flesh of 1 large orange, 2 pieces of finely chopped preserved stem ginger and 2 teaspoons of ground ginger. As this mixture contains no dried fruit, it can be put straight into the preserving pan without soaking.

Warm this richly flavoured preserve until bubbling then thin it with a little water to make a pourable sauce for hot sponge puddings or pancakes. Of course, it can also be served cold with scones or bread.

Lemon Curd

MAKES 500G/1LB 2OZ

225g/8oz golden caster sugar
115g/4oz unsalted butter, diced
grated rind and juice of 3 large lemons
3 large eggs, beaten

Put the sugar, butter, lemon rind and juice in a double pan or a non-metallic bowl set over a pan of simmering water. Stir until the sugar has dissolved and the butter has melted.

Strain the beaten eggs into the pan and cook, stirring constantly, over a low heat until the mixture thickens – do not boil or the mixture will scramble. Pour into warm jars then cover. When cold, store the curd in the refrigerator and use within 1 month.

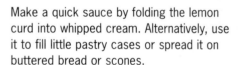

Make a quick sauce by folding the lemon curd into whipped cream. Alternatively, use it to fill little pastry cases or spread it on buttered bread or scones.

Oranges in Red Wine

A good recipe for summer parties as most of the preparation can be done in advance.

SERVES 6

425ml/¾ pint light red wine
1 vanilla pod
1 cinnamon stick
2 cloves
80g/3oz golden granulated sugar
150ml/5fl oz water
6 thin-skinned sweet oranges
250g/9oz strawberries

Put the wine, vanilla, cinnamon, cloves, sugar and water into a large non-aluminium saucepan. Heat gently, stirring constantly, until the sugar completely dissolves then bring the mixture to a boil and simmer until the liquid has reduced to a syrup measuring about 300ml/½ pint.

Meanwhile, hold the oranges over a large heatproof bowl to catch the juice and peel them with a sharp knife to remove the skin and all the white pith. Slice the oranges thinly, removing any pips. Arrange the slices in the heatproof bowl and, when it is ready, strain the hot wine sauce over the oranges. Leave them until completely cold then stir well, cover and leave to macerate in the refrigerator overnight.

An hour before serving, thinly slice the strawberries and stir them into the orange and wine mixture. Return the mixture to the refrigerator to continue macerating.

Serve alone or with ice-cream.

Crêpes Suzette

This dish of delicate pancakes in an orange liqueur sauce used to be a *coup de théâtre* in grand French restaurants where the *maître d'* would finish the dish at the table by igniting the alcohol to applause from the diners. Crêpes Suzette is thought to have been created by accident at the Café de Paris in Monte Carlo when the Prince of Wales, later Edward VII, dined there with friends. The nervous chef ignited the sauce and the spectacular result was named in honour of the youngest member of the party. In my version the sauce is less sweet and sticky and more refreshingly fruity. There is no need to set fire to the final dish, it will only set off the smoke alarm and do nothing for the taste of the recipe.

SERVES 4

FOR THE CRÊPES:
110g/4oz plain flour
large pinch of salt
1 large egg plus 1 large egg yolk
300ml/½ pint milk
20g/¾oz unsalted butter, melted
1 teaspoon Grand Marnier or other orange liqueur
extra melted butter or oil for frying
FOR THE FILLING:
10 demerara sugar cubes
2 large oranges
1 tablespoon Grand Marnier or other orange liqueur
125g/4½oz unsalted butter, softened
FOR THE SAUCE:
juice of the 2 oranges above
3 tablespoons Grand Marnier or other orange liqueur

Make the crêpe batter by sifting the flour and salt into a large bowl and making a well in the centre. Place the whole egg, yolk and milk in the well and gradually stir in the flour. Whisk in the melted butter and liqueur then cover and leave to stand for 30 minutes.

Heat a 15cm/6in crêpe pan and grease it lightly with kitchen paper dipped in the extra melted butter or oil. Put a good spoonful of the batter in the pan, swirling it around until the base of the pan is covered with a thin layer. Cook over a medium heat until golden brown then use a palette knife to loosen the edges of the crêpe and flip it over to brown the other side. Turn out the cooked crêpe and keep it warm while cooking the rest of the batch: you will need 16 crêpes. When necessary, grease the pan as before. If you want to cook the crêpes in advance, stack them on a plate interleaved with greaseproof paper, then cover tightly with foil.

To make the filling, rub the sugar cubes over the oranges until they absorb all the oils from the skin. Put the sugar cubes into a small bowl, add the liqueur and stir until dissolved. Beat the butter until creamy then gradually beat in the sugar and liqueur mixture. Reserve a tablespoon of the flavoured butter to fry the crêpes later.

Above: fresh orange juice and orange liqueur combine in a buttery sauce for Crêpes Suzette, here garnished with a little zest from the fruit.

Spread a teaspoon of flavoured butter on each crêpe then fold them in quarters. The filled crêpes can be covered and chilled for up to 6 hours before finishing.

When ready to serve, heat a large, heavy and preferably non-stick frying pan. Add the reserved butter then quickly fry the folded crêpes in batches for 2 minutes on each side until they are thoroughly heated and lightly browned. Keep the crêpes warm on a serving dish while frying the remainder.

When all the crêpes have been fried, add the orange juice to the pan and bring it to a boil, stirring over a medium heat to dissolve the sugary pan juices. Cook until reduced to a thin, syrupy sauce. Remove the pan from the heat and stir in the liqueur. Spoon a little sauce over the crêpes and pour the rest into a warmed sauce boat. Serve immediately.

Fruit Sauces

Variation: fill the crêpes with Crème Pâtissière (see page 130) and heat through gently before serving with the sauce.

Cherries Jubilee

Use your choice of fresh, canned, bottled or frozen black cherries for this quick sauce. Make sure they are drained thoroughly before use. Any excess juice can be used another time for a red fruit salad.

SERVES 4

15g/½oz unsalted butter
300g/10½oz pitted, drained black cherries
4 tablespoons golden caster sugar
grated rind and juice of 1 orange
4 tablespoons brandy, cherry brandy, kirsch or
   orange liqueur

Heat the butter in a heavy non-aluminium frying pan or sauté pan. When it begins to foam, add the cherries, shaking the pan so that they are well coated with butter, then sprinkle the sugar over the fruit. Cook over a medium-high heat for 2-3 minutes until the sugar just begins to caramelize.

Carefully add the orange rind and juice to the pan, then lower the heat and stir gently until the mixture boils and makes a syrupy sauce. Add the brandy or liqueur and ignite the pan with a match so that the sauce flames. Shake the pan until the flames die down then serve immediately.

Variations: white peaches, fresh or bottled, can also be used for this recipe. You can then replace the brandy with peach liqueur.

Cherries Jubilee is delicious with vanilla ice-cream and crisp biscuits. It also makes an unusual sauce for sweet batter puddings and adds a luxurious richness to chocolate cakes and puddings.

Hot Blackberry Sauce

SERVES 4-6

250g/9oz blackberries, fresh or frozen
60g/2¼oz light muscovado sugar, or to taste
2 tablespoons water
squeeze of lemon juice (optional)

Put the fruit (there is no need to defrost frozen fruit) and sugar into a medium-sized non-aluminium pan. Add the water and simmer the fruit for 5 minutes or until soft. Pass the fruit mixture through a fine nylon or stainless steel sieve into a clean pan. Taste the sauce and adjust the sweetness if necessary. If it is not tart enough, add a squeeze of lemon juice. Reheat and serve.

This sauce can be served with sorbets and sponge puddings as well as ice-cream.

Hot Strawberry and Orange Sauce

A good recipe for using strawberries that are slightly past their best.

SERVES 4

450g/1lb strawberries, hulled and halved
100g/3½oz golden caster sugar
4 tablespoons freshly squeezed orange juice
2-3 tablespoons orange liqueur

Sprinkle the fruit with half the sugar. Put the remaining sugar into a heavy non-aluminium sauté or frying pan and heat carefully until it melts and starts to caramelize. Remove the pan from the heat and stir in the orange juice, then return it to the heat and simmer until the sauce is syrupy.

Add about 50g/1¾oz of the prepared fruit to the sauce, stirring and mashing using a wooden spoon until the fruit has become a pulp. Add the rest of the fruit and the liqueur to the sauce. Reheat gently, stirring constantly, then serve.

Crêpes and pancakes are delicious with this sauce. Serve them with a dollop of cream or thick yogurt too, if you like.

Variation: add some chopped rhubarb to the pan and cook it gently for 10 minutes before adding the strawberries.

Red Fruit Slump

Another hot fruit sauce for which the fruit can be fresh or frozen. The name refers to the way the soft summer berries break down during cooking.

SERVES 4-6

500g/1lb 2oz red fruits such as blackberries,
   stoned cherries, red and blackcurrants,
   loganberries, raspberries or strawberries,
   fresh or frozen
3-4 tablespoons golden caster sugar, to taste
2 tablespoons water or crème de cassis

Put the fruit into a deep non-aluminium sauté pan or frying pan (any cherries and red or blackcurrants should be put in the pan first) and heat gently for about 2 minutes or until the juices start to run.

Stir in the softer fruit, the sugar and water or crème de cassis. Simmer the mixture for 5 minutes over a gentle heat until the fruit starts to soften, then cover the pan and continue simmering for another 4-5 minutes until the fruit is tender. Serve the sauce hot.

Sweet dumplings flavoured with a pinch of ground cinnamon can be poached in the simmering fruit sauce after it has been cooking for 5 minutes. Serve with generous spoonfuls of Greek yogurt or ice-cream.

ℰGG AND ℭREAM ℐAUCES

Crème Pâtissière

MAKES 350ML/12FL OZ

300ml/½ pint rich creamy milk
1 vanilla pod, split, or 1 tablespoon vanilla
  essence
4 medium egg yolks
60g/2¼oz caster sugar or vanilla sugar
2 tablespoons plain flour
½ teaspoon sugar

Put the milk and the vanilla pod (but not the essence, if using) into a heavy pan and heat slowly until scalding hot. Turn off the heat, cover, and leave to infuse for 20 minutes.

In a medium-sized bowl, whisk the egg yolks and sugar until light and thick, then whisk in the flour. Remove the vanilla from the pan and whisk the milk into the eggs.

Return the mixture to the pan and bring it to a boil, whisking constantly. Lower the heat and cook the mixture gently, whisking, for 2-3 minutes until the flour no longer tastes raw. Remove from the heat and stir in the essence, if using. Sprinkle with sugar to prevent a skin forming, then leave to cool.

The pastry cream can be stored, covered, in the refrigerator for up to 2 days.

Variations: flavour with brandy or liqueur to taste, with 100g/3½oz of melted chocolate or with 1½ tablespoons of instant coffee which you have dissolved in the milk.

Crème Pâtissière is the traditional cream filling for French pastries and tarts.

Crème Chantilly

MAKES 400ML/14FL OZ

200ml/7fl oz whipping cream, well chilled
½ teaspoon vanilla essence, or 1 tablespoon
  sweet sherry
1½ tablespoons caster sugar

Chill a whisk and mixing bowl for 1 hour in the refrigerator or freezer. Use them to whisk the chilled cream until just thickened, then add the sugar, vanilla or sherry and whip again until the cream almost forms stiff peaks. Beware: the cream will stiffen further as you come to use it and will separate later if you overwork it at this stage.

Use this whipped, sweetened cream to fill and decorate meringues, cakes and pastries as well as profiteroles and éclairs.

Honey Yogurt Cream

SERVES 6-8

125ml/4fl oz double cream
1 tablespoon clear honey
125ml/4fl oz Greek yogurt

In a large bowl, whip the cream until it forms soft peaks. Stir the honey into the yogurt then use a large metal spoon to fold the yogurt into the whipped cream. Cover and leave to chill before serving.

Serve this cream on top of juicy fruit salads flavoured with a dash of fruit liqueur or eau-de-vie. Alternatively, you can dollop it onto waffles and pancakes spread with jam. It also goes well with muesli.

Cinnamon and Mascarpone Cream

SERVES 8

100ml/3½fl oz cream
200g/7oz mascarpone cheese
1 tablespoon icing sugar
½ teaspoon ground cinnamon

In a large bowl, whip the cream until it forms soft peaks. In a separate bowl, beat the mascarpone cheese with the icing sugar and cinnamon until soft and creamy.

Fold the mascarpone mixture into the whipped cream and chill until ready to serve.

Variation: add 1 tablespoon of brandy, masala or madeira wine to the mascarpone before you beat it.

Best served in small quantities alongside pastry and fruit desserts or with steamed fruit puddings or toffee puddings. For an attractive presentation, shape into quenelles.

Orange Custard Sauce

MAKES 250ML/9FL OZ

25g/1oz unsalted butter, softened
grated rind and juice of 1 orange
2 teaspoons plain flour
50g/1¾oz caster sugar
1 egg

In a small saucepan, beat the butter until it is creamy then gradually stir in the orange rind, flour, sugar and then the egg until you have a thick paste. Measure the orange juice in a jug and make it up to 150ml/5fl oz with some cold water.

Gradually stir the diluted orange juice into the paste and, when it is thoroughly combined, place the pan over a low heat. Cook the sauce, stirring constantly, until it thickens and the taste of the flour has cooked out, adding a little extra water if necessary to keep the sauce at a pouring consistency. Serve warm.

Use as you would custard, with puddings and pastry desserts, especially those made with fruit. Also delicious with meringues.

Layered Fruit Bavarois

A bavarois is a crème anglaise lightened with whipped cream then set with gelatine. It has a smooth, creamy texture, different from the fluffy lightness of a mousse. The custard used for a bavarois is prepared in the same way as a pouring custard (see page 24), however the proportions of the ingredients need to be a little different in order to make a superior dessert: simply adding whipped cream and gelatine to a pouring custard would give the bavarois a heavy texture. To make this bavarois you will need a 1.2 litre/2 pint terrine, oiled and lined with some non-stick parchment or cling-film.

SERVES 8

15g/½oz powdered gelatine
3 tablespoons cold water
200ml/7fl oz double cream
175g/6oz raspberries, loganberries, or
**   tayberries**
175g/6oz strawberries or blackberries
2 small or 1 large peach or nectarine
FOR THE CRÈME ANGLAISE:
300ml/½ pint creamy milk
3 large egg yolks
85g/3oz caster sugar
grated rind of ½ orange
1-2 tablespoons orange liqueur, or to taste

Make the crème anglaise as on page 24, omitting the vanilla. Stir in the orange rind and liqueur then leave the custard to cool.

In a small heatproof bowl, sprinkle the gelatine over the cold water and leave it to soak for 5 minutes. Stand the bowl in a pan of simmering water and dissolve the gelatine, stirring gently. Cool it slightly, then stir the gelatine into the cooled custard.

Whip the cream until it forms soft peaks and, using a large metal spoon, fold it into the custard. Chill the mixture until it has almost set but is still smooth and soft.

Meanwhile, pick over the berries and wash them only if they are sandy or dusty. Pour some boiling water over the peaches or nectarine, steep for 30 seconds, then drain and peel. Halve, remove the stones and finely dice or slice the flesh.

Spread a third of the bavarois mixture in the base of the prepared terrine and chill it for 30 minutes or until set. Cover the set bavarois with half the fruit: you can layer the fruit separately or mix them together. Spoon over half the remaining bavarois mixture, smooth the surface then chill again until set. Top this layer with the remaining fruit and smooth on the final layer of bavarois. Cover the tin and chill the bavarois for 4 hours or until it has thoroughly set.

Turn out the bavarois and serve it in slices accompanied by Raspberry Coulis (see page 126). The bavarois can be made up to 1 day in advance but it cannot be frozen.

Below: Layered Fruit Bavarois features fresh red berries and juicy, tender peaches set in a thick, orange-flavoured Crème Anglaise to give a stunning dinner-party dessert.

*W*INE AND *S*PIRIT *S*AUCES

Brandy Sauce

MAKES 300ML/½ PINT

1 tablespoon cornflour
300ml/½ pint creamy milk
1 tablespoon caster sugar
2 tablespoons brandy

In a small bowl, blend the cornflour to a smooth paste with a little of the milk. Put the remaining milk into a small saucepan and heat, watching carefully, until it comes to the boil. Remove the pan from the heat and slowly pour in the cornflour paste, stirring constantly until it is thoroughly combined.

Return the pan to the heat, add the sugar and brandy and cook, stirring frequently, for 2-3 minutes until thick and smooth.

———— ∽ ————

This sauce is a reasonably light alternative to custard that can be served with traditional steamed fruit puddings and pies.

Red Wine Sauce

Wine sauces are often thickened with cornflour but this relies on simple reduction.

SERVES 4

350ml/12fl oz red wine
100g/3½oz caster sugar
1 cinnamon stick

In a small saucepan, stir the red wine and sugar together, add the cinnamon stick and bring to a boil, stirring occasionally. Lower the heat and simmer until the liquid has reduced by half and the mixture is syrupy.

Discard the cinnamon stick and serve the sauce hot, warm or at room temperature.

———— ∽ ————

Adds a rich, adults-only flavour to ice-cream, set vanilla custards and lemon tarts.

Rum Butter

Hard butter sauces are too often over-rich and cloyingly sweet, thus overwhelming the pudding they accompany. I have added lemon rind and juice as well as some honey to the recipe to lighten this traditional British festive season favourite.

SERVES 6

100g/3½oz unsalted butter, at room
temperature
80g/3oz light muscovado sugar
1 tablespoon honey
grated rind and juice of ½ lemon
3 tablespoons rum

Beat the butter until it is very light and creamy then beat in the sugar a tablespoon at a time until the mixture is fluffy. Beat in the honey and lemon rind, then add the lemon juice and rum a teaspoon at a time, beating well after each addition – this is important to stop the mixture from curdling.

Spoon the sauce into a dish, then cover and chill until firm. You can store it tightly covered in the refrigerator for up to 1 week, or freeze it for up to 1 month.

Beating the butter until light and fluffy: start with the butter at room temperature and dice it so that it breaks down quickly. Beat vigorously until the butter is like thick whipped cream.

Variations: replace the rum with brandy. For a richer hard sauce, replace the light muscovado sugar with dark brown sugar.

———— ∽ ————

Serve well chilled with some mince pies or Christmas pudding. This sauce is also good with other steamed or baked puddings, baked apples, crêpes and thick pancakes.

Syllabub

Another traditional British favourite that should not be forgotten.

SERVES 4

pared rind and juice of ½ lemon
175ml/6fl oz sweet sherry
3 tablespoons brandy
115g/4oz caster sugar
425ml/¾ pint double cream, well chilled
freshly grated nutmeg

Put the lemon rind, juice, sherry, brandy and sugar into a china or glass jug and leave the mixture to infuse for about 20 minutes, then remove and discard the strips of lemon rind.

Pour the cream into a large, well-chilled bowl. Start whisking, then gradually pour in the sherry mixture, whisking well as you go. Continue whisking until it is very thick and light. Spoon the syllabub into chilled glasses and decorate with a light dusting of freshly grated nutmeg. Serve immediately, or cover and chill for up to 4 hours.

Variation: stir in some toasted slivered almonds and pomegranate seeds.

———— ∽ ————

Syllabub can be served on its own with ratafias or sponge fingers for dipping. Or use it to make a trifle, with layers of thick egg custard, and sponge cake soaked with lashings of sherry and spread with jam.

Wine and Spirit Sauces

Zabaglione

SERVES 2-4

4 egg yolks
4 tablespoons caster sugar
6 tablespoons marsala wine
2 tablespoons water

Set all the ingredients in a heatproof bowl over a pan of just simmering – but not boiling – water. Whisk the mixture constantly for about 5 minutes until it turns light in colour and becomes very thick; it should leave a ribbon-like trail when the whisk is lifted from the bowl.

Remove the bowl from the heat and continue whisking the mixture until it cools. Serve the zabaglione warm or at room temperature within 1 hour.

Variations: replace the marsala wine with 4 tablespoons of kirsch, or you can replace it with 125ml/4fl oz of dry white wine or champagne. Alternatively, leave the mixture to cool then fold in 100ml/3½fl oz of lightly whipped cream.

Zabaglione is a marvellous sauce for sponge cakes, fresh fruit, fruit desserts, trifles and parfaits. You can also serve it the traditional way, in tall glasses accompanied by Italian biscuits such as crostini which are dipped into the sauce before eating.

Left: a tempting plate of luscious mixed berries, currants and crunchy Italian crostini is topped with generous spoonfuls of creamy Zabaglione to make a luxurious but simple treat.

CHOCOLATE SAUCES

Chocolate Sauce

For the best flavour, use chocolate with a cocoa solids content of over 70 per cent. These days such high quality chocolate is available in large supermarkets as well as specialist food shops.

MAKES 200ML/7FL OZ

100g/3½oz plain dark chocolate, chopped
60g/2oz unsalted butter, diced
100ml/3½fl oz water

Put the chopped chocolate, butter and water in a heatproof bowl and set it over a pan of steaming water. Stir the mixture frequently until the chocolate melts and the sauce is very smooth. Remove the bowl from the heat and stir well until the sauce is glossy and slightly thickened. As the sauce cools it will thicken further. Serve warm.

Variations: for a creamier sauce, replace the water with an equal quantity of cream; for a flavoured sauce, replace a tablespoon or two of the water with brandy or rum.

Profiteroles

SERVES 6

FOR THE CHOUX PASTRY:
115g/4oz plain flour
185ml/6fl oz cold water
large pinch of salt
large pinch of sugar
80g/3oz unsalted butter, diced
3 medium eggs, beaten
extra beaten egg, for brushing
FOR THE FILLING:
Crème Chantilly or Crème Pâtissière (see page 130)
TO SERVE:
Chocolate Sauce (see above), Toffee Sauce (see page 137), Creamy Caramel Sauce (see page 27), or Raspberry Coulis (see page 126)

To make the choux pastry, sieve the flour onto a piece of paper. Put the water, salt, sugar and butter into a medium-sized saucepan and heat gently until the butter has completely melted. Rapidly bring the mixture to a boil, then immediately remove the saucepan from the heat and tip in all the flour. Beat the mixture vigorously with a wooden spoon until it comes together to make a smooth, heavy clump of dough.

Return the pan to the heat and beat the mixture over a low heat for 30 seconds to dry the dough slightly. It should come away from the sides of the pan to form a smooth ball. Tip the dough into a large mixing bowl and leave to cool until tepid.

Using an electric mixer (you can use a wooden spoon but it is hard work), gradually add the beaten eggs to the mixture, beating well after each addition to make a smooth and shiny paste-like dough that falls from the spoon when lightly shaken. Cover the pastry until ready to use.

Preheat the oven to 190°C/375°F/Gas 5 and grease and dampen two baking trays. Put the choux pastry into a piping bag fitted with a 1.5cm/⅝in plain tube, and pipe rounded mounds, about 2.5cm/1in wide and 1.5cm/⅝in high, spacing them well apart on the trays. Lightly brush the profiteroles with beaten egg, making sure it does not drip down and glue the pastry to the tray. Bake

Below: luscious dark Chocolate Sauce oozes temptingly over a pile of cream-filled Profiteroles, giving a stunning special occasion dessert.

$\mathscr{C}$HOCOLATE $\mathscr{S}$AUCES

for about 20 minutes until crisp and golden. Wash and dry the piping bag.

Remove the profiteroles from the oven and, using a skewer or cocktail stick, make a small hole in the side of each profiterole to let out the steam. Return them to the oven and bake for a further 3-4 minutes. Transfer to a wire rack to cool.

To fill the profiteroles, spoon the Crème Chantilly or Crème Pâtissière into the dry, clean piping bag fitted with the plain tube. Pipe the filling into the profiteroles through the steam hole, enlarging it if necessary. Filled profiteroles can be kept in a cool spot for up to 2 hours before serving.

When you are ready to serve, pile the filled profiteroles in a dish, pour over your choice of sauce and pass the remainder separately in a jug for people to help themselves.

Profiteroles without filling can be kept in an airtight container for 2 days or frozen for up to 1 month. Frozen profiteroles may need to be crisped for 5 minutes or so in a hot oven before use.

Variation: if you do not have a piping bag, use a teaspoon to make the small mounds of pastry on the baking tray. To fill the profiteroles, split them in two and use a teaspoon to spoon in the filling. When using this method you can use slightly softened ice-cream to fill the profiteroles instead of Crème Chantilly or Crème Pâtissière.

Chocolate Cream Sauce

This is a really quick, rich sauce.

SERVES 4

125ml/4fl oz double cream
80g/3oz plain dark chocolate, finely chopped
½ teaspoon pure vanilla essence

Gently heat the cream in a small heavy-based saucepan, stirring frequently. When the cream comes to a boil, remove the pan from the heat and stir in the chopped chocolate. Stir the sauce gently until it is smooth then stir in the vanilla at the last moment and serve immediately.

Variations: just before serving, the sauce can be flavoured with rum, brandy or coffee liqueur to taste. For a thinner sauce, use single cream or mix the double cream with a little milk or coffee.

Best served with ice-cream, profiteroles and steamed sponge puddings. Garnish the sauce with grated chocolate, if you like.

Chocolate Ginger Sauce

Chocolate-coated stem ginger is usually more popular with adults than with children. This recipe takes the delicious combination and turns it into a rich but simple sauce.

SERVES 6

125g/4½oz dark chocolate, chopped
2 tablespoons single cream
1 tablespoon whisky
6 pieces stem ginger, finely chopped
2 tablespoons stem ginger syrup

Place all the ingredients in the top of a double boiler or in a heatproof bowl set over a pan of steaming water. Do not let the water come into contact with the chocolate or the mixture could sieze. Stir constantly until the chocolate melts and forms a silky sauce. Serve the sauce hot.

Variation: omit the whisky, if you prefer.

Serve with strawberries or other red berries, with bananas or apricots, over ice-cream or with meringue-based desserts.

Chocolate Self-Saucing Pudding

A pudding that comes with its own sauce, hidden underneath a pecan-studded sponge.

SERVES 4

125g/4½oz unsalted butter, softened
125g/4½oz golden caster sugar
4 large eggs, beaten
80g/3oz self-raising flour
½ teaspoon real vanilla essence
30g/1oz cocoa powder, sifted
30g/1oz pecan pieces
40g/1½oz plain dark chocolate, roughly chopped
1 tablespoon milk
FOR THE SAUCE:
30g/1oz cocoa powder, sifted
125g/4½oz light brown muscovado sugar
300ml/½ pint very hot water

Preheat the oven to 180°C/350°F/Gas 4 and grease a 1.7 litre/3 pint baking dish.

Beat the butter until creamy using a wooden spoon or electric mixer. Add the sugar and beat until light and fluffy. Gradually beat in the eggs, stirring well after each addition. Stir in a little flour when you add the last egg – this mixture will look curdled.

Stir in the vanilla followed by the rest of the flour and the cocoa. When the mixture is thoroughly combined, fold in the nuts, chopped chocolate, then the milk and spoon the mixture into the buttered dish.

To make the sauce, mix the cocoa and sugar in a medium-sized heatproof bowl or wide-necked jug. Stir in the very hot water until you have a smooth, thin sauce then gently pour it on top of the pudding. Bake it for 30-35 minutes until the sponge is cooked in the centre and the sauce beneath is thick and bubbling. Serve immediately.

This pudding needs no accompaniment but you could serve it with cream, if you like.

*C*HOCOLATE *S*AUCES AND *F*UDGE

In a small saucepan, heat the cream and the milk just to boiling point then remove the pan from the heat and whisk the mixture into the melted white chocolate.

When the sauce is smooth, pour it into a warmed jug and serve immediately. Or you can leave the sauce to cool then chill it for up to 48 hours. Stir well before serving.

Serve the sauce hot with steamed puddings or ice-cream. When chilled it is an excellent accompaniment to fresh red berries or cherries as well as chocolate desserts.

Chocolate Fudge

In this recipe, the darker the chocolate you choose, the deeper the flavour of the final sauce. However, if your taste is for milk chocolate, use the plain variety in this recipe as, once it is combined with the cream, the sauce will taste quite milky.

MAKES 250ML/9FL OZ

175ml/6fl oz double cream
3 tablespoons golden syrup
200g/7oz sugar
pinch of salt
90g/3¼oz plain or dark chocolate
25g/1oz butter, diced
½ teaspoon vanilla extract, or to taste (optional)

Put the cream, golden syrup, sugar and salt into a small saucepan and heat, stirring, until the sugar dissolves completely and the mixture is very smooth.

Meanwhile, chop the chocolate and, when the sauce is smooth, add it to the pan. Bring the mixture to a boil then lower the heat and simmer it gently for 20 minutes, stirring frequently, until the sauce is very thick.

Remove the saucepan from the heat and gradually whisk in the pieces of butter, then stir in the vanilla extract, if using. This sauce

White Chocolate Sauce

The flavour of this simple sauce depends on the quality of the chocolate, so choose the best available rather than children's bars.

MAKES 350ML/12FL OZ

200g/7oz white chocolate
200ml/7fl oz double cream
80ml/3fl oz milk

Above: a light, delicate pool of White Chocolate Sauce makes a dramatic complement to this rich dark chocolate roulade filled with thick cream.

Break the white chocolate into even-sized pieces and melt it very gently in a heatproof bowl set over a saucepan of steaming water. Remove the bowl from the heat and stir the chocolate until smooth.

*F*UDGE AND *T*OFFEE *S*AUCES

can be kept for 2 days in the refrigerator, where it will set to a thick paste. Gently reheat it before serving.

———— ⟋ ————

Ice-cream will encourage this hot sauce to set to an indulgent, chewy fudge.

Coffee Chocolate Fudge

If you want to boost the coffee flavour of this sauce with the instant coffee, make sure you choose powder and not granules as the powder will dissolve much more easily.

MAKES 175ML/6FL OZ

75ml/2½fl oz freshly brewed strong coffee
75g/2½oz dark brown sugar
115g/4oz cocoa powder
pinch of salt
25g/1oz butter, diced
50ml/2fl oz double cream
1 teaspoon instant espresso coffee powder (optional)

Put the hot coffee and the sugar into a small saucepan over a medium heat and stir until the sugar has completely dissolved. Use a whisk to blend the cocoa powder into the mixture, then the salt, and continue whisking until the sauce is smooth.

Lower the heat under the pan. Gradually whisk in the diced butter, then the cream and finally the instant coffee powder, if using. Keep whisking until the coffee powder has completely dissolved.

This sauce can be served immediately or left to cool and then stored covered in the refrigerator for up to 2 weeks.

———— ⟋ ————

Makes a rich adult treat of plain vanilla ice-cream. Alternatively, you can serve it with desserts of meringue and cream and perhaps some flavoursome strawberries.

Butterscotch Fudge

One of the thickest, richest, most indulgent sauces you will ever taste.

MAKES 300ML/½ PINT

90g/3¼oz butter
200g/7oz dark brown sugar
2 tablespoons golden syrup
75ml/2½fl oz double cream

Combine the butter, sugar and golden syrup in a small saucepan and stir them constantly with a wooden spoon over a gentle heat until the sugar dissolves completely – this may take as long as 10 minutes.

When the mixture is velvety smooth, stir in the cream and heat the sauce until it is piping hot. Pour into a jug and serve. The sauce can be poured into a heatproof bowl and allowed to cool until quite firm then stored in the refrigerator for up to 1 week. It will need to be reheated to a pouring consistency before serving.

———— ⟋ ————

A rich, chewy caramelized sauce that is particularly good with ice-cream and sundaes, especially banana splits.

Toffee Sauce

SERVES 6

200g/7oz dark or light muscovado sugar
90ml/3fl oz double cream
100g/3½oz unsalted butter
½ teaspoon vanilla extract

In a medium-sized bowl, crush the sugar with a wooden spoon to remove any lumps, then put it into a heavy pan with the cream and butter and stir together over a low heat until the butter has melted.

Bring the mixture to a boil and simmer gently for 2-3 minutes until toffee-coloured.

Remove the pan from the heat, stir in the vanilla extract and serve immediately.

The cooled sauce can be kept, covered, in the refrigerator for up to 1 week. Warm it through gently before serving.

———— ⟋ ————

Good with ice-cream, crêpes, pancakes, sponge puddings or profiteroles.

Thick Toffee Cream

This rich, creamy caramel toffee is similar to the South American treat *dulce de leche* in which a tin of condensed milk is boiled, but this is no longer considered a safe process.

SERVES 8

75g/2¾oz butter
50g/1¾oz brown sugar
225g/8oz condensed milk
2-4 tablespoons single cream

In a small saucepan, melt the butter then stir in the sugar. Slowly bring the mixture to a boil, stirring constantly until the sugar dissolves, then simmer for 1 minute.

Remove the pan from the heat and stir in the condensed milk and 2 tablespoons of the cream, blending thoroughly to give a smooth sauce. Return the pan to the heat and bring the mixture to a boil. Lower the heat and simmer, stirring constantly, for 2 minutes or until rich and thick. If you would like a thinner sauce, stir in the remaining cream. Serve warm or at room temperature.

———— ⟋ ————

Made with the smaller quantity of cream, this sauce can be used to fill pastry cases and to make banoffee pie, in which it is topped with bananas and whipped cream. Use the thinner version in ice-cream sundaes or serve it alongside apple desserts such as baked apples and apple pie.

Mint Syrup

MAKES 750ML/1⅓ PINTS

250g/9oz caster sugar
500ml/18fl oz water
juice of 1 lemon
15g/½oz mint

Put the sugar and water into a small non-aluminium saucepan and slowly bring to the boil, stirring frequently. Simmer until the sugar has completely dissolved and the liquid is clear, then stir in the lemon juice (there is no need to strain it). Turn off the heat under the pan.

Meanwhile, remove the mint leaves from their stems and roughly chop the leaves. Place them in a heatproof bowl and pour the hot syrup onto the leaves. Set the syrup aside to infuse.

When the syrup is cold, strain it through a fine-meshed sieve and discard the solids. Store it in a bottle or jar in the refrigerator for no more than 1 week.

Variation: *Vanilla and Basil Syrup*
Replace the lemon juice and mint with 3 split vanilla pods and a bunch of chopped basil.

Use the syrup to flavour fruit salads or pour it over chocolate cakes.

Lemon Syrup Sauce

MAKES 350ML/12FL OZ

2 teaspoons arrowroot
150ml/¼ pint water
4 tablespoons golden syrup
2 tablespoons lemon juice

In a small saucepan, blend the arrowroot with the water then stir in the golden syrup and lemon juice until the mixture is smooth. Slowly bring the sauce to a boil over a low

heat, stirring constantly. After simmering for 1-2 minutes it will be thick enough to coat the back of a spoon. Serve hot or warm.

This is an excellent sauce to serve with steamed puddings and hot cakes fresh from the oven. Leave it to cool slightly if you want to serve it with ice-cream and sundaes, pancakes or waffles.

Passion Fruit Syrup

A recipe from Brazil – a pretty, well-textured and intensely flavoured cold fruit sauce. Make sure you choose ripe passion fruit, which look really wrinkled.

MAKES 400ML/14FL OZ

10 passion fruit, halved
75ml/3fl oz water
50g/2oz golden caster sugar

Scoop the flesh and seeds from the passion fruit and set aside. Put the water and sugar into a small pan and heat gently, stirring frequently until the sugar is dissolved. Bring

Removing the pulp from a passion fruit: use a teaspoon to scoop out all the edible seeds, pith and juices from each half of the fruit.

the mixture to a boil and simmer for about 2 minutes to make a thin syrup.

Remove the saucepan from the heat, allow the syrup to cool for 1 minute then stir in the passion fruit flesh and seeds. Beat the sauce well for about 1 minute to break down the fleshy fibres of the fruit. Leave the sauce until cold then cover and chill before serving.

The sauce can be kept covered in the refrigerator for up to 24 hours.

Serve with cakes (the Mediterranean cake made from whole fresh oranges and ground almonds is particularly good), as well as with ice-cream and chocolate desserts.

Pineapple Syrup

SERVES 4

250g/9oz pineapple
100ml/4fl oz water
50g/2oz caster sugar
50ml/2fl oz pineapple juice
2-3 teaspoons rum, or to taste
squeeze of lemon juice

Cut 90g/3oz of the pineapple into chunks and purée it in a blender or food processor. Strain through a sieve then set aside. Finely dice the remaining pineapple.

Put the water and sugar into a medium-sized saucepan and bring the mixture to a boil. Simmer until the sugar has completely dissolved then add the diced pineapple and cook gently for 2-3 minutes.

Stir in the pineapple juice and reserved purée and remove the pan from the heat. Leave to cool then stir in the rum and lemon juice to taste. Chill before serving.

Pour over lightly flavoured cakes or dark chocolate cakes, coconut ice-cream or a rice pudding made from coconut milk.

Raisin and Honey Syrup

SERVES 4

125g/4oz raisins
75ml/3fl oz brandy
250ml/9fl oz freshly squeezed orange juice
75ml/3fl oz clear honey

Place the raisins and brandy in a small bowl and set them aside to marinate for 3 hours.

When the raisins have plumped up, put them into a small saucepan with the soaking liquid and add the orange juice and honey. Bring the mixture to a boil and simmer for 8-10 minutes or until the syrup is of a light coating consistency. Remove the sauce from the heat and serve it warm or chilled.

Spoon over vanilla ice-cream or serve as an accompaniment to apple pie or rice pudding.

Maple Pecan Sauce

SERVES 4-6

2 small dessert apples, quartered and cored
150ml/5fl oz maple syrup
50g/2oz pecan halves

Peel the apples only if the skin is very thick and tasteless. Cut the fruit into medium dice. Gently warm the maple syrup in a small saucepan then mix in the apple and pecan halves and serve immediately.

Best with pancakes or crêpes, ice-cream or steamed sponge puddings.

Below: three simple ingredients, crunchy pecans, maple syrup and sweet apples, are gently heated to give a speedy Maple Pecan Sauce. For the best results, make sure the pecans are very fresh.

$\mathscr{I}$NDEX BY $\mathscr{A}$CCOMPANIMENT

GENERAL INDEX

GENERAL INDEX

GENERAL INDEX

ACKNOWLEDGMENTS

The author and publisher would like to thank the following for their help: Alan Hertz, Annette Hertz, Yvonne Jenkins, Sharon Turner, Barbara Levy, Norma MacMillan, Jenni Muir, Sue Storey, Meg Jansz, Patrice de Villiers, Helen Ridge, Tanya Robinson, Victoria Richards, Alison Bolus, Simon Le Fevre.